Charles Latimer Marson

The Psalms at Work

Being the English Church Psalter, With a Few Short Notes on the Use of... Second Edition

Charles Latimer Marson

The Psalms at Work
Being the English Church Psalter, With a Few Short Notes on the Use of... Second Edition

ISBN/EAN: 9783337021603

Printed in Europe, USA, Canada, Australia, Japan

Cover: Foto ©Lupo / pixelio.de

More available books at **www.hansebooks.com**

THE PSALMS AT WORK.

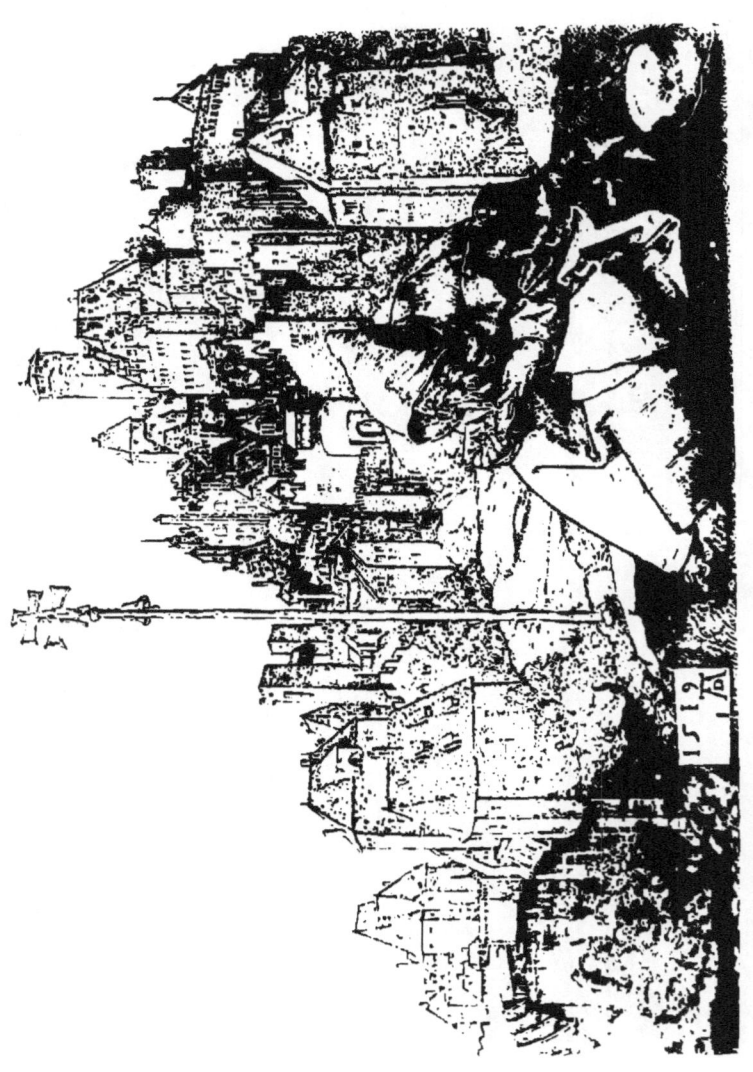

THE
PSALMS AT WORK.

BEING

THE ENGLISH CHURCH PSALTER, WITH A FEW SHORT NOTES ON THE USE OF THE PSALMS, GATHERED TOGETHER

BY

CHARLES L. MARSON.

SECOND EDITION, REVISED.

PHILADELPHIA:
GEORGE W. JACOBS AND CO.,
103, SOUTH 15TH STREET.
1895.

To

S. J. P.,

WITH AN OLD FRIEND'S GRATEFUL LOVE.

PREFACE TO THE SECOND EDITION.

THE public and the press have so kindly entertained this little book that, contrary to the expectation of the compiler, it has been encored. It now reappears somewhat amended and a little grown in stature. Hence the editor begs to thank his many friends and reviewers, and at the same time to ask the pardon of such readers as have sent him hints or material which he has been unable to use. The fact is that out of a considerable mass of notes only a few have been selected for publication. Mere citations, anecdotes of private and local interest have been left out, of set purpose; so have the too recondite instances, which might indeed have helped the editor to simulate learning, but would have acted only as soporifics to the 'general.'

Without doubt the warmest praise of the book has come from its elder readers, and for these the editor is sure that it is still entirely suitable. He may be allowed to say this with less immodesty, because it has generally been found (upon inquiry) that the eyes of such students did not suffer them to read the small print, and that it is to David therefore that their thanks, and his, are wholly due.

156, SEYMOUR STREET,
    ST. PANCRAS, N.W.

Feast of St. Lucian, 1895.

PREFACE TO THE FIRST EDITION.

This little collection of notes was gathered chiefly in the highways; and is meant to set the reader gathering for himself. If he does so, the Psalms will not only interest him more, but will unfold themselves to him in many new and deeper meanings. The melody of the Psalter will be all the sweeter when he hears it harmonized with the music of noble and varied human life. Its greatness will be better set forth, and its beauty will be brought home to him, not by tedious homily, but by that antiphonal method which makes a landscape seem doubly beautiful when it is reflected in a clear lake. Perhaps even a handful of instances can help one dimly to understand how enormously this one little book of poems has affected the life of mankind; and that, because the Psalmists have reached the common bed-rock of our human nature.

December, 1893,
   13, Soho Square.

DAY 1.

MORNING PRAYER.

PSALM I. *Beatus vir, qui non abiit, etc.*

BLESSED is the man that hath not walked in the counsel of the ungodly, nor stood in the way of sinners : and hath not sat in the seat of the scornful.

2 But his delight is in the law of the Lord : and in his law will he exercise himself day and night.

3 And he shall be like a tree planted by the waterside : that will bring forth his fruit in due season.

4 His leaf also shall not wither : and look, whatsoever he doeth, it shall prosper.

5 As for the ungodly, it is not so with them : but they are like the chaff, which the wind scattereth away from the face of the earth.

6 Therefore the ungodly shall not be able to stand in the judgement : neither the sinners in the congregation of the righteous.

7 But the Lord knoweth the way of the righteous : and the way of the ungodly shall perish.

This psalm is a " short introduction " to the whole book, as St. Basil calls it, and is chiefly used as such. The whole Psalter is chanted through, with us monthly, among the Latins and Greeks weekly. By many pious souls (for instance, by St. Margaret of Scotland and George Herbert) it was recited once daily. The importance of singing psalms has been insisted upon from the very first in the Church of England. It is one of the early instructions given by St. Gregory to St. Augustine, that those under the ecclesiastical rule should " sing psalms early and late " (A.D. 601). At the Cloves Hoo Council (747) psalmody is classed with prayer and fasting. By St. Dunstan's canons, indeed, infirm men might use the Psalter instead of fasting— " 200 psalms " or the fine of a penny (a day's pay) for each fast-day. The working people in the early Church knew the Psalms so well, that they could and did chant and hum them in field and house and street.

Our translation is, in its base, the joint work of Tyndale and Coverdale, which was made out of the Greek, during the sweating sickness at Antwerp and in exile. The notes were erased, the mistakes corrected, and the language improved by Cranmer and the bishops, and the book set forth in 1541. Bonner gave six chained copies to St. Paul's, which perished in the Great Fire. The Bishops' Bible version was retained for the Psalms partly because it was better known to choirs, partly because it was more rhythmic, and perhaps partly because the Puritans were militantly bitter against it in the seventeenth century. The translators were accustomed to the measured roll of the Latin version; and Bishop Cosin —thanks to whom we retain our Prayer-Book version—had a fine ear for the now almost forgotten art of sonorous and organ-like prose. The version was therefore started by extreme Protestants, revised by bishops, "mostly popish," defended and kept by English Churchmen with almost unanimous consent, after it had run the gauntlet of the severest criticism.

Verse 1. Erasmus in 1516 dedicated his commentary on this psalm to Beatus Rhenanus, the corrector of Froben's press, whose character was aptly described by the text.

Verse 2. One of St. Jerome's most favourite texts; it is woven in and out of his writings, and he may almost have been said to have moulded his life upon it. Robert Burton also quotes it as one of the cures of melancholy, in his "Anatomy" "that maze of remedies for a labyrinth of diseasements," as Lamb calls it.

Liturgical use.—Introit to Mass, 1st Sunday in Advent (e).*
Latins.—Sunday Matins; Easter Day Matins; Martyrs and All Saints Matins.
Greeks.—Saturday at Vespers.

PSALM II. *Quare fremuerunt gentes?*

WHY do the heathen so furiously rage together : and why do the people imagine a vain thing?

2 The kings of the earth stand up, and the rulers take counsel together : against the Lord, and against his Anointed.

3 " Let us break their bonds asunder : and cast away their cords from us."

4 He that dwelleth in heaven shall laugh them to scorn : the Lord shall have them in derision.

5 Then shall he speak unto them in his wrath : and vex them in his sore displeasure.

(e) means in the first Prayer-Book of Edward VI., 1549.

6 "Yet have I set my King : upon my holy hill of Sion."

7 "I will preach the law, whereof the Lord hath said unto me : Thou art my Son, this day have I begotten thee.

8 "Desire of me, and I shall give thee the heathen for thine inheritance : and the utmost parts of the earth for thy possession.

9 "Thou shalt bruise them with a rod of iron : and break them in pieces like a potter's vessel."

10 Be wise now therefore, O ye kings : be learned, ye that are judges of the earth.

11 Serve the Lord in fear : and rejoice unto him with reverence.

12 Kiss the Son, lest he be angry, and so ye perish from the right way : if his wrath be kindled, (yea, but a little,) blessed are all they that put their trust in him.

This has been from the earliest days a psalm of good heart in hard times. When the Apostles, SS. Peter and John, had drawn upon themselves the threats of Jewish persecution, by their use of that miracle done on the lame man at the Beautiful Gate, they heartened the little church by chanting this psalm. It was sung by the Jews at the siege of Jerusalem. It inspired many martyrs ; it called the people to the first Crusade.

It was a favourite psalm of Savonarola, and he used it on two great occasions : once to cheer the Florentines, when they were in fear at the French invasion ; and again (1496) to rally the Republic when the Plague, the Pisan War, the death of Piero Capponi, and the Imperial League seemed to overwhelm everything, when the people were "furiously raging in streets, houses, shops, and markets" against the preacher and his followers. St. Athanasius, in the fourth century, had used it as a trumpet-call against the enemies of the Faith ; and Luther, in the sixteenth, found consolation in the notion that the gathering of princes and "rage of our enemies is not aimed at us, but at the Lord and His Christ."

Verse 4. Sir Thomas Browne with this verse confutes the " vulgar error that our Lord never laughed," " nor need we be afraid to ascribe that unto the incarnate Son, which sometimes is attributed to the uncarnate Father."

Verse 7. St. Paul uses this verse in his sermon at Antioch to illustrate his teaching that the Godhead of Christ was part of historical Jewish teaching. It is used on the same lines in the Epistle to the Hebrews ; and consequently was a Catholic motto in the Arian, Socinian and Deist controversies.

These words, "Thou art," etc., were heard and a bright

light shone at Christ's baptism.

Verse 9. Not only used in the Revelation of St. John to the Church at Thyatira; of the child of the woman clothed with the sun; and of him who rode on the white horse; but a constant answer of Churchmen to those who asserted that the Faith had no political side to it, and of Puritans to those who doubted their right to govern the nations.

Verses 10-12. Baxter, preaching at Worcester Cathedral before the judges in 1654, wished "that each man present could, when he forgot Christ, see written on the wall, 'Kiss the Son, lest He be angry, and thou perish,' and on the tester of his bed, as often as he lay down in an unregenerate state."

Liturgical use.—English proper psalm for Easter Morning.
Latins.—Sunday Matins; Christmas; Circumcision; Good Friday; Easter; Martyrs.
Greeks.—Saturday at Vespers.

PSALM III. *Domine, quid multiplicati.*

LORD, how are they increased that trouble me: many are they that rise against me.

2 Many one there be that say of my soul: "There is no help for him in his God."

3 But thou, O Lord, art my defender: thou art my worship, and the lifter up of my head.

4 I did call upon the Lord with my voice: and he heard me out of his holy hill.

5 I laid me down and slept, and rose up again: for the Lord sustained me.

6 I will not be afraid for ten thousands of the people: that have set themselves against me round about.

7 Up, Lord, and help me, O my God: for thou smitest all mine enemies upon the cheek-bone; thou hast broken the teeth of the ungodly.

8 Salvation belongeth unto the Lord: and thy blessing is upon thy people.

At the Synod of Haba (1010) Archbishop Elphege ordered that in all churches, every day and at each of the hours of prayer, the whole congregation should prostrate themselves and sing *Domine, quid multiplicati sunt* by reason of the fury of the Norsemen.

This was one of the psalms appointed to be sung after the defeat of the Spanish Armada, before the extent of the victory was fully realized, and when England was still nervous about those who had set themselves against her. It was one of the psalms most dwelt upon by Churchmen in the trying time between the fall of the Rump Parliament and the Restoration of the English Church.

Liturgical use.—Second Mass, Easter Day (1549).
Latins.—Sunday Matins; Martyrs; the daily morning hymn in monasteries.
Greeks.—Saturday Vespers.

PSALM IV. *Cum invocarem.*

HEAR me when I call, O God of my righteousness : thou hast set me at liberty when I was in trouble; have mercy upon me, and hearken unto my prayer.

2 O ye sons of men, how long will ye blaspheme mine honour : and have such pleasure in vanity, and seek after leasing?

3 Know this also, that the Lord hath chosen to himself the man that is godly : when I call upon the Lord he will hear me.

4 Stand in awe, and sin not : commune with your own heart, and in your chamber, and be still.

5 Offer the sacrifice of righteousness : and put your trust in the Lord.

6 There be many that say : "Who will shew us any good?"

7 Lord, lift thou up : the light of thy countenance upon us.

8 Thou hast put gladness in my heart : since the time that their corn, and wine, and oil, increased.

9 I will lay me down in peace, and take my rest : for it is thou, Lord, only, that makest me dwell in safety.

This is the evening psalm of Christendom.

St. Augustine, made glad by his conversion to the Catholic Faith, wished the Manichæans could witness his delight as he read this psalm, and was glad at corn, wine, oil, and all such things as they falsely thought to be "Satan in solution," the work, not of God, but of the devil.

Verse 7. This verse was a text for Charlemagne, in his struggle against images in churches. His *Capitulare* on the subject is almost a series of sermons, pleading against things which "dim instead of reveal the light of God's countenance."

Verse 9. St. Gregory Nazianzen tells a story of his sister, St. Gorgonia, when she was dying : "Her father, marking her lips a little to move, put his ear near to (for his virtue and compassion made him bold and hardy), and, listening, he heard it was a verse of a psalm which she muttered, and such a verse as was most

Day 1   PSALM V   *Morning Prayer*

agreeable to such as were departing, and in her a testimony wherewith she left this life. And blessed be that person who yieldeth up his life with those words of hers, which were these: 'I will lay me down in peace, and take my rest: for it is Thou, Lord, only, that makest me dwell in safety.'"

This psalm, used by Christians every evening of their lives, is naturally and beautifully used last, in the evening of life.

Liturgical use.—Introit for 3rd Sunday in Advent (e).
Latins.—Compline and the proper psalm for Easter Eve.
Greeks.—Saturday Vespers and late Evensong.

PSALM V. *Verba mea auribus.*

PONDER my words, O Lord : consider my meditation.

2 O hearken thou unto the voice of my calling, my King, and my God : for unto thee will I make my prayer.

3 My voice shalt thou hear betimes, O Lord : early in the morning will I direct my prayer unto thee, and will look up.

4 For thou art the God that hast no pleasure in wickedness : neither shall any evil dwell with thee.

5 Such as be foolish shall not stand in thy sight : for thou hatest all them that work vanity.

6 Thou shalt destroy them that speak leasing : the Lord will abhor both the blood-thirsty and deceitful man.

7 But as for me, I will come into thine house, even upon the multitude of thy mercy : and in thy fear will I worship toward thy holy temple.

8 Lead me, O Lord, in thy righteousness, because of mine enemies : make thy way plain before my face.

9 For there is no faithfulness in his mouth : their inward parts are very wickedness.

10 Their throat is an open sepulchre : they flatter with their tongue.

11 Destroy thou them, O God; let them perish through their own imaginations : cast them out in the multitude of their ungodliness ; for they have rebelled against thee.

12 And let all them that put their trust in thee rejoice : they shall ever be giving of thanks, because

thou defendest them : they that love thy Name shall be joyful in thee :

13 For thou, Lord, wilt give thy blessing unto the righteous : and with thy favourable kindness wilt thou defend him as with a shield.

This psalm is the first of the book which comes into the English Dirge for the Dead, authorized in 1545. This began with, " In the name of the Father," etc. Then were said Psalms cxvi., xli., and cxlvi., without *Gloria*. Then, after some versicles and prayers, came Psalms v., xxvii., and xlii., without *Gloria*, but with the antiphon, " I believe verily to see the goodness of the Lord in the land of the living." The three lessons followed, with anthems ; and after them Psalm xxx., Isaiah xxxviii. (10-20), and Psalm lxxi. These had *Gloria*, and the antiphon, " I am the Resurrection," etc. Prayers and the Grace concluded the Dirge. Of course there were many other Dirges, even in England.

Verse 5. St. Athanasius presses the Arians with this verse, to prove to them that Wisdom (or Christ) was of the Divine Substance, even before the Incarnation.

Verse 8. The very name Dirge (or Dirige) is from *Dirige in conspectu tuo viam meam*, the second half of this verse, the usual antiphon in dirges.

Liturgical use.—Introit on 4th Sunday in Advent (e).
Latins.—Lauds on Monday : Martyrs.
Greeks.—Saturday Vespers.

PSALM VI. *Domine, ne in furore.*

O LORD, rebuke me not in thine indignation : neither chasten me in thy displeasure.

2 Have mercy upon me, O Lord, for I am weak : O Lord, heal me, for my bones are vexed.

3 My soul also is sore troubled : but, Lord, how long wilt thou punish me ?

4 Turn thee, O Lord, and deliver my soul : O save me for thy mercy's sake.

5 For in death no man remembereth thee : and who will give thee thanks in the pit ?

6 I am weary of my groaning ; every night wash I my bed : and water my couch with my tears.

7 My beauty is gone for very trouble : and worn away because of all mine enemies.

8 Away from me, all ye that work vanity : for the Lord hath heard the voice of my weeping.

9 The Lord hath heard my petition : the Lord will receive my prayer.

10 All mine enemies shall be confounded, and sore vexed : they shall be turned back, and put to shame suddenly.

The penitential psalms are vi., xxxii., xxxviii., li., cii., cxxx., and cxliii.

The beautiful petition in our Litany, "Remember not, Lord, our offences, nor the offences of our forefathers... for ever," was usually sung as an antiphon before and after these psalms. By these, "the Seven Psalms," as they were called, has been expressed most of the lamentation and mourning and woe of the Christian Church. Fast days, times of public penance, times of humiliation, and the like, have always been the fitting season for the "seven sobs," as William Hunnis, chapel-master to Queen Elizabeth, used to call them. He turned them into "metre," as was fashionable in his time—very doggerel metre, too—and named them the "Seven Sobs of a sorrowful Soul for Sin." Each of the seven psalms was used in the Middle Ages as a remedy against one of the seven deadly sins. This one was "*contra Iram*" (against Wrath), and was recited by many bearded lips in penance for that vice, during the ages of wrath, and is still used by the pious of our times against their tamer angers. St. Ambrose, who loved simplicity, severity, and restraint in poetry, had an especial love of this psalm. Henry II. sang it, at his penance for the murder of St. Thomas of Canterbury, as he walked barefoot in the rain from St. Dunstan's Church to the scene of the martyrdom. Bishop Fisher, who meditated upon the same psalm in his lifetime, preached upon it at length to the " most excellent Princess Margaret, Countess of Richmond and Derby, and mother to our Sovereign Lord King Henry the Seventh," who also much delighted in these psalms. The same psalm naturally comforted Fisher in the Tower, and prepared him for death.

The fierce Catherine de Medici called it her favourite psalm.

Verse 1. *Domine, ne in furore arguas me* is the motto Edward III. chose for the English florins of 1344. He was then in great commercial difficulties.

Verses 2 and 3 are inserted in the pathetic journal of Jane Carlyle (1855), at a time when she was so ill and unhappy that "sleep has come to look to me the highest virtue and the greatest happiness."

Verse 3 was the usual expression of Calvin, when he was in any trouble of mind.

Verse 5. A verse often used to deepen men's horror of hell, but St. Cyprian gave it a pleasanter turn when he made it a basis for readmitting the lapsed to communion, against the Puritan Novatians. This verse is quoted by St. Boniface,

Wilfrid of Crediton, in his circular letter to the English, asking for their help in the work of evangelizing Germany, reminding them that the aid should be sent "while it is day." The letter was well responded to.

Liturgical use.—This is the first penitential psalm, and therefore a proper psalm for Ash Wednesday. Introit for the Ash Wednesday Mass (e).
Latins.—Sunday Matins and Visitation of the Sick.
Greek.—Saturday Vespers.

PSALM VII. *Domine, Deus meus.*

O LORD my God, in thee have I put my trust : save me from all them that persecute me, and deliver me ;

2 Lest he devour my soul, like a lion, and tear it in pieces : while there is none to help.

3 O Lord my God, if I have done any such thing : or if there be any wickedness in my hands ;

4 If I have rewarded evil unto him that dealt friendly with me : yea, I have delivered him that without any cause is mine enemy ;

5 Then let mine enemy persecute my soul, and take me : yea, let him tread my life down upon the earth, and lay mine honour in the dust.

6 Stand up, O Lord, in thy wrath, and lift up thyself, because of the indignation of mine enemies : arise up for me in the judgement that thou hast commanded.

7 And so shall the congregation of the people come about thee : for their sakes therefore lift up thyself again.

8 The Lord shall judge the people ; give sentence with me, O Lord : according to my righteousness, and according to the innocency that is in me.

9 O let the wickedness of the ungodly come to an end : but guide thou the just.

10 For the righteous God : trieth the very hearts and reins.

11 My help cometh of God : who preserveth them that are true of heart.

12 God is a righteous Judge, strong, and patient : and God is provoked every day.

13 If a man will not turn, he will whet his sword : he hath bent his bow, and made it ready.

14 He hath prepared for him the instruments of death : he ordaineth his arrows against the persecutors.

15 Behold, he travaileth with mischief : he hath conceived sorrow, and brought forth ungodliness.

16 He hath graven and digged up a pit : and is fallen himself into the destruction that he made for others.

17 For his travail shall come upon his own head : and his wickedness shall fall on his own pate.

18 I will give thanks unto the Lord, according to his righteousness : and I will praise the name of the Lord most High.

This psalm was a favourite with the Fifth Monarchy men. Sir Harry Vane uses it in his "Valley of Jehoshaphat" to support their belief in an immediate advent of Christ and His Monarchy. says also that anyone with his five wits ought to blush if he does not end his day with psalmody, for even the tiniest birds mark the coming of both night and day with holy devoutness and sweet song.

Verses 3 and 4. St. Ambrose comments on these verses, as the chief Old Testament example of the spirit of patience, expressed in a way that both foresees and anticipates the New Testament spirit. He

Verse 12. Deux iudex iustus fortis patiens is the motto chosen by Edward the Black Prince for the coins of 1362.

Verse 16. This is Capgrave's commentary upon the fate of King Richard II.

Latins.—Matins on Sunday.
Greeks.—Saturday at Vespers.

PSALM VIII. *Domine, Dominus noster.*

O LORD our Governour, how excellent is thy Name in all the world : thou that hast set thy glory above the heavens !

2 Out of the mouth of very babes and sucklings hast thou ordained strength, because of thine enemies : that thou mightest still the enemy, and the avenger.

3 For I will consider thy heavens, even the works of thy fingers : the moon and the stars, which thou hast ordained.

4 What is man, that thou art mindful of him : and the son of man, that thou visitest him ?

5 Thou madest him lower than the angels : to crown him with glory and worship.

6 Thou makest him to have dominion of the works of thy hands : and thou hast put all things in subjection under his feet :

7 All sheep and oxen : yea, and the beasts of the field ;

8 The fowls of the air, and the fishes of the sea : and whatsoever walketh through the paths of the seas.

9 O Lord our Governour : how excellent is thy Name in all the world!

St. Paul uses this whole psalm in his great resurrection passage (1 Cor. xv.), the lesson which has been read at the burial of our fathers since 1549, and will probably be read over our own bodies ; and which Bishop Ken so loved that his Greek Testament opens to this day at this very passage. Bishop Berkeley was also talking to his family on the same when he died.

Fuller calls this psalm "A Nocturnal," and says of it : "When I cannot sleep, may I with this psalmist entertain my waking with good thoughts! Not to use them as opium, to invite my corrupt nature to slumber, but to bolt out bad thoughts, which otherwise would possess my soul."

Verse 2. This is quoted by Christ against the Pharisees in defence of the little children (St. Matt. xxi. 16).

This was the verse which overruled Bishop Defensor's objections to the election of St. Martin at Tours. He despised the saint for his mean and unkempt appearance. At the Mass the sub-deacon came in late, and could not find the Epistle for the day, so opened a Psalter and read the eighth psalm. At the words "Still the enemy and avenger" (*Defensorem*), the people all shouted together, and regarded it as an augury from Heaven, and forthwith elected St. Martin to the see.

Verse 5. Quoted by the writer of the Hebrews in defence of our Lord's superiority to the angels (Heb. ii. 6-9).

Gloriâ et honore eum coronasti Domine. Philip Howard inscribed these words on the mantelpiece in his dungeon, June 1587. He added, "*In memoria æterna erit justus.*" He died in 1597, having been kept a prisoner in the Tower for his zeal in the Roman Catholic cause.

Verse 6. The motto of the Butcher's Company is *Omnia subjecisti sub pedibus, oves et boves.*

Liturgical use.—First psalm for Ascension Day at Matins. Introit for 2nd Mass on Christmas morning (e).

Latins.—Ascension Day : Adult Baptism ; Martyrs ; Our Lady ; All Saints and Trinity-tide.

Greeks.—Saturday evening.

PSALM IX. *Confitebor tibi.*

I WILL give thanks unto thee, O Lord, with my whole heart : I will speak of all thy marvellous works.

2 I will be glad, and rejoice in thee : yea, my songs will I make of thy Name, O thou most Highest.

3 While mine enemies are driven back : they shall fall and perish at thy presence.

4 For thou hast maintained my right and my cause : thou art set in the throne that judgest right.

5 Thou hast rebuked the heathen, and destroyed the ungodly : thou hast put out their name for ever and ever.

6 O thou enemy, destructions are come to a perpetual end : even as the cities which thou hast destroyed ; their memorial is perished with them.

7 But the Lord shall endure for ever : he hath also prepared his seat for judgement.

8 For he shall judge the world in righteousness : and minister true judgement unto the people.

9 The Lord also will be a defence for the oppressed : even a refuge in due time of trouble.

10 And they that know thy Name will put their trust in thee : for thou, Lord, hast never failed them that seek thee.

11 O praise the Lord which dwelleth in Sion : shew the people of his doings.

12 For, when he maketh inquisition for blood, he remembereth them : and forgetteth not the complaint of the poor.

13 "Have mercy upon me, O Lord ; consider the trouble which I suffer of them that hate me : thou that liftest me up from the gates of death.

14 "That I may shew all thy praises within the ports of the daughter of Sion : I will rejoice in thy salvation."

15 The heathen are sunk down in the pit that they made : in the same net which they hid privily, is their foot taken.

16 The Lord is known to execute judgement : the ungodly is trapped in the work of his own hands.

17 The wicked shall be turned into hell : and all the people that forget God.

18 For the poor shall not always be forgotten : the patient abiding of the meek shall not perish for ever.

19 Up, Lord, and let not man have the upper hand : let the heathen be judged in thy sight.

20 Put them in fear, O Lord : that the heathen may know themselves to be but men.

Psalms ix. and x. are united in the Vulgate.

Psalms ix., x., and xi. were said as the proper psalms for King Charles the Martyr, on the morning of January 30th.

Verse 5. In one of St. Anthony's sermons there is a curious tale of how a huge phantom came and complained that he, the devil, was abused overmuch by monks, and unjustly, for that Christ had made him weak, rebuked, destroyed, and " his name was put out," for the world was being filled with the Gospel. St. Anthony agreed that he had spoken the truth for once, and told his hearers that, unless we co-operate with the devil, he has no real power at all over us, and that many so-called struggles with the devil are but our own disorders.

Verse 10. Dante quotes this to St. James in Paradise.

Verse 11. This verse stirred up De Bérulle to found the Oratorian order.

Verse 12. Poor little old Bishop Laud quoted this verse in his last speech upon the scaffold on Tower Hill, January 10, 1644. He read his speech with his clear eye, and his face so ruddy, that his enemies falsely declared he had painted it, so as not to show fear. Fuller quotes of him : " He pluckt down Puritans and Property, to build up Paul's and Privilege."

Latins.—Sunday Matins.
Greeks.—Sunday morning.

PSALM X. *Ut quid, Domine?*

WHY standest thou so far off, O Lord : and hidest thy face in the needful time of trouble ?

2 The ungodly for his own lust doth persecute the poor : let them be taken in the crafty wiliness that they have imagined.

3 For the ungodly hath made boast of his own heart's desire : and speaketh good of the covetous, whom God abhorreth.

4 The ungodly is so proud, that he careth not for God : neither is God in all his thoughts.

5 His ways are always grievous : thy judgements are far above out of his sight, and therefore defieth he all his enemies.

6 For he hath said in his heart, "Tush, I shall never be cast down : there shall no harm happen unto me."

7 His mouth is full of cursing, deceit, and fraud : under his tongue is ungodliness and vanity.

8 He sitteth lurking in the thievish corners of the streets : and privily in his lurking dens doth he murder the innocent ; his eyes are set against the poor.

9 For he lieth waiting secretly, even as a lion lurketh he in his den : that he may ravish the poor.

10 He doth ravish the poor : when he getteth him into his net.

11 He falleth down and humbleth himself : that the congregation of the poor may fall into the hands of his captains.

12 He hath said in his heart, "Tush, God hath forgotten : he hideth away his face, and he will never see it."

13 Arise, O Lord God, and lift up thine hand : forget not the poor.

14 Wherefore should the wicked blaspheme God : while he doth say in his heart, "Tush, thou God carest not for it."

15 Surely thou hast seen it : for thou beholdest ungodliness and wrong.

16 That thou mayest take the matter into thine hand : the poor committeth himself unto thee ; for thou art the helper of the friendless.

17 Break thou the power of the ungodly and malicious : take away his ungodliness, and thou shalt find none.

18 The Lord is King for ever and ever : and the heathen are perished out of the land.

19 Lord, thou hast heard the desire of the poor : thou preparest their heart, and thine ear hearkeneth thereto.

20 To help the poor and fatherless unto their right : that the man of the earth be no more exalted against them.

Sir Philip Sidney's rendering of part of this psalm is worth contrasting with some others, which do not "carve and polish the edges of the text, axe-hewn in the Hebrew."

"But nak'd before Thine eyes
All wrong and mischief lies,
For of them in Thine hands
The balance ev'nly stands :
But who aright poor minded be,
Commit their cause—themselves—to Thee, [less,
The Succour of the succour-
The Father of the fatherless."

Here is Waddell's racy version: "Ye hae seen 't yersel: for yersel can baith cark and care, till tak a' i' yer han'. Till yersel the puir man leuks an' lippens: the frien' o' the faitherless yerlane are Thou."

Here is Tate and Brady's poor bald rendering:

"Thou dost the humble suppliants hear
That to Thy throne repair,
Thou first preparest their hearts to pray,
And then accept'st their prayer.

Thou in Thy righteous judgment weigh'st
The fatherless and poor."

This is both the hardest psalm for mediæval commentators and for modern critics; its prophetic darkness puzzled the one and its title the others.

Verse 20. This verse inspired St. Hugh of Lincoln to rebuke and defy Jordan of the Tower, a powerful Londoner, who had wronged two orphan children, and threatened violence to all who opposed him.

The *Latins* make it a part of Psalm ix., and use it at Matins on Sundays.

Greeks.—On Sunday morning.

PSALM XI. *In Domino confido.*

IN the Lord put I my trust : how say ye then to my soul, that she should flee as a bird unto the hill?

2 For lo, the ungodly bend their bow, and make ready their arrows within the quiver : that they may privily shoot at them which are true of heart.

3 For the foundations will be cast down : and what hath the righteous done?

4 The Lord is in his holy temple : the Lord's seat is in heaven.

5 His eyes consider the poor : and his eye-lids try the children of men.

6 The Lord alloweth the righteous : but the ungodly, and him that delighteth in wickedness, doth his soul abhor.

7 Upon the ungodly he shall rain snares, fire and brimstone, storm and tempest : this shall be their portion to drink.

8 For the righteous Lord loveth righteousness : his countenance shall behold the thing that is just.

This is one of the psalms which helped the Abolitionist movement in America. Verse 8 is quoted in one of President Lincoln's anti-slavery manifestoes. The next psalm was similarly used.

Verse 8. Charles, King of Navarre, "the bad," preached a sermon to the Parisians in

1357, after Poictiers, from this text. He stood on a kind of platform outside St. Germain's Abbey, and spoke eloquently of the woes and wrongs of France, and his desire to right them, so that his audience wept. He thus crept into the hearts of the men of Paris, who, under Marcel, favoured him in the Civil War which followed.

Liturgical use.—Introit to Mass of St. John, Evangelist (e).
Latins.—Sunday Matins; Matins of Martyrs.
Greeks.—Sunday morning.

PSALM XII. *Salvum me fac.*

HELP me, Lord, for there is not one godly man left : for the faithful are minished from among the children of men.

2 They talk of vanity every one with his neighbour : they do but flatter with their lips, and dissemble in their double heart.

3 The Lord shall root out all deceitful lips : and the tongue that speaketh proud things;

4 Which have said, "With our tongue will we prevail : we are they that ought to speak; who is lord over us?"

5 Now for the comfortless troubles' sake of the needy : and because of the deep sighing of the poor;

6 "I will up," saith the Lord : "and will help every one from him that swelleth against him, and will set him at rest."

7 The words of the Lord are pure words : even as the silver, which from the earth is tried, and purified seven times in the fire.

8 Thou shalt keep them, O Lord : thou shalt preserve him from this generation for ever.

9 The ungodly walk on every side : when they are exalted, the children of men are put to rebuke.

This is the psalm used by modern Jews at circumcision.

There is an interesting old picture of this psalm to be found in the Utrecht Eadwine and Harley psalters. A number of maimed and ragged men are singing it, and the angels with them. Christ is coming out of heaven with a long crossed spear, which he presents to St. Michael. He falls upon a jeering and armed crowd of knights, who are standing idle while some labourers grind a mill. At a forge the words of the Lord are being tried, and the ungodly are also going round and round in a profitless circle (*in circuitu*).

St. Bernard describes (and it was a common belief in the Middle Ages, derived from St. Augustine) how "the angels and the spirits of just men made perfect cannot but join with the Church on earth" in her rapture of worship, when the Psalms are sung, "when hands smite the breast and knees the floor, when altars are heaped with devout prayers, when cheeks are stained with tears, and groans and sighs resound on all sides, when with the pleading of spiritual songs the roof shakes; that is what the heavenly citizens love best to behold; that is the sweetest sight to the King of kings. What else did He mean who said, 'Whoso offereth me thanks and praise, he honoureth me'? O that one could have the open eyes which Elisha's prayers gave to his servant! Without doubt such an one would see the Princes joined to them that sing psalms, in the midst of the damsels playing on the timbrels. He would behold how carefully, how rhythmically, they join the singers, attend those who pray, supply those who meditate, help those who wait, guide those who order and arrange. Well do the higher powers know their fellow-citizens; and when these possess their heritage of salvation, they rejoice lovingly with them, they share their lot, they educate, they shield, they aid them all, wholly and everywhere."

Latins.—Sunday Matins.
Greeks.—Sunday morning.

PSALM XIII. *Usque quo, Domine?*

HOW long wilt thou forget me, O Lord, for ever: how long wilt thou hide thy face from me?

2 How long shall I seek counsel in my soul, and be so vexed in my heart: how long shall mine enemies triumph over me?

3 Consider, and hear me, O Lord, my God: lighten mine eyes, that I sleep not in death.

4 Lest mine enemy say, "I have prevailed against him": for if I be cast down, they that trouble me will rejoice at it.

5 But my trust is in thy mercy: and my heart is joyful in thy salvation.

6 I will sing of the Lord, because he hath dealt so lovingly with me: yea, I will praise the Name of the Lord most Highest.

A commendatory psalm for the dying.

"In spite of his manifold afflictions," says Beza of Calvin, "he uttered no syllable save what was worthy of a

Christian, but just raised his eyes to heaven and said, *Usque quo, Domine?* And even this was in his mouth but a mark of the sorrow he felt for the calamities of the brethren rather than for any of his own."

Verse 3. St. Gregory of Decapolis tells a pathetic story of a noble Saracen who beheld the Lamb of God in a vision, and sought out the Christians to learn from them their Way. He was christened and abode three years at Decapolis, where he learnt the Psalter by heart. He then returned to his own people and professed his faith. He was heard with fury, and first thrown out of the house, and was at last stoned to death, using the prayers of David: Psalms xxxi., li., and these words, " Lighten mine eyes."

Illumina oculos meos begins the " verses of St. Bernard," which Cranmer, Marshall, and other reformers denounce, as so superstitious in use.

Liturgical use.—Introit for 1st Sunday after Epiphany (e).
Latins.—Sunday at Matins.
Greeks.—Late Evensong in Lent.

PSALM XIV. *Dixit insipiens.*

THE fool hath said in his heart : " There is no God."

2 They are corrupt, and become abominable in their doings : there is none that doeth good, no not one.

3 The Lord looked down from heaven upon the children of men : to see if there were any that would understand, and seek after God.

4 But they are all gone out of the way, they are altogether become abominable : there is none that doeth good, no not one.

5 Their throat is an open sepulchre ; with their tongues have they deceived : the poison of asps is under their lips.

6 Their mouth is full of cursing and bitterness : their feet are swift to shed blood.

7 Destruction and unhappiness is in their ways, and the way of peace have they not known : there is no fear of God before their eyes.

8 Have they no knowledge, that they are all such workers of mischief : eating up my people as it were bread, and call not upon the Lord ?

9 There were they brought in great fear, even where no fear was : for God is in the generation of the righteous.

10 As for you, ye have made a mock at the counsel of the poor : because he putteth his trust in the Lord.

11 Who shall give salvation unto Israel out of Sion ? When the Lord turneth the captivity of his people : then shall Jacob rejoice, and Israel shall be glad.

This psalm is quoted by Bacon in his essay, "Of Atheism" in the sense that the fool "rather saith it by rote to himselfe, as he that would have then that he can throughly beleeve it, or be persuaded of it." So the *Meditationes Sacræ* on the same subject.

This psalm was one in which Queen Elizabeth took a delight; probably it expressed her view of the stormy and ungodly age in which she lived, and also promised better things to come. She put it into verse and, added, "Prayse to God" at the end.

Verse 11. "The captivity of Sion," a phrase much used by the persecuted English Churchmen for the outlawry of our liturgy by Cromwell. John Evelyn went to church on Christmas Day, 1652, and wrote : "No more notice taken of Christmas Day in churches. I went to London, where Dr. Wild preach'd the funeral sermon of Preaching, this being the last day, after which Cromwell's Proclamation was to take place, that none of the Church of England should dare either to preach or administer Sacraments, teache schoole, etc., on paine of imprisonment or exile. So this was the mournfullest day that in my life I had seene, or the Church of England herselfe since the Reformation; to the greate rejoicing both of Papist and Presbyter. So pathetic was his discourse, that it drew many teares from the auditory. Myself, wife and some of our family receiv'd the Communion ; God make me thankfull, who hath hitherto provided for us the food of our soules as well as bodies ! The Lord Jesus pity our distress'd Church, and bring back the Captivity of Sion !'

Latins.—Sunday Matins.
Greeks.—Sunday morning.

PSALM XV. *Domine, quis habitabit ?*

LORD, who shall dwell in thy tabernacle : or who shall dwell upon thy holy hill ?

2 Even he, that leadeth an uncorrupt life : and doeth the thing which is right, and speaketh the truth from his heart.

3 He that hath used no deceit in his tongue, nor done evil to his neighbour : and hath not slandered his neighbour.

4 He that setteth not by himself, but is lowly in his

own eyes : and maketh much of them that fear the Lord.

5 He that sweareth unto his neighbour, and disappointeth him not : though it were to his own hindrance.

6 He that hath not given his money upon usury : nor taken reward against the innocent.

7 Whoso doeth these things : shall never fail.

This has been called the gentleman's psalm, for it describes that character. It was one of St. Basil the Great's favourites.

One of the last books Erasmus wrote was a commentary upon this psalm, with mystical interpretations and exhortations. It was printed at Basle, 1536, and was called, "Concerning the Purity of the Christian Church." This is the more interesting because for some time the leaders of the New Learning did not lay much emphasis upon the Psalms, regarding these rather as the stronghold of their enemies. This commentary therefore means, in some sense, a rediscovery of the use of the Psalter.

Verse 6. This verse is in the forefront of the long fight against usury which the Church has maintained. St. Augustine constantly appeals to it. The Council of Cealchythe, 785 A.D., instance it, and so does every writer on the subject, down to the last great battle, when in the times of Jeremy Bentham the protest against usury practically ceased, and the civilization begins which Renan accused the Church of putting back for a thousand years.

Liturgical use.—Introt to 3rd Sunday after Epiphany (e) ; on Ascension Day morning.
Latins.—Sunday Matins ; Easter Eve ; Matins of Martyrs ; Michaelmas ; All Saints, etc.
Greeks.—Sunday morning.

PSALM XVI. *Conserva me, Domine.*

PRESERVE me, O God : for in thee have I put my trust.

2 O my soul, thou hast said unto the Lord : "Thou art my God, my goods are nothing unto thee.

3 "All my delight is upon the saints, that are in the earth : and upon such as excel in virtue."

4 But they that run after another god : shall have great trouble.

5 Their drink-offerings of blood will I not offer : neither make mention of their names within my lips.

6 The Lord himself is the portion of mine inheritance, and of my cup : thou shalt maintain my lot.

7 The lot is fallen unto me in a fair ground : yea, I have a goodly heritage.

8 I will thank the Lord for giving me warning : my reins also chasten me in the night-season.

9 I have set God always before me : for he is on my right hand, therefore I shall not fall.

10 Wherefore my heart was glad, and my glory rejoiced : my flesh also shall rest in hope.

11 For why? thou shalt not leave my soul in hell : neither shalt thou suffer thy Holy One to see corruption.

12 Thou shalt shew me the path of life; in thy presence is fulness of joy : at thy right hand there is pleasure for evermore.

This was Pico della Mirandola's favourite. His comments upon it were Englished by Sir Thomas More.

This was the last psalm used by Sir Walter Scott's Hugh M'Kail, a Genevan minister, who was tortured by the boot in Claverhouse's time.

Verse 7. The Beauchamp family have for their motto *Fortuna mea in bello campo,* which seems to refer to this verse.

Verses 9 and 10. The enemy of mankind often takes radiant Christ-like form, and appears as an angel of light. He tempted St. Martin thus; but the saint looked hard for the print of the nails. In this form he also tempted a boy at a Benedictine school to idle away his time. The boy, in his perplexity, made the holy sign, sang these verses, and overcame the sin : and became the learned Bishop Oswald, the second saint of that name.

Verse 10. St. Paul argued from this verse of the prophetic nature of this psalm (Acts xiii. 35).

Liturgical use.—Introit for first Mass on Easter Day (e).
Latins.—Sunday morning ; Many Martyrs ; Visitation of the Sick.
Greeks.—Sunday Matins.

PSALM XVII. *Exaudi, Domine.*

HEAR the right, O Lord, consider my complaint : and hearken unto my prayer, that goeth not out of feigned lips.

2 Let my sentence come forth from thy presence : and let thine eyes look upon the thing that is equal.

3 Thou hast proved and visited mine heart in the night-season : thou hast tried me, and shalt find no

wickedness in me : for I am utterly purposed that my mouth shall not offend.

4 Because of men's works, that are done against the words of thy lips : I have kept me from the ways of the destroyer.

5 O hold thou up my goings in thy paths : that my footsteps slip not.

6 I have called upon thee, O God, for thou shalt hear me : incline thine ear to me, and hearken unto my words.

7 Show thy marvellous loving-kindness, thou that art the Saviour of them which put their trust in thee : from such as resist thy right hand.

8 Keep me as the apple of an eye : hide me under the shadow of thy wings,

9 From the ungodly that trouble me : mine enemies compass me round about to take away my soul.

10 They are inclosed in their own fat : and their mouth speaketh proud things.

11 They lie waiting in our way on every side : turning their eyes down to the ground;

12 Like as a lion that is greedy of his prey : and as it were a lion's whelp, lurking in secret places.

13 Up, Lord, disappoint him, and cast him down : deliver my soul from the ungodly, which is a sword of thine;

14 From the men of thy hand, O Lord, from the men, I say, and from the evil world : which have their portion in this life, whose bellies thou fillest with thy hid treasure.

15 They have children at their desire : and leave the rest of their substance for their babes.

16 But as for me, I will behold thy presence in righteousness : and when I awake up after thy likeness, I shall be satisfied with it.

St. Jerome says that this is the psalm to which the Church betakes herself when her enemies begin to persecute her.

Verse 7. Captain Allen Gardiner left England in 1850 on a mission to Patagonia. After a year's gallant effort, he and his five companions were starved to death at Spanish Harbour, and this verse was in his mind as he made his last entry in his diary. " Great and marvellous are the loving kindnesses of my gracious God unto me. He has preserved me hitherto, and for four days, although without bodily food, without any feelings of hunger and thirst."

Verse 8. *Custodi me ut pupillum oculi* was the motto of Pope Anastasius IV. (1153).

Verse 16. A favourite quotation with the Seraphic doctor, St. Bonaventura, the author of " In the Lord's Atoning Grief " (1221-1274). Also with many moderns, *e.g.*, Archbishop Tait, Julius Hare, and others.

Latins.—Sunday Matins.
Greeks.—Sunday morning ; Saturday in Lent at noon.

PSALM XVIII. *Diligam te, Domine.*

I WILL love thee, O Lord, my strength ; the Lord is my stony rock, and my defence : my Saviour, my God, and my might, in whom I will trust, my buckler, the horn also of my salvation, and my refuge.

2 I will call upon the Lord, which is worthy to be praised : so shall I be safe from mine enemies.

3 The sorrows of death compassed me : and the overflowings of ungodliness made me afraid.

4 The pains of hell came about me : the snares of death overtook me.

5 In my trouble I will call upon the Lord : and complain unto my God.

6 So shall he hear my voice out of his holy temple : and my complaint shall come before him, it shall enter even into his ears.

7 The earth trembled and quaked : the very foundations also of the hills shook, and were removed, because he was wroth.

8 There went a smoke out in his presence : and a consuming fire out of his mouth, so that coals were kindled at it.

9 He bowed the heavens also, and came down : and it was dark under his feet.

10 He rode upon the cherubims, and did fly : he came flying upon the wings of the wind.

11 He made darkness his secret place : his pavilion round about him with dark water, and thick clouds to cover him.

12 At the brightness of his presence his clouds removed : hail-stones, and coals of fire.

13 The Lord also thundered out of heaven, and the Highest gave his thunder : hail-stones, and coals of fire.

14 He sent out his arrows and scattered them : he cast forth lightnings, and destroyed them.

15 The springs of water were seen, and the foundations of the round world were discovered, at thy chiding, O Lord : at the blasting of the breath of thy displeasure.

16 He shall send down from on high to fetch me : and shall take me out of many waters.

17 He shall deliver me from my strongest enemy, and from them which hate me : for they are too mighty for me.

18 They prevented me in the day of my trouble : but the Lord was my upholder.

19 He brought me forth also into a place of liberty : he brought me forth, even because he had a favour unto me.

20 The Lord shall reward me after my righteous dealing : according to the cleanness of my hands shall he recompense me.

21 Because I have kept the ways of the Lord : and have not forsaken my God, as the wicked doth.

22 For I have an eye unto all his laws : and will not cast out his commandments from me.

23 I was also uncorrupt before him : and eschewed mine own wickedness.

24 Therefore shall the Lord reward me after my righteous dealing : and according unto the cleanness of my hands in his eye-sight.

25 With the holy thou shalt be holy : and with a perfect man thou shalt be perfect.

26 With the clean thou shalt be clean : and with the froward thou shalt learn frowardness.

27 For thou shalt save the people that are in adversity : and shalt bring down the high looks of the proud.

28 Thou also shalt light my candle : the Lord my God shall make my darkness to be light.

29 For in thee I shall discomfit an host of men : and with the help of my God I shall leap over the wall.

30 The way of God is an undefiled way : the way of the Lord also is tried in the fire; he is the defender of all them that put their trust in him.

31 For who is God, but the Lord : or who hath any strength, except our God?

32 It is God, that girdeth me with strength of war : and maketh my way perfect.

33 He maketh my feet like harts' feet : and setteth me up on high.

34 He teacheth mine hands to fight : and mine arms shall break even a bow of steel.

35 Thou hast given me the defence of thy salvation : thy right hand also shall hold me up, and thy loving correction shall make me great.

36 Thou shalt make room enough under me for to go : that my footsteps shall not slide.

37 I will follow upon mine enemies, and overtake them : neither will I turn again till I have destroyed them.

38 I will smite them, that they shall not be able to stand : but fall under my feet.

39 Thou hast girded me with strength unto the battle : thou shalt throw down mine enemies under me.

40 Thou hast made mine enemies also to turn their backs upon me : and I shall destroy them that hate me.

41 They shall cry, but there shall be none to help them : yea, even unto the Lord shall they cry, but he shall not hear them.

42 I will beat them as small as the dust before the wind : I will cast them out as the clay in the streets.

43 Thou shalt deliver me from the strivings of the people : and thou shalt make me the head of the heathen.

44 A people whom I have not known : shall serve me.

45 As soon as they hear of me, they shall obey me : but the strange children shall dissemble with me.

46 The strange children shall fail : and be afraid out of their prisons.

47 The Lord liveth, and blessed be my strong helper : and praised be the God of my salvation.

48 Even the God that seeth that I be avenged : and subdueth the people unto me.

49 It is he that delivereth me from my cruel enemies, and setteth me up above mine adversaries : thou shalt rid me from the wicked man.

50 For this cause will I give thanks unto thee, O Lord, among the Gentiles : and sing praises unto thy Name.

51 Great prosperity giveth he unto his King : and sheweth loving-kindness unto David his Anointed, and unto his seed for evermore.

Verse 10. Kirke White challenged any other translator to excel Sternhold and Hopkins' spirited version of these words:
"On cherubs and on cherubims
   Full royally he rode,
And on the wings of mighty winds
   Came flying all abroad."
But Pope ridiculed the lines by his reference to them in the Prologue to his Satires. Shakespeare has the verse in his mind in Macbeth's
"Pity, like a new born naked babe
   Striding the blast, or heaven's cherubin, horsed
   Upon the sightless couriers of the air,
Shall blow the horrid deed in every eye,
That tears shall drown the wind."
He has several other allusions to this psalm ; for instance :
"O war ! thou son of hell,
Whom angry heavens do make their minister,
Throw in the frozen bosoms of our part
Hot coals of vengeance."
Verse 11. A stronghold of the Mystics. Theodore (of Mopsuestia), for instance, dwells on this verse as showing that God's light is so intense that it is dark to us, not from its own nature, but from our limitations. So many others, from Molinos' enthusiastic comment, "See now if darkness be not to be esteemed and embraced," to John Norris's lines :

"Tho' Light and Glory be th' Almighty's throne,
Darkness is his Pavilion."

Verses 13 *and* 14. Bede relates that St. Chad used to remain prostrate in prayer in church during great gales and storms, interceding for those in danger. He gave these verses as his reason.

Verse 29. "By the help of God and your holiness," wrote Mary Queen of Scots to the Pope, "I shall leap over the wall" of English opposition to the ecclesiastical domination of the Italian Church ; but the gallant lady broke her neck in the leap.

Verse 39. When Clovis sent to St. Martin's tomb to ask for an omen in his conflict with Alaric, his messengers heard the monks chanting these words (507 A.D.). The augury proved correct.

Latins.—Sunday Matins.
Greeks.—Sunday morning.

PSALM XIX. *Cœli enarrant.*

THE heavens declare the glory of God : and the firmament sheweth his handy-work.

2 One day telleth another : and one night certifieth another.

3 There is neither speech nor language : but their voices are heard among them.

4 Their sound is gone out into all lands : and their words into the ends of the world.

5 In them hath he sat a tabernacle for the sun : which cometh forth as a bridegroom out of his chamber, and rejoiceth as a giant to run his course.

6 It goeth forth from the uttermost part of the heaven, and runneth about unto the end of it again : and there is nothing hid from the heat thereof.

7 The law of the Lord is an undefiled law, converting the soul : the testimony of the Lord is sure, and giveth wisdom unto the simple.

8 The statutes of the Lord are right, and rejoice the heart : the commandment of the Lord is pure, and giveth light unto the eyes.

9 The fear of the Lord is clean, and endureth for ever : the judgements of the Lord are true, and righteous altogether.

10 More to be desired are they than gold, yea, than much fine gold : sweeter also than honey, and the honey-comb.

11 Moreover, by them is thy servant taught : and in keeping of them there is great reward.

12 Who can tell how often he offendeth : O cleanse thou me from my secret faults.

13 Keep thy servant also from presumptuous sins, lest they get the dominion over me : so shall I be undefiled, and innocent from the great offence.

14 Let the words of my mouth, and the meditation of my heart : be alway acceptable in thy sight,

15 O Lord : my strength, and my redeemer.

This psalm was one of St. Augustine's favourites. Its use at Christmas is from the mystical interpretation of the giant and other imagery. In the Sarum hymn, *Veni Redemptor*, attributed sometimes to St. Ambrose, we have this reference:

Procedens e thalamo suo
Pudoris aula regia
Geminæ gigas substatiæ
Alacris ut currat viam.

Mr. Ruskin in vol. v. of "Modern Painters," while treating of the Angel of the Sea, Rain, speaks to us of the "parts of the Bible we are intended to make specially our own"—the Psalms—and writes quite a commentary on this one.

Verse 1. *Cæli enarrant gloriam Dei et operationem manuum ejus annunciat firmamentum*—a common sundial motto.

Verse 2. *Dies Diem docet—Disce!* is the dial motto in Barniston Church, Yorks. *Nox nocti indicat scientiam* is the motto of one of William Habington's most beautiful poems (xvii. cent.), "When I survey the bright celestial sphere."

Verse 4. Justinianus of Genoa, in his polyglot Psalter of 1562, cannot resist enlarging upon this verse, *In fines orbis terræ verba eorum*, in praise of his fellow-countryman, Christopher Columbus, who, though born of the meanest of the people, had discovered the ends of the world in America. His digression is the most interesting part of his book.

Verse 5. This is a favourite verse with the poets. St. Ambrose, Milton, Addison, Thomson, Wordsworth, etc., embody it in their verses. Spenser alludes to it:

"Phœbus, fresh as bridegroom to his mate,
Came dancing forth, shaking his dewy hair."

And Shakespeare (with whom it seems a favourite):

"See how the morning opes her golden gates,
And takes her farewell of the glorious sun!
How well resembles it the pride of youth,
Trimmed like a younker, prancing to his love."

And perhaps these—

"Night's candles are burnt out, and jocund day
Stands tiptoe on the misty mountain-top."

And—

"The glorious sun
Stays in his course and plays the alchemist;
Turning with splendour of his precious eye
The meagre cloddy earth to glittering gold."

But certainly he has an echo of this psalm in his mind in—

"Look! how the floor of heaven
Is thick inlaid with patines of bright gold;
There's not the smallest orb which thou behold'st
But in his motion like an angel sings,
Still quiring to the young-ey'd cherubins:
Such harmony is in immortal souls;
But, whilst this muddy vesture of decay
Doth grossly close us in, we cannot hear it."

Liturgical use.—First psalm Christmas Matins.
Latins.—Matins Sundays ; Christmas ; Circumcision ; Ascension-tide ; Trinity ; Matins of Our Lady.
Greeks.—Sunday morning.

PSALM XX. *Exaudiat te Dominus.*

THE Lord hear thee in the day of trouble : the Name of the God of Jacob defend thee ;

2 Send thee help from the sanctuary : and strengthen thee out of Sion ;

3 Remember all thy offerings : and accept thy burnt-sacrifice ;

4 Grant thee thy heart's desire : and fulfil all thy mind.

5 We will rejoice in thy salvation, and triumph in the Name of the Lord our God : the Lord perform all thy petitions.

6 Now know I, that the Lord helpeth his Anointed, and will hear him from his holy heaven : even with the wholesome strength of his right hand.

7 Some put their trust in chariots, and some in horses : but we will remember the Name of the Lord our God.

8 They are brought down, and fallen : but we are risen, and stand upright.

9 Save, Lord, and hear us, O King of heaven : when we call upon thee.

Verse 7. Both Hilarion and St. Anthony of the Desert, when assailed by the mistrust and malice of Satan, defeated him with these words. The same have been used often enough in spiritual conflicts, but they have also been a battle-cry in actual conflict. They were the war-cry of the Byzantines in the ninth century. When their city was besieged, Michael Balbus successfully defended them and gave them this motto. The words were often used in the Byzantine wars afterwards, up till the terrible disaster of May, 1453, when the infidels took Constantinople.

Verse 9. The Latin version, *Domine salvum fac regem*, is the origin of the versicle, "O Lord, save the Queen," and, of course, of our National Anthem.

Liturgical use.—Introit for 5th Sunday after Epiphany (e) ; Queen's Accession.
Latins.—Sunday morning ; Visitation of the Sick.
Greeks.—Sunday morning ; Dawn in Lent.

PSALM XXI. *Domine, in virtute tua.*

THE King shall rejoice in thy strength, O Lord : exceeding glad shall he be of thy salvation.

2 Thou hast given him his heart's desire : and hast not denied him the request of his lips.

3 For thou shalt prevent him with the blessings of goodness : and shalt set a crown of pure gold upon his head.

4 He asked life of thee, and thou gavest him a long life : even for ever and ever.

5 His honour is great in thy salvation : glory and great worship shalt thou lay upon him.

6 For thou shalt give him everlasting felicity : and make him glad with the joy of thy countenance.

7 And why? because the King putteth his trust in the Lord : and in the mercy of the most Highest he shall not miscarry.

8 All thine enemies shall feel thy hand : thy right hand shall find out them that hate thee.

9 Thou shalt make them like a fiery oven in time of thy wrath : the Lord shall destroy them in his displeasure, and the fire shall consume them.

10 Their fruit shalt thou root out of the earth : and their seed from among the children of men.

11 For they intended mischief against thee : and imagined such a device as they are not able to perform.

12 Therefore shalt thou put them to flight : and the strings of thy bow shalt thou make ready against the face of them.

13 Be thou exalted, Lord, in thine own strength : so will we sing, and praise thy power.

Carlyle's book of "Heroes" contains this passage : "David's life and history, as written for us in those Psalms of his, I consider to be the truest emblem ever given of a man's moral progress and warfare here below. All earnest souls will ever discern in it the faithful struggle of an earnest human soul towards what is good and best. Struggle often baffled, sore baffled, down as into entire wreck ; yet a struggle never ended ; ever with tears, repentance, true unconquerable purpose, begun anew. Poor human nature! Is not a man's walking, in truth, always that : "a succession of falls"? Man can do no other. In this wild element of a life he has to struggle onwards ; now fallen, deep-abased ; and ever, with tears, repentance, with bleeding heart, he has to rise again, struggle again still onwards." *Verses 6 and 7.* Laud's text for the accession sermon of King James I.

Liturgical use.—Ascension Day Matins ; Queen's Accession.
Latins.—Sunday Matins ; Martyrs ; Ascension-tide.
Greeks.—Sunday Morning and Dawn in Lent.

PSALM XXII. *Deus, Deus meus.*

MY God, my God, look upon me; why hast thou forsaken me : and art so far from my health, and from the words of my complaint?

2 O my God, I cry in the day-time, but thou hearest not : and in the night-season also I take no rest.

3 And thou continuest holy : O thou worship of Israel.

4 Our fathers hoped in thee : they trusted in thee, and thou didst deliver them.

5 They called upon thee, and were holpen : they put their trust in thee, and were not confounded.

6 But as for me, I am a worm, and no man : a very scorn of men, and the outcast of the people.

7 All they that see me laugh me to scorn : they shoot out their lips, and shake their heads, saying,

8 He trusted in God, that he would deliver him : let him deliver him, if he will have him.

9 But thou art he that took me out of my mother's womb : thou wast my hope, when I hanged yet upon my mother's breasts.

10 I have been left unto thee ever since I was born : thou art my God even from my mother's womb.

11 O go not from me, for trouble is hard at hand : and there is none to help me.

12 Many oxen are come about me : fat bulls of Basan close me in on every side.

13 They gape upon me with their mouths : as it were a ramping and a roaring lion.

14 I am poured out like water, and all my bones are out of joint : my heart also in the midst of my body is even like melting wax.

15 My strength is dried up like a potsherd, and my tongue cleaveth to my gums : and thou shalt bring me into the dust of death.

16 For many dogs are come about me : and the counsel of the wicked layeth siege against me.

17 They pierced my hands and my feet; I may tell all my bones : they stand staring and looking upon me.

18 They part my garments among them : and cast lots upon my vesture.

19 But be not thou far from me, O Lord : thou art my succour, haste thee to help me.

20 Deliver my soul from the sword : my darling from the power of the dog.

21 Save me from the lion's mouth : thou hast heard me also from among the horns of the unicorns.

22 I will declare thy Name unto my brethren : in the midst of the congregation will I praise thee.

23 O praise the Lord, ye that fear him : magnify him, all ye of the seed of Jacob, and fear him, all ye seed of Israel :

24 For he hath not despised, nor abhorred, the low estate of the poor : he hath not hid his face from him, but when he called unto him he heard him.

25 My praise is of thee in the great congregation : my vows will I perform in the sight of them that fear him.

26 The poor shall eat, and be satisfied : they that seek after the Lord shall praise him ; your heart shall live for ever.

27 All the ends of the world shall remember themselves, and be turned unto the Lord : and all the kindreds of the nations shall worship before him.

28 For the kingdom is the Lord's : and he is the Governour among the people.

29 All such as be fat upon the earth : have eaten, and worshipped.

30 All they that go down into the dust shall kneel before him : and no man hath quickened his own soul.

31 My seed shall serve him : they shall be counted unto the Lord for a generation.

32 They shall come, and the heavens shall declare his righteousness : unto a people that shall be born, whom the Lord hath made.

Verse 1. The greatest association this psalm can have is that our Lord Himself quoted it on the Cross. It has been suggested that perhaps He quoted the Psalter from this up to Psalm xxxi. 6, at which He gave up the ghost. The mere possibility of this, invests this part of the Psalter with a peculiar interest; but the Church has never authorized this view, and has even by implication denied it, by the small liturgical use she has made of some of the intervening psalms.

Richard Cœur de Lion had this psalm in his mind when he ordered out the crusaders to battle and scarce a fifth came out, and he saw that the crusade had failed. He cried out, "My God, why hast Thou forsaken me? Oh, how unwilling should I be to forsake Thee in so forlorn and dreadful a position were I Thy Lord and Advocate, as Thou art mine."

This psalm was formerly sung by the African Church at the Easter Communion, as it is still used by Scottish Presbyterians.

Verses 2 *and* 3 were the dying meditation of Dr. Thomas Newton, the art-loving Bishop of Bristol (1781). He was the mouthpiece of Reynolds, West, and others for their request that they might be allowed to decorate the interior of St. Paul's. The Dean and Chapter refused.

Verses 4 *and* 5 were used by Notker, the monk of St. Gall, in his great antiphon, "In the midst of life we are in death," which he composed as he watched boys trying to "gather samphire, dreadful trade," on a cliff. The antiphon is used in our Burial Service.

Verse 12. Shakespeare makes Antony allude to this psalm, and Psalm lxviii. 15, in "Antony and Cleopatra," iii. 13.

Verse 18. Applied by St. John (xix. 24) to the soldiers at the Crucifixion.

Verse 21. Evidently alluded to in the Lion and Unicorn of the Royal Arms. This is the verse which Bishop Burnet selected when he preached before the King at the Rolls Chapel, and thereby obtained his dismissal.

Liturgical use.—Good Friday morning; Introit for Good Friday Mass (e).
Latins.—Friday at Prime; Good Friday Matins.
Greeks.—Sunday morning.

PSALM XXIII. *Dominus regit me.*

THE Lord is my shepherd: therefore can I lack nothing.

2 He shall feed me in a green pasture: and lead me forth beside the waters of comfort.

3 He shall convert my soul: and bring me forth in the paths of righteousness, for his Name's sake.

4 Yea, though I walk through the valley of the shadow of death, I will fear no evil: for thou art with me; thy rod and thy staff comfort me.

5 Thou shalt prepare a table before me against them

that trouble me : thou hast anointed my head with oil, and my cup shall be full.

6 But thy loving-kindness and mercy shall follow me all the days of my life : and I will dwell in the house of the Lord for ever.

Mr. Ruskin tells us that this psalm was the first he learnt at his mother's knee ; and the rest she gave him as a solid foundation for life and learning, were Nos. xxxii , xc., xci., ciii., cxii., cxix., cxxxix.

This was the last psalm of Edward Irving, who recited it in Hebrew on his death-bed before his great disappointment and death.

It was a favourite with most of our poets. George Herbert, John Byrom, Addison, and Sir Henry Baker, are not the least among those who have translated it into well-known verse. "The God of Love my Shepherd is," "The Lord is my shepherd, His goodness my song," "The Lord my pasture shall prepare," and "The King of Love my Shepherd is," are their renderings. Sir Henry Baker died repeating his verse, " Perverse and foolish oft I strayed."

Verse 2. One of the last poems of Heine quotes this verse.

Verse 4. This is the verse which St. Francis of Assisi chanted when he went alone, bare-headed and bare-footed, to convert the Sultan and to Christianize the Saracens, instead of crusading against them. He was warned that he was going to certain death, as a price had been set on every Christian's head. His sincerity and zeal so impressed the heathen that he was courteously treated, and sent home.

Liturgical use.—Introit for Septuagesima (e).
Latins.—Thursday at Prime.
Greeks.—On Sunday morning ; Visitation of the Sick ; Burial of Priests.

PSALM XXIV. *Domini est terra.*

THE earth is the Lord's, and all that therein is : the compass of the world, and they that dwell therein.

2 For he hath founded it upon the seas : and prepared it upon the floods.

3 Who shall ascend into the hill of the Lord : or who shall rise up in his holy place ?

4 Even he that hath clean hands and a pure heart : and that hath not lift up his mind unto vanity, nor sworn to deceive his neighbour.

5 He shall receive the blessing from the Lord : and righteousness from the God of his salvation.

6 This is the generation of them that seek him: even of them that seek thy face, O Jacob.

7 Lift up your heads, O ye gates, and be ye lift up, ye everlasting doors : and the King of glory shall come in.

8 " Who is the King of glory " : " it is the Lord strong and mighty, even the Lord mighty in battle."

9 Lift up your heads, O ye gates, and be ye lift up, ye everlasting doors : and the King of glory shall come in.

10 " Who is the King of glory " : " even the Lord of hosts, he is the King of glory."

This was a burial psalm in St. Chrysostom's time, and that gives particular point to his use of it, when he defied the Empress Eudoxia, who threatened him for his sermon against her. " Let her banish me, if she will, ' The earth is the Lord's ': let her have me sawn asunder, Isaiah suffered so," etc.

This psalm is the foundation of that glorious old drama of the " Harrowing of Hell " (found in the " Gospel of Nicodemus," the " Parliament of Devils," and elsewhere). On Good Friday the spirits and souls of the men of old time were sitting in the land of Darkness, when they saw a purple light break into the sky. They looked at one and another, and each quoted from his writings a prophecy of this time. But Satan bade make fast the great doors of brass, and bar them with the iron bars of Cruelty. But presently Christ and His knights were seen, and they shouted, " Lift up your heads," and Satan with his men replied scornfully, " Who is the King of Glory ?" At the last Christ burst the brazen gates, and taking Adam by the hand, delivered him to the tender care of the angels. To this old drama allusion is made in the custom of singing verse 7, etc., on Palm Sunday, outside the Rood-screen. Handel also refers to this legend in his " Messiah." But Dionysius the Areopagite says that as Christ ascended the lower angels in wonder asked of the mid ones above them, " Who is the King of Glory ?" This also explains some of its ritual uses, e.g., on Ascension Day.

The Ven. Bede quotes it in his Ascension hymn.

On Christmas Eve, 1669, Bishop Hacket reconsecrated the restored cathedral of Lichfield, and " reconciled it from much bloodshed and confusion according to piety and best antiquity" with these psalms : in the south aisle, xxiv. ; north, c. ; upper nave, cii. ; south chancel, cxxii. ; north chancel, cxxxii.

Dean Milman selected the opening words of the psalm for the legend under the figure of Commerce in the Stock Exchange.

Liturgical use.—Ascension Day evening; Introit for Sexagesima (e).
Latins.—Monday at Prime; Matins for Martyrs; 2nd Matins Easter Eve; Trinity Sunday; Dedication of a Church; St. Mary; St. Michael; All Saints; Burial of Children, at the Churching of Women.
Greeks.—Sunday morning; Burial of Priests.

PSALM XXV. *Ad te, Domine, levavi.*

UNTO thee, O Lord, will I lift up my soul; my God, I have put my trust in thee: O let me not be confounded, neither let mine enemies triumph over me.

2 For all they that hope in thee shall not be ashamed: but such as transgress without a cause shall be put to confusion.

3 Shew me thy ways, O Lord: and teach me thy paths.

4 Lead me forth in thy truth, and learn me: for thou art the God of my salvation; in thee hath been my hope all the day long.

5 Call to remembrance, O Lord, thy tender mercies: and thy loving-kindnesses, which have been ever of old.

6 O remember not the sins and offences of my youth: but according to thy mercy think thou upon me, O Lord, for thy goodness.

7 Gracious and righteous is the Lord: therefore will he teach sinners in the way.

8 Them that are meek shall he guide in judgement: and such as are gentle, them shall he learn his way.

9 All the paths of the Lord are mercy and truth: unto such as keep his covenant, and his testimonies.

10 For thy Name's sake, O Lord: be merciful unto my sin, for it is great.

11 What man is he, that feareth the Lord: him shall he teach in the way that he shall choose.

12 His soul shall dwell at ease: and his seed shall inherit the land.

13 The secret of the Lord is among them that fear him: and he will shew them his covenant.

14 Mine eyes are ever looking unto the Lord: for he shall pluck my feet out of the net.

15 Turn thee unto me, and have mercy upon me: for I am desolate, and in misery.

16 The sorrows of my heart are enlarged : O bring thou me out of my troubles.

17 Look upon my adversity and misery : and forgive me all my sin.

18 Consider mine enemies, how many they are : and they bear a tyrannous hate against me.

19 O keep my soul, and deliver me : let me not be confounded, for I have put my trust in thee.

20 Let perfectness and righteous dealing wait upon me : for my hope hath been in thee.

21 Deliver Israel, O God : out of all his troubles.

This was part of the private daily prayers given to the clergy by Archbishop Elfric, with Ps. xxvi. and li.

Joinville notices that St. Louis of France was crowned on 1st Sunday in Advent, "when the Mass begins with *Ad te levavi animam meam*, and what follows is this: Fair Sire God, I will lift up my soul unto Thee, I put my trust in Thee ;" words which seemed to strike the keynote of the reign of that noble Prince, pious Crusader and Defender of the poor : for " he had perfect trust in God, even to his death, for at the moment of his dying, in his last words, he invoked God and His saints, especially Monseigneur St. James and Madame Ste. Genevieve."

Strafford repeated the psalm on the scaffold.

From *verse* 5, the Introit, the 2nd Sunday in Lent, is called *Reminiscere :* and from *verse* 14, the 3rd Sunday, is called *Oculi.*

Latins.—Prime on Tuesday.

Greeks.—On Monday morning, 3rd hour ; late Evensong in Lent.

PSALM XXVI. *Judica me, Domine.*

BE thou my Judge, O Lord, for I have walked innocently : my trust hath been also in the Lord, therefore shall I not fall.

2 Examine me, O Lord, and prove me : try out my reins and my heart.

3 For thy loving-kindness is ever before mine eyes : and I will walk in thy truth.

4 I have not dwelt with vain persons : neither will I have fellowship with the deceitful.

5 I have hated the congregation of the wicked : and will not sit among the ungodly.

6 I will wash my hands in innocency, O Lord : and so will I go to thine altar ;

7 That I may shew the voice of thanksgiving : and tell of all thy wondrous works.

8 Lord, I have loved the habitation of thy house : and the place where thine honour dwelleth.

9 O shut not up my soul with the sinners : nor my life with the bloodthirsty;

10 In whose hands is wickedness : and their right hand is full of gifts.

11 But as for me, I will walk innocently : O deliver me, and be merciful unto me.

12 My foot standeth right : I will praise the Lord in the congregations.

This psalm (with xxv. and li.) was given for daily use by Archbishop Elfric to his clergy in 995 A.D. He followed Theodulf's *Capitula* in recommending it for this use.

Verse 4. Both that "unpitying Phrygian sect," the Montanists, and the Donatists laid great stress upon this verse, and used it to uphold their schisms, forgetting that the admission to the Church Catholic is not given us because we love Christ and are good, but because He loves us. The Baptists, who have been called "Donatists new dipt," occupy now some of the ground once held by the earlier sects.

Verse 6 to the end. These words are the *Lavabo*, the words the priest uses at Mass, when he washes his finger-tips, after the oblation of the alms, bread, and wine, before the Canon or essential part of the service.

Verse 8. A favourite verse of Charlemagne's (*Domine dilexi decorem domûs tuæ*), though he was careful to insist that *decorem* in church does not mean statues. He took great interest in psalm-singing and reformed it carefully, and "although he was a master at reading and psalming, yet he would not read aloud in church, nor sing in his resonant voice, save with all the rest, and in obedience to the precentor"— no small virtue in his day.

Verse 11. *In innocentiâ meâ ingressus sum.* This was Innocent VIII.'s motto, and it was also his epitaph, 1484. He was a friend of Lorenzo dei Medici. It was also a favourite saying of Pico della Mirandola.

Liturgical use.—Introit for Mass on Quinquagesima Sunday (e).
Latins.—Prime on Wednesday.
Greeks.—On Monday morning.

PSALM XXVII. *Dominus illuminatio.*

THE Lord is my light, and my salvation; whom then shall I fear : the Lord is the strength of my life; of whom then shall I be afraid?

2 When the wicked, even mine enemies, and my foes, came upon me to eat up my flesh : they stumbled and fell.

3 Though an host of men were laid against me, yet shall not my heart be afraid : and though there rose up war against me, yet will I put my trust in him.

4 One thing have I desired of the Lord, which I will require : even that I may dwell in the house of the Lord all the days of my life, to behold the fair beauty of the Lord, and to visit his temple.

5 For in the time of trouble he shall hide me in his tabernacle : yea, in the secret place of his dwelling shall he hide me, and set me up upon a rock of stone.

6 And now shall he lift up mine head : above mine enemies round about me.

7 Therefore will I offer in his dwelling an oblation with great gladness : I will sing, and speak praises unto the Lord.

8 Hearken unto my voice, O Lord, when I cry unto thee : have mercy upon me, and hear me.

9 My heart hath talked of thee, "Seek ye my face" : "Thy face, Lord, will I seek."

10 O hide not thou thy face from me : nor cast thy servant away in displeasure.

11 Thou hast been my succour : leave me not, neither forsake me, O God of my salvation.

12 When my father and my mother forsake me : the Lord taketh me up.

13 Teach me thy way, O Lord : and lead me in the right way, because of mine enemies.

14 Deliver me not over into the will of mine adversaries : for there are false witnesses risen up against me, and such as speak wrong.

15 I should utterly have fainted : but that I believe verily to see the goodness of the Lord in the land of the living.

16 O tarry thou the Lord's leisure : be strong, and he shall comfort thine heart ; and put thou thy trust in the Lord.

This was one of the psalms with which St. Anselm cheered himself in his exile.

Lady Lawrence, in her diary for January, 1858, records that she read this psalm just before parting with her husband in India.

Verse 1. *Dominus illuminatio mea* is the Charles II. motto of Oxford University.

Verse 4. The last words of many of the saints, *e.g.*, SS. Peter Balsam, Magloire of Brittany, etc.

Verse 12. This verse inspired and comforted Mary Bosanquet (afterwards Mrs. Fletcher of Madeley), when, at the age of twenty-two, she was cast out of her father's house for Methodism.

Verse 15. "I believe to see," etc., were the Requiem words with which Richard Reynolds received his sentence of execution at Tyburn in 1535, for his adhesion to the autocracy of the Pope. He has been 'beatified' in our own time. Like many of the Psalms it has been said by those appointed to die, as they were carried along the old Tyburn Road from Newgate, which is now Holborn and Oxford Street. The gallows stood where 43, Connaught Square is now, near the Marble Arch.

Liturgical use.—A dirge psalm (see note on Ps. v.).
Latins.—Matins on Monday; Good Friday morning; Easter Eve.
Greeks.—Monday morning and Visitation of the Sick.

PSALM XXVIII. *Ad te, Domine.*

UNTO thee will I cry, O Lord my strength: think no scorn of me; lest, if thou make as though thou hearest not, I become like them that go down into the pit.

2 Hear the voice of my humble petitions, when I cry unto thee: when I hold up my hands towards the mercy-seat of thy holy temple.

3 O pluck me not away, neither destroy me with the ungodly and wicked doers: which speak friendly to their neighbours, but imagine mischief in their hearts.

4 Reward them according to their deeds: and according to the wickedness of their own inventions.

5 Recompense them after the work of their hands: pay them that they have deserved.

6 For they regard not in their mind the works of the Lord, nor the operation of his hands: therefore shall he break them down, and not build them up.

7 Praised be the Lord: for he hath heard the voice of my humble petitions.

8 The Lord is my strength, and my shield; my heart hath trusted in him, and I am helped: therefore my heart danceth for joy, and in my song will I praise him.

9 The Lord is my strength : and he is the wholesome defence of his Anointed.

10 O save thy people, and give thy blessing unto thine inheritance : feed them, and set them up for ever.

Verses 1 *and* 2. These were the verses which Albertus Magnus regarded as the type and model of all prayer. He was a Suabian by birth, became a Dominican, and was so learned that it was commonly said of him that "God had never divulged so many of His secrets to one of His creatures," and he must have practised evil arts to get them. He died in 1280.

Verse 8. *Dominus adiutor meus et protector meus: in ipso speravit cor meum.* These words were chosen by Edward the Black Prince as the motto for the silver coins he struck in Guienne, after his victories in France.

Verse 10. The last quarter of the *Te Deum* is wholly compiled from the Psalms, this verse forming vv. 22 and 23 of that hymn.

Latins.—Matins on Monday.
Greeks.—On Monday morning.

PSALM XXIX. *Afferte Domino.*

BRING unto the Lord, O ye mighty, bring young rams unto the Lord : ascribe unto the Lord worship and strength.

2 Give the Lord the honour due unto his Name : worship the Lord with holy worship.

3 It is the Lord, that commandeth the waters : it is the glorious God, that maketh the thunder.

4 It is the Lord, that ruleth the sea; the voice of the Lord is mighty in operation : the voice of the Lord is a glorious voice.

5 The voice of the Lord breaketh the cedar-trees : yea, the Lord breaketh the cedars of Libanus.

6 He maketh them also to skip like a calf : Libanus also, and Sirion, like a young unicorn.

7 The voice of the Lord divideth the flames of fire ; the voice of the Lord shaketh the wilderness : yea, the Lord shaketh the wilderness of Cades.

8 The voice of the Lord maketh the hinds to bring forth young, and discovereth the thick bushes : in his temple doth every man speak of his honour.

9 The Lord sitteth above the water-flood : and the Lord remaineth a King for ever.

10 The Lord shall give strength unto his people : the Lord shall give his people the blessing of peace.

This was the psalm sung at the baptism of Clovis, and of Ethelbert, and of all the converts from paganism in the warfare of the Church with Western and Northern barbarism.

Verse 8. " In his temple doth every man speak of his honour." These words are the motto, and suggested as the title, of George Herbert's "Sacred Poems and Private Ejaculations," which were published at Cambridge in 1633, and called " The Temple."

Latins.—Monday at Matins ; Epiphany Matins ; Adult Baptism.
Greeks.—Monday morning.

PSALM XXX. *Exaltabo te, Domine.*

I WILL magnify thee, O Lord, for thou hast set me up : and not made my foes to triumph over me.

2 O Lord my God, I cried unto thee : and thou hast healed me.

3 Thou, Lord, hast brought my soul out of hell : thou hast kept my life from them that go down to the pit.

4 Sing praises unto the Lord, O ye saints of his : and give thanks unto him for a remembrance of his holiness.

5 For his wrath endureth but the twinkling of an eye, and in his pleasure is life : heaviness may endure for a night, but joy cometh in the morning.

6 And in my prosperity I said, I shall never be removed : thou, Lord, of thy goodness hast made my hill so strong.

7 Thou didst turn thy face from me : and I was troubled.

8 Then cried I unto thee, O Lord : and gat me to my Lord right humbly.

9 " What profit is there in my blood : when I go down to the pit ?

10 " Shall the dust give thanks unto thee : or shall it declare thy truth ?

11 " Hear, O Lord, and have mercy upon me : Lord, be thou my helper."

12 Thou hast turned my heaviness into joy : thou hast put off my sackcloth, and girded me with gladness.

13 Therefore shall every good man sing of thy praise without ceasing : O my God, I will give thanks unto thee for ever.

This is the first of the musical psalms, as they are called from their titles. The others are xlviii., lxvii., lxviii., lxxv., xcii.

Verse 5. A common mediæval text for Easter Day, "alluded to in many of the Latin Easter hymns"; hence its Latin use on Easter Eve.

Liturgical use.—A dirge psalm (see Ps. v.).
Latins.—Monday Matins ; Easter Eve.
Greeks.—Monday morning ; Mesorion of third hour.

PSALM XXXI. *In te, Domine, speravi.*

IN thee, O Lord, have I put my trust : let me never be put to confusion, deliver me in thy righteousness.

2 Bow down thine ear to me : make haste to deliver me.

3 And be thou my strong rock, and house of defence : that thou mayest save me.

4 For thou art my strong rock, and my castle : be thou also my guide, and lead me for thy Name's sake.

5 Draw me out of the net, that they have laid privily for me : for thou art my strength.

6 Into thy hands I commend my spirit : for thou hast redeemed me, O Lord, thou God of truth.

7 I have hated them that hold of superstitious vanities : and my trust hath been in the Lord.

8 I will be glad, and rejoice in thy mercy : for thou hast considered my trouble, and hast known my soul in adversities.

9 Thou hast not shut me up into the hand of the enemy : but hast set my feet in a large room.

10 Have mercy upon me, O Lord, for I am in trouble : and mine eye is consumed for very heaviness ; yea, my soul and my body.

11 For my life is waxen old with heaviness : and my years with mourning.

12 My strength faileth me, because of mine iniquity: and my bones are consumed.

13 I became a reproof among all mine enemies, but especially among my neighbours : and they of mine acquaintance were afraid of me ; and they that did see me without conveyed themselves from me.

14 I am clean forgotten, as a dead man out of mind : I am become like a broken vessel.

15 For I have heard the blasphemy of the multitude : and fear is on every side, while they conspire together against me, and take their counsel to take away my life.

16 But my hope hath been in thee, O Lord : I have said, Thou art my God.

17 My time is in thy hand; deliver me from the hand of mine enemies : and from them that persecute me.

18 Shew thy servant the light of thy countenance : and save me for thy mercy's sake.

19 Let me not be confounded, O Lord, for I have called upon thee : let the ungodly be put to confusion, and be put to silence in the grave.

20 Let the lying lips be put to silence : which cruelly, disdainfully, and despitefully, speak against the righteous.

21 O how plentiful is thy goodness, which thou hast laid up for them that fear thee : and that thou hast prepared for them that put their trust in thee, even before the sons of men !

22 Thou shalt hide them privily by thine own presence from the provoking of all men : thou shalt keep them secretly in thy tabernacle from the strife of tongues.

23 Thanks be to the Lord : for he hath shewed me marvellous great kindness in a strong city.

24 And when I made haste, I said : I am cast out of the sight of thine eyes.

25 Nevertheless, thou heardest the voice of my prayer : when I cried unto thee.

26 O love the Lord, all ye his saints : for the Lord preserveth them that are faithful, and plenteously rewardeth the proud doer.

27 Be strong, and he shall establish your heart : all ye that put your trust in the Lord.

The fact that our Lord's last words were contained in this psalm would have given it a greater universal prominence, if it had not been that he inserted the word "Father," which makes it improbable that he meant merely to cite David's words. The enormous number of eminent and obscure Christians who have died with verse 6 on their lips is beyond all possible calculation. Even King Arthur, in the old romances, says his *In manus tuas*. Most of the earlier Saints, Christian Fathers, Schoolmen, even the heretics, the greater Reformers, and the victims of hatred or persecution on either side, used the psalm thus, *e.g.*, SS. Polycarp, Epiphanius Nicholas, Basil, Charlemagne, Louis and Bernard. Also Conradine and Mary Queen of Scots, and Northumberland, Suffolk, and Essex, at their executions. If Huss, Luther, Ridley, and Knox said the words when they were dying, so did the blessed Cuthbert Maine, John Nelson and Father Campion, in Elizabeth's time ; and John Houghton, Robert Lawrence, and Austin Webster, in 1535. Many only reached the first verse when the end came, *In te, Domine, speravi, non con-* *fundar in æternum*, were the last words of the heroic author of the hymn, "My God, I love Thee," Francis Xavier, the Jesuit missionary, who died on the sand of the island of Sancian, leaning on his crucifix. He was bent on reaching China, when death cut him off in 1552. Savonarola had meditated upon this psalm between his cruel torture and his judicial murder in 1498 (*vide* Ps. cxlviii.).

Verse 1. *In te, Domine, speravi*, is the heraldic motto of the House of Strathmore ; and *Esperance en Dieu* is that of the Percies of Northumberland.

Verse 6. *In manus tuas Domine, commendo spiritum meum* were the last words also of Columbus, as he died heartbroken at Valladolid, in 1506 ; as also of poor mad Tasso, in the monastery of St. Onofrio (1594) ; and of gentle George Herbert, at Bemerton, in 1632, etc.

Verse 7. On July 27th, 1628, Dr. Peter Smart preached from this a violent tirade against Cosin for ritualism, and stirred up the people to madness against a most moderate ritual. He was at once imprisoned and fined ; and this was made much of in Parliament as "the English counter-Reformation."

Latins.—Monday at Matins ; Compline daily (verses 1-6).
Greeks.—Monday morning ; late Lent Evensong.

PSALM XXXII. *Beati quorum.*

BLESSED is he whose unrighteousness is forgiven : and whose sin is covered.

2 Blessed is the man unto whom the Lord imputeth no sin : and in whose spirit there is no guile.

3 For while I held my tongue : my bones consumed away through my daily complaining.

4 For thy hand is heavy upon me day and night : and my moisture is like the drought in summer.

5 I will acknowledge my sin unto thee : and mine unrighteousness have I not hid.

6 I said, I will confess my sins unto the Lord : and so thou forgavest the wickedness of my sin.

7 For this shall everyone that is godly make his prayer unto thee, in a time when thou mayest be found : but in the great water-floods they shall not come nigh him.

8 Thou art a place to hide me in, thou shalt preserve me from trouble : thou shalt compass me about with songs of deliverance.

9 I will inform thee, and teach thee in the way wherein thou shalt go : and I will guide thee with mine eye.

10 Be ye not like to horse and mule, which have no understanding : whose mouths must be held with bit and bridle, lest they fall upon thee.

11 Great plagues remain for the ungodly : but whoso putteth his trust in the Lord, mercy embraceth him on every side.

12 Be glad, O ye righteous, and rejoice in the Lord ! and be joyful all ye that are true of heart.

The penitential psalms are vi., xxxii., xxxviii., li., cii., cxxx., cxliii.

This was the psalm prescribed against the deadly sin of pride.

St. Augustine of Hippo, to whom much was forgiven, used to repeat this weeping. He wrote it over his bed, that he might see it the first thing in the morning. At the end of his life, during the siege of Hippo, he had all Seven written in four columns over his bed, gazed on them, read and wept as he lay dying.

When St. Louis of France was dying, he repeated its verses in turn as best he could (1270) ; and Sir Thomas More read it, before his execution, with his daughter.

Piers Ploughman heard Hope blow his horn with it, and set all the saints in heaven a singing.

Verse 2. Izaak Walton's great hope was that he should attain to this "guileless spirit" before he died ; and, indeed, no man had more of it.

Verse 4. On Nov. 21st, 1693, Henry Wharton visited the meek, deprived Archbishop Sancroft, the non-juror, at Fressingfield, and found him, though he was old, poor, and dying, busy preparing Archbishop Laud's papers for publication. "That which came nearest to a complaint" was that he said this verse, but immediately added, "Though He slay me, yet will I trust in Him."

Verse 10. One cannot but remember here racy old Bishop Latimer's third sermon before King Edward VI., and his use of the verse, anent "the stout skorneful gentil man" and his mule, who said they both had absolution at Paul's Cross.

Luther declared that the best psalms were xxxii., li., cxxx., and cxliii., which he called the Pauline Psalms.

Liturgical use.—Ash Wednesday morning; Introit on 1st Sunday in Lent (e); the second penitential psalm.
Latins.—Monday Matins; All Saints' Day; Visitation of the Sick.
Greeks.—On Monday morning; Mesorion of third hour: after Baptism.

PSALM XXXIII. *Exultate, justi.*

REJOICE in the Lord, O ye righteous: for it becometh well the just to be thankful.

2 Praise the Lord with harp: sing praises unto him with the lute, and instrument of ten strings.

3 Sing unto the Lord a new song: sing praises lustily unto him with a good courage.

4 For the word of the Lord is true: and all his works are faithful.

5 He loveth righteousness and judgement: the earth is full of the goodness of the Lord.

6 By the word of the Lord were the heavens made: and all the host of them by the breath of his mouth.

7 He gathered the waters of the sea together, as it were upon an heap: and layeth up the deep, as in a treasure-house.

8 Let all the earth fear the Lord: stand in awe of him, all ye that dwell in the world.

9 For he spake, and it was done: he commanded, and it stood fast.

10 The Lord bringeth the counsel of the heathen to nought: and maketh the devices of the people to be of none effect, and casteth out the counsels of princes.

11 The counsel of the Lord shall endure for ever: and the thoughts of his heart from generation to generation.

12 Blessed are the people, whose God is the Lord

Jehovah : and blessed are the folk, that he hath chosen to him to be his inheritance.

13 The Lord looked down from heaven, and beheld all the children of men : from the habitation of his dwelling he considereth all them that dwell on the earth.

14 He fashioneth all the hearts of them : and understandeth all their works.

15 There is no king that can be saved by the multitude of an host : neither is any mighty man delivered by much strength.

16 A horse is counted but a vain thing to save a man : neither shall he deliver any man by his great strength.

17 Behold, the eye of the Lord is upon them that fear him : and upon them that put their trust in his mercy.

18 To deliver their soul from death : and to feed them in the time of dearth.

19 Our soul hath patiently tarried for the Lord : for he is our help, and our shield.

20 For our heart shall rejoice in him : because we have hoped in his holy Name.

21 Let thy merciful kindness, O Lord, be upon us : like as we do put our trust in thee.

St. Augustine fixed this as a hymn for martyrs.

Verse 2. It is probably to this verse we owe the fact that St. Gregory allowed the use of organs in the Western Church, and St. Thomas Aquinas did not condemn them. The mysteriousness of the decachord, regarded as the type of a heavenly instrument, kept the imagination and invention on the alert, and possibly resulted in that series of instruments, the last of which is the piano.

Liturgical use.—Introit for Whit Sunday (e),
Latins.—Monday morning ; for many Martyrs.
Greeks.—Monday morning.

PSALM XXXIV. *Benedicam Domino.*

I WILL alway give thanks unto the Lord : his praise shall ever be in my mouth.

2 My soul shall make her boast in the Lord : the humble shall hear thereof, and be glad.

3 O praise the Lord with me : and let us magnify his name together.

4 I sought the Lord, and he heard me : yea, he delivered me out of all my fear.

5 They had an eye unto him, and were lightened : and their faces were not ashamed.

6 Lo, the poor crieth, and the Lord heareth him : yea, and saveth him out of all his troubles.

7 The angel of the Lord tarrieth round about them that fear him : and delivereth them.

8 O taste, and see, how gracious the Lord is : blessed is the man that trusteth in him.

9 O fear the Lord, ye that are his saints : for they that fear him lack nothing.

10 The lions do lack, and suffer hunger : but they who seek the Lord shall want no manner of thing that is good.

11 Come, ye children, and hearken unto me : I will teach you the fear of the Lord.

12 What man is he that lusteth to live : and would fain see good days?

13 Keep thy tongue from evil : and thy lips, that they speak no guile.

14 Eschew evil, and do good : seek peace, and ensue it.

15 The eyes of the Lord are over the righteous : and his ears are open unto their prayers.

16 The countenance of the Lord is against them that do evil : to root out the remembrance of them from the earth.

17 The righteous cry, and the Lord heareth them : and delivereth them out of all their troubles.

18 The Lord is nigh unto them that are of a contrite heart : and will save such as be of an humble spirit.

19 Great are the troubles of the righteous : but the Lord delivereth him out of all.

20 He keepeth all his bones : so that not one of them is broken.

21 But misfortune shall slay the ungodly : and they that hate the righteous shall be desolate.

22 The Lord delivereth the souls of his servants : and

all they that put their trust in him shall not be destitute.

St. Theodore, the Martyr, was scourged to death singing this psalm.

Whatever be the weakness of Tate and Brady's version, their hymn of "Through all the changing scenes of life" (Ps. xxxiv.) is a very noble one.

Verse 5. When Bishop Fisher was on the scaffold, the southeast sun shined very brightly upon him, and he was heard to say, *Accedite ad eum et illuminamini et facies vestræ non confundentur.*

Verse 10. This is the last verse transcribed by St. Columba on Saturday, June 8, 597 A.D. He had a presentiment of his approaching end, walked out with some of the brethren, and thanked God, as he looked in at the granary, for the corn he had been able to lay up for the winter. Then he began to transcribe Ps. xxxiv., but coming to the tenth verse, remarked he might as well stop there. "The next words belong," said he, "rather to my successor than to myself." At the midnight Matins he was found on the altar step dying indeed, but smiling and blessing the brethren, and "doubtless seeing the holy angels coming to meet him."

Latins.—Monday Matins; for many Martyrs; All Saints' Day.
Greeks.—Monday morning.

PSALM XXXV. *Judica Domine.*

PLEAD thou my cause, O Lord, with them that strive with me : and fight thou against them that fight against me.

2 Lay hand upon the shield and buckler : and stand up to help me.

3 Bring forth the spear, and stop the way against them that persecute me : say unto my soul, I am thy salvation.

4 Let them be confounded, and put to shame, that seek after my soul : let them be turned back, and brought to confusion, that imagine mischief for me.

5 Let them be as the dust before the wind : and the angel of the Lord scattering them.

6 Let their way be dark and slippery : and let the angel of the Lord persecute them.

7 For they have privily laid their net to destroy me without a cause : yea, even without a cause have they made a pit for my soul.

8 Let a sudden destruction come upon him unawares, and his net, that he hath laid privily, catch himself: that he may fall into his own mischief.

9 And, my soul, be joyful in the Lord: it shall rejoice in his salvation.

10 All my bones shall say, "Lord, who is like unto thee, who delivereth the poor from him that is too strong for him: yea, the poor, and him that is in misery from him that spoileth him?"

11 False witnesses did rise up: they laid to my charge things that I knew not.

12 They rewarded me evil for good: to the great discomfort of my soul.

13 Nevertheless, when they were sick, I put on sackcloth, and humbled my soul with fasting: and my prayer shall turn into mine own bosom.

14 I behaved myself as though it had been my friend, or my brother: I went heavily, as one that mourneth for his mother.

15 But in mine adversity they rejoiced, and gathered themselves together: yea, the very abjects came together against me unawares, making mouths at me, and ceased not.

16 With the flatterers were busy mockers: who gnashed upon me with their teeth.

17 Lord, how long wilt thou look upon this: O deliver my soul from the calamities which they bring on me, and my darling from the lions.

18 So will I give thee thanks in the great congregation: I will praise thee among much people.

19 O let not them that are mine enemies triumph over me ungodly: neither let them wink with their eyes that hate me without a cause.

20 And why? their communing is not for peace: but they imagine deceitful words against them that are quiet in the land.

21 They gaped upon me with their mouths, and said: "Fie on thee, fie on thee, we saw it with our eyes."

22 This thou hast seen, O Lord: hold not thy tongue, then, go not far from me, O Lord.

23 Awake, and stand up to judge my quarrel: avenge thou my cause, my God, and my Lord.

24 Judge me, O Lord my God, according to thy righteousness : and let them not triumph over me.

25 Let them not say in their hearts, "There, there, so would we have it" : neither let them say, "We have devoured him."

26 Let them be put to confusion and shame together, that rejoice at my trouble : let them be clothed with rebuke and dishonour, that boast themselves against me.

27 Let them be glad and rejoice, that favour my righteous dealing : yea, let them say alway, "Blessed be the Lord, who hath pleasure in the prosperity of his servant."

28 And as for my tongue, it shall be talking of thy righteousness : and of thy praise all the day long.

"What is there necessary for man to know, which the Psalms are not able to teach? They are, to beginners, an easy and familiar introduction ; a mighty augmentation of all virtue and knowledge, in such as are entered before ; a strong confirmation to the most perfect amongst others. Heroical magnanimity, exquisite justice, grave moderation, exact wisdom, patience unfeigned, unwearied patience, the mysteries of God, the sufferings of Christ, the terrors of wrath, the comforts of grace, the works of Providence over this world, and the promised joys of the world which is to come, all good necessarily to be either known, or done, or had, this one celestial fountain yieldeth. Let there be any grief or disease incident unto the soul of man, any wound or sickness named, for which there is not in this treasure-house a present comfortable remedy at all times ready to be found. Hereof it is that we covet to make the Psalms especially familiar unto us all" (Hooker).

This celebrated passage is a witness to the power of the Psalter in yet another way ; for though it is quoted even by the extremest Protestant, it was originally derived from the exposition of Torquemada, the Dominican Inquisitor (1420-98).

Verse 19. The words, "They hated me without a cause," are quoted by Christ in His last discourses to His disciples (St. John xv. 25).

Latins.—Monday Matins.
Greeks.—Monday morning.

PSALM XXXVI. *Dixit injustus.*

MY heart showeth me the wickedness of the ungodly : that there is no fear of God before his eyes.

2 For he flattereth himself in his own sight : until his abominable sin be found out.

3 The words of his mouth are unrighteous and full

of deceit : he hath left off to behave himself wisely, and to do good.

4 He imagineth mischief upon his bed, and hath set himself in no good way : neither doth he abhor anything that is evil.

5 Thy mercy, O Lord, reacheth unto the heavens : and thy faithfulness unto the clouds.

6 Thy righteousness standeth like the strong mountains : thy judgements are like the great deep.

7 Thou, Lord, shalt save both man and beast ; How excellent is thy mercy, O God : and the children of men shall put their trust under the shadow of thy wings.

8 They shall be satisfied with the plenteousness of thy house : and thou shalt give them drink of thy pleasures, as out of the river.

9 For with thee is the well of life : and in thy light shall we see light.

10 O continue forth thy loving-kindness unto them that know thee : and thy righteousness unto them that are true of heart.

11 O let not the foot of pride come against me : and let not the hand of the ungodly cast me down.

12 There are they fallen, all that work wickedness : they are cast down, and shall not be able to stand.

Verse 5. Mr. Ruskin uses this verse to instance the fact that in those psalms which most distinctly set forth the power of God, clouds and heavens are used as interchangeable words, and as constant revelations of Him. And so, " by accepting the words in their simple sense, we are led to apprehend the immediate presence of the Deity and His purpose of manifesting Himself as near us whenever the storm-cloud stoops upon its course ; while, by our vague and inaccurate acceptance of the words, we remove the idea of His presence far from us into a region which we can neither see nor know ; and gradually from the close realization of a living God who ' maketh the clouds His chariot,' we refine and explain ourselves into dim and distant suspicion of an inactive God, inhabiting inconceivable places, and fading into the multitudinous formalisms of the laws of nature."

Verse 7. Piers Ploughman heard all the saints in heaven sing this at once, for joy over sinners that repent.

Verse 9. The expression *Lumen de Lumine* (Light of Light) in the Nicene Creed was adopted from this verse.

Latins.—Monday Matins.
Greeks.—Monday morning.

PSALM XXXVII. *Noli æmulari.*

FRET not thyself because of the ungodly : neither be thou envious against the evil doers.

2 For they shall soon be cut down like the grass : and be withered even as the green herb.

3 Put thou thy trust in the Lord, and be doing good : dwell in the land, and verily thou shalt be fed.

4 Delight thou in the Lord : and he shall give thee thy heart's desire.

5 Commit thy way unto the Lord, and put thy trust in him : and he shall bring it to pass.

6 He shall make thy righteousness as clear as the light : and thy just dealing as the noonday.

7 Hold thee still in the Lord, and abide patiently upon him : but grieve not thyself at him, whose way doth prosper, against the man that doeth after evil counsels.

8 Leave off from wrath, and let go displeasure : fret not thyself, else shalt thou be moved to do evil.

9 Wicked doers shall be rooted out : and they that patiently abide the Lord, those shall inherit the land.

10 Yet a little while, and the ungodly shall be clean gone : thou shalt look after his place, and he shall be away.

11 But the meek-spirited shall possess the earth : and shall be refreshed in the multitude of peace.

12 The ungodly seeketh counsel against the just : and gnasheth upon him with his teeth.

13 The Lord shall laugh him to scorn : for he hath seen that his day is coming.

14 The ungodly have drawn out the sword, and have bent their bow : to cast down the poor and needy, and to slay such as are of a right conversation.

15 Their sword shall go through their own heart : and their bow shall be broken.

16 A small thing that the righteous hath : is better than great riches of the ungodly.

17 For the arms of the ungodly shall be broken : and the Lord upholdeth the righteous.

18 The Lord knoweth the days of the godly : and their inheritance shall endure for ever.

19 They shall not be confounded in the perilous time : and in the days of dearth they shall have enough.

20 As for the ungodly, they shall perish ; and the enemies of the Lord shall consume as the fat of lambs : yea, even as the smoke, shall they consume away.

21 The ungodly borroweth, and payeth not again : but the righteous is merciful, and liberal.

22 Such as are blessed of God shall possess the land : and they that are cursed of him shall be rooted out.

23 The Lord ordereth a good man's going : and maketh his way acceptable to himself.

24 Though he fall, he shall not be cast away : for the Lord upholdeth him with his hand.

25 I have been young, and now am old : and yet saw I never the righteous forsaken, nor his seed begging their bread.

26 The righteous is ever merciful, and lendeth : and his seed is blessed.

27 Flee from evil, and do the thing that is good : and dwell for evermore.

28 For the Lord loveth the thing that is right : he forsaketh not his that be godly, but they are preserved for ever.

29 The unrighteous shall be punished : as for the seed of the ungodly, it shall be rooted out.

30 The righteous shall inherit the land : and dwell therein for ever.

31 The mouth of the righteous is exercised in wisdom : and his tongue will be talking of judgement.

32 The law of his God is in his heart : and his goings shall not slide.

33 The ungodly seeth the righteous : and seeketh occasion to slay him.

34 The Lord will not leave him in his hand : nor condemn him when he is judged.

35 Hope thou in the Lord, and keep his way, and he shall promote thee, that thou shalt possess the land : when the ungodly shall perish, thou shalt see it.

36 I myself have seen the ungodly in great power : and flourishing like a green bay-tree.

37 I went by, and lo, he was gone : I sought him, but his place could nowhere be found.

38 Keep innocency, and take heed unto the thing that is right : for that shall bring a man peace at the last.

39 As for the transgressors, they shall perish together : and the end of the ungodly is, they shall be rooted out at the last.

40 But the salvation of the righteous cometh of the Lord : who is also their strength in the time of trouble.

41 And the Lord shall stand by them, and save them : he shall deliver them from the ungodly, and shall save them, because they put their trust in him.

Verse 3. *Spera in Domino.* Don Manuel of Portugal took this as his motto, and spelt it *sphera.* Hence all the churches of his time are capped by a sphere, for hope, instead of a cross.

Verse 5. A favourite verse of Dr. Livingstone, the great African traveller.

Verse 11. Fuller's "mixed contemplation" on this, which he calls "Good Auguries," comforted many distressed souls in the confusions and hopes which came with the decline of the Commonwealth. "I was much affected with reading that distich in Ovid, as having something extraordinary therein :

'*Tarpeia quondam prædixit ab ilice cornix,*
Est bene non potuit dicere dixit erit.'

'The crow sometimes did sit and spell on top of Tarpie Hall;
She could not say, All's well! all's well! but said, It shall! it shall!'

But what do I listen to the language of the crow, whose black colour hath a cast of hell therein, in superstitious soothsaying? Let us hearken to what the Dove of the Holy Spirit saith, promising God's servants that, though the present times be bad, the future will be better. Ps. xxxvii. 11 : 'The meek shall inherit the earth, and shall delight themselves in the abundance of peace.'"

Verse 23. One cannot but remember here Thackeray's picture in "The Newcomes" of the old colonel in the Grey Friars' Almshouse, in the black gown of the pensioners and the order of the Bath on his breast, standing among the Poor Brethren and repeating the responses of the Founder's psalm.

Verse 24. This was Henry de Blois, the Bishop of Winchester's, comment, when he heard of the martyrdom of St. Thomas of Canterbury; as it was St. Gregory Nazianzen's when his sister Gorgonia died.

Verse 25. Piers Ploughman concluded from this that " the Book banneth beggary."
Verse 27. Benedict of Aniane (821 A.D.), who braved the hostility of the nobles by his fearless championship of the poor, used often to say, " If it seems to you impossible to keep many commandments, then keep only this one little commandment, 'Flee from evil, and do the thing that is good.'"

Latins.—Monday Matins.
Greeks.—Monday morning.

PSALM XXXVIII. *Domine, ne in furore.*

PUT me not to rebuke, O Lord, in thine anger : neither chasten me in thy heavy displeasure.

2 For thine arrows stick fast in me : and thy hand presseth me sore.

3 There is no health in my flesh, because of thy displeasure : neither is there any rest in my bones, by reason of my sin.

4 For my wickednesses are gone over my head : and are like a sore burden, too heavy for me to bear.

5 My wounds stink, and are corrupt : through my foolishness.

6 I am brought into so great trouble and misery : that I go mourning all the day long.

7 For my loins are filled with a sore disease : and there is no whole part in my body.

8 I am feeble, and sore smitten : I have roared for the very disquietness of my heart.

9 Lord, thou knowest all my desire : and my groaning is not hid from thee.

10 My heart panteth, my strength hath failed me : and the sight of mine eyes is gone from me.

11 My lovers and my neighbours did stand looking upon my trouble : and my kinsmen stood afar off.

12 They also that sought after my life laid snares for me : and they that went about to do me evil talked of wickedness, and imagined deceit all the day long.

13 As for me, I was like a deaf man, and heard not : and as one that is dumb, who doth not open his mouth.

14 I became even as a man that heareth not : and in whose mouth are no reproofs.

15 For in thee, O Lord, have I put my trust : thou shalt answer for me, O Lord my God.

16 I have required that they, even mine enemies, should not triumph over me : for when my foot slipped, they rejoiced greatly against me.

17 And I, truly, am set in the plague : and my heaviness is ever in my sight.

18 For I will confess my wickedness : and be sorry for my sin.

19 But mine enemies live, and are mighty : and they that hate me wrongfully are many in number.

20 They also that reward evil for good are against me : because I follow the thing that good is.

21 Forsake me not, O Lord my God : be not thou far from me.

22 Haste thee to help me : O Lord God of my salvation.

The third penitential psalm. These are, vi., xxxii., xxxviii., li., cii., cxxx., and cxliii. This is the antidote against the deadly sin of gluttony (*contra Gulam*).

St. Louis of France, when death was at hand, "received the last sacraments of the Church with a full consciousness, as appeared by this, that while they were anointing him with holy oil and saying the seven psalms, he repeated the verses in his turn."

Sir Thomas Wyatt, "the delight of the Muses and of mankind," the poet of the dawn of English poetry,

"Amid great storms, whom grace assured so
To live upright and smile at fortune's choice,"

(1503-1542) wrote in his youth a book of "the vii. penytentiall psalmes, drawen into Englyshe meter," which Sir John Harrington edited and dedicated to the brother of Queen Catharine Parr. Sir Thomas was a close student of Dante. He depicts David singing this psalm to his harp in a cave, with great and many tears—

" But who had been without the cave's mouth,
And heard the tears and sighs that him did strain,
He would have sworn, there had out of the south,
A lukewarm wind brought forth a smoky rain."

Edmund Spenser also wrote a paraphrase upon the penitential psalms, which is lost.

Verse 15. "Thou shalt answer for me, O Lord my God," suggested to George Herbert his matchless and most characteristic poem, "The Quip," the burden of which is—

"Thou shalt answer, Lord, for me." The World with Beauty, Money, Glory, and Wit in turn jeered at the poet—

"Yet when the houre of Thy designe
To answer these fine things shall come,

Speak not at large, say, I am thine,
And then they have their answer home."

The same text was one of the last recorded sayings of John Wesley.

Liturgical use.—Ash Wednesday morning.
Latins.—Monday Matins; Good Friday Matins; Visitation of the Sick.
Greeks.—Monday evening; Dawn in Lent.

PSALM XXXIX. *Dixi, custodiam.*

I SAID, " I will take heed to my ways : that I offend not in my tongue.

2 " I will keep my mouth as it were with a bridle : while the ungodly is in my sight."

3 I held my tongue, and spake nothing : I kept silence, yea, even from good words; but it was pain and grief to me.

4 My heart was hot within me, and while I was thus musing the fire kindled : and at the last I spake with my tongue ;

5 " Lord, let me know mine end, and the number of my days : that I may be certified how long I have to live.

6 " Behold, thou hast made my days as it were a span long : and mine age is even as nothing in respect of thee ; and verily every man living is altogether vanity.

7 " For man walketh in a vain shadow, and disquieteth himself in vain : he heapeth up riches, and cannot tell who shall gather them.

8 " And now, Lord, what is my hope : truly my hope is even in thee.

9 " Deliver me from all mine offences : and make me not a rebuke unto the foolish.

10 " I became dumb, and opened not my mouth : for it was thy doing.

11 " Take thy plague away from me : I am even consumed by means of thy heavy hand.

12 " When thou with rebukes dost chasten man for sin, thou makest his beauty to consume away, like as it were a moth fretting a garment : every man therefore is but vanity.

13 " Hear my prayer, O Lord, and with thine ears consider my calling : hold not thy peace at my tears.

14 "For I am a stranger with thee : and a sojourner, as all my fathers were.

15 "O spare me a little, that I may recover my strength : before I go hence, and be no more seen."

Archbishop Leighton's favourite psalm.

St. Ambrose was stirred up by this psalm to write his book of Offices, being much moved by its holy tone, patience, apt speech, and its contempt of riches, which is the foundation of all virtue.

Verse 1. Socrates Scholasticus tells us that Isidore gave this as the first lesson to St. Pambo. After nineteen years the pupil complained that he had not yet been able to learn it, in spite of the most diligent study ; so that he was not yet ready for the second lesson. See, also, Browning's "Jocoseria."

Verse 4. Keble used to say that this verse contained the secret of all poetry — strong feeling, meditative reason, and lastly, expression.

Verse 10. John Calvin passed the last of his days "almost wholly in prayers. His voice was chokt with the asthma, and his eyes, which to the end shone clearly, were raised to heaven, and his face was as composed as the ardour of prayer allowed. Often in his pain he groaned out David's words, ' I became dumb, Lord, for it was Thy doing,' and sometimes Isaiah's ' I mourned as a dove.' He was also heard to say, ' Thou afflictest me, O Lord, but it is fully enough for me that it is Thy hand.'"

Liturgical use.—Burial psalm.
Latins.—Tuesday morning.
Greeks.—Monday evening.

PSALM XL. *Expectans expectavi.*

I WAITED patiently for the Lord : and he inclined unto me, and heard my calling.

2 He brought me also out of the horrible pit, out of the mire and clay : and set my feet upon the rock, and ordered my goings.

3 And he hath put a new song in my mouth : even a thanksgiving unto our God.

4 Many shall see it, and fear : and shall put their trust in the Lord.

5 Blessed is the man that hath set his hope in the Lord : and turned not unto the proud, and to such as go about with lies.

6 O Lord, my God, great are the wondrous works which thou hast done, like as be also thy thoughts

which are to us-ward : and yet there is no man that ordereth them unto thee.

7 If I should declare them, and speak of them : they should be more than I am able to express.

8 Sacrifice, and meat offering, thou wouldest not : but mine ears hast thou opened.

9 Burnt offerings, and sacrifice for sin, hast thou not required : then said I, " Lo, I come.

10 " In the volume of the book it is written of me, that I should fulfil thy will, O my God : I am content to do it ; yea, thy law is within my heart."

11 I have declared thy righteousness in the great congregation : lo, I will not refrain my lips, O Lord, and that thou knowest.

12 I have not hid thy righteousness within my heart : my talk hath been of thy truth, and of thy salvation.

13 I have not kept back thy loving mercy and truth : from the great congregation.

14 Withdraw not thou thy mercy from me, O Lord : let thy loving-kindness and thy truth alway preserve me.

15 For innumerable troubles are come about me ; my sins have taken such hold upon me that I am not able to look up : yea, they are more in number than the hairs of my head, and my heart hath failed me.

16 O Lord, let it be thy pleasure to deliver me : make haste, O Lord, to help me.

17 Let them be ashamed, and confounded together, that seek after my soul to destroy it : let them be driven backward, and put to rebuke, that wish me evil.

18 Let them be desolate, and rewarded with shame : that say unto me, " Fie upon thee, fie upon thee."

19 Let all those that seek thee be joyful and glad in thee : and let such as love thy salvation say alway, " The Lord be praised."

20 As for me, I am poor and needy : but the Lord careth for me.

21 Thou art my helper and redeemer : make no long tarrying, O my God.

Among the smallest books in the British Museum are two little volumes the size of a postage stamp (64mo). They were published in Birmingham in 1855, and contain one this psalm and one P's. cxlv. The words are clearly printed, but without note or comment. The catalogue number is 1221. i. Each psalm is the cry of a poor man, and the little volumes are but driftweed, which tells of a whole continent—small tokens of the love which the unknown many have had for these poems.

There is a beautiful legend of David, quoted by the old *Guardian* (No. 138), from the Rabbins, that Adam saw the spirits of all his sons pass before him. The most beautiful of all, he was told, was but to live one year. He prayed and obtained his prayer, that threescore and ten of his own years should be given to this spirit, and thus Adam fell short of one thousand years by David's seventy. The story not only "shows the high opinion that the Rabbins entertained of the sweet Psalmist of Israel," but also tells that the Psalms seemed to them to fulfil human life.

Verses 1 and 2 were the last words of St. Francis de Sales, and to them he added only *Advesperascit et inclinata est jam dies.*

Liturgical use.—Good Friday morning.
Latins.—Tuesday Matins; Good Friday.
Greeks.—Monday evening.

PSALM XLI. *Beatus qui intelligit.*

BLESSED is he that considereth the poor and needy : the Lord shall deliver him in the time of trouble.

2 The Lord preserve him, and keep him alive, that he may be blessed upon earth : and deliver not thou him into the will of his enemies.

3 The Lord comfort him, when he lieth sick upon his bed : make thou all his bed in his sickness.

4 I said, "Lord, be merciful unto me : heal my soul, for I have sinned against thee."

5 Mine enemies speak evil of me : "When shall he die, and his name perish?"

6 And if he come to see me, he speaketh vanity : and his heart conceiveth falsehood within himself, and when he cometh forth he telleth it.

7 All mine enemies whisper together against me : even against me do they imagine this evil.

8 "Let the sentence of guiltiness proceed against him : and now that he lieth, let him rise up no more."

9 Yea, even mine own familiar friend, whom I trusted : who did also eat of my bread, hath laid great wait for me.

10 But be thou merciful unto me, O Lord : raise thou me up again, and I shall reward them.

11 By this I know thou favourest me : that mine enemy doth not triumph against me.

12 And when I am in my health, thou upholdest me : and shalt set me before thy face for ever.

13 Blessed be the Lord God of Israel : world without end. Amen.

It has been the text of many famous political sermons, *e.g.*, Bishop Hacket upon the Gowrie Conspiracy (verse 9), and Dr. T. Laurie upon the Victory of Waterloo (verses 1-3).

This is a dirge psalm, because St. Augustine interprets it (with Psalms iii., xvi., and lxviii.) as prophetic of the resurrection.

Verse 6. St. Ambrose calls this Judas Iscariot's verse, and indeed this whole psalm used always to be applied to him. Hence at Milan it was always used on Wednesday, the day of the betrayal.

Verse 9. Our Lord Himself applies this verse to Judas (St. John xiii. 18).

Liturgical use.—English dirge (see Ps. v.).
Latins.—Tuesday Matins.
Greeks.—Monday evening.

PSALM XLII. *Quemadmodum.*

LIKE as the hart desireth the water-brooks : so longeth my soul after thee, O God.

2 My soul is athirst for God, yea, even for the living God : when shall I come to appear before the presence of God ?

3 My tears have been my meat day and night : while they daily say unto me, Where is now thy God ?

4 Now when I think thereupon, I pour out my heart by myself : for I went with the multitude, and brought them forth into the house of God ;

5 In the voice of praise and thanksgiving : among such as keep holy-day.

6 Why art thou so full of heaviness, O my soul : and why art thou so disquieted within me ?

7 Put thy trust in God; for I will yet give him thanks for the help of his countenance.

8 My God, my soul is vexed within me : therefore will I remember thee concerning the land of Jordan, and the little hill of Hermon.

9 One deep calleth another, because of the noise of

the water-pipes : all thy waves and storms are gone over me.

10 The Lord hath granted his loving-kindness in the daytime : and in the night-season did I sing of him, and made my prayer unto the God of my life.

11 I will say unto the God of my strength, "Why hast thou forgotten me : why go I thus heavily, while the enemy oppresseth me?"

12 My bones are smitten asunder as with a sword : while mine enemies that trouble me cast me in the teeth;

13 Namely, while they say daily unto me : "Where is now thy God?"

14 Why art thou so vexed, O my soul : and why art thou so disquieted within me?

15 O put thy trust in God : for I will yet thank him, which is the help of my countenance, and my God.

This psalm was formerly used in the English Burial Service: and because it was said over the bodies of our fathers for many generations it is very appropriate as a devotion in the presence of the dead. It acquires a new and tender significance in this use.

"As pants the hart for cooling streams" is perhaps the most successful of Tate and Brady's version of the Psalter.

In reference to this psalm, the hart appears often upon the walls of the catacombs and in later Christian art and heraldry.

"From the time of" Lord William Russell's "imprisonment, he looked upon himself as a dead man, and turned his thoughts wholly to another world. He read much in the Scriptures, particularly in the Psalms, and read Baxter's 'Dying Thoughts,'" in which Ps. xlii. is very prominent. "Be not cast down, O departing soul, nor by unbelief disquieted within me. Trust in God, for thou shalt quickly by experience be taught to give Him thanks and praise, who is the health of my countenance and my God." Lord Russell on his way to the scaffold in Lincoln's Inn Fields "was singing psalms a great part of the way, and said he hoped to sing better very soon."

The psalm was one of Bede's favourites, and he turned it into Latin verse.

Verse 8. St. Maur used to retire from the busy cares of his bishopric, when the troubles of his office vexed him, to a little grove where he had a cell, his "little hill of Hermon," with as much delight as if he were going to a banquet. He was buried there at the last, and his shrine raised where his Hermon once stood.

Verse 9. The mediæval explanation of this was always mystical. "The deep of misery to the deep of mercy" is the usual comment upon it.

Liturgical use.—In the dirge (see Ps. v.); Requiem (e).
Latins.—Matins on Tuesday; Baptism of Adults.
Greeks.—On Monday evening.

PSALM XLIII. *Judica me, Deus.*

GIVE sentence with me, O God, and defend my cause against the ungodly people : O deliver me from the deceitful and wicked man.

2 For thou art the God of my strength, why hast thou put me from thee : and why go I so heavily, while the enemy oppresseth me?

3 O send out thy light and thy truth, that they may lead me : and bring me unto thy holy hill, and to thy dwelling.

4 And that I may go unto the altar of God, even unto the God of my joy and gladness : and upon the harp will I give thanks unto thee, O God, my God.

5 Why art thou so heavy, O my soul : and why art thou so disquieted within me?

6 O put thy trust in God : for I will yet give him thanks, which is the help of my countenance, and my God.

This psalm belongs to the *Secreta* at Mass, and has been for centuries the psalm by which the priest prepares himself for the celebration of the great Christian service.

It was sung at the baptism of St. Augustine by St. Ambrose, at which time the *Te Deum* is said to have been composed.

When Henry of Richmond landed at Milford Haven (in 1485), he straightway knelt upon the shore, raised his gray eyes to heaven, and recited *Judica me, Deus* all through. His fine fair hair, long neck, bright complexion, and smiling mouth had not yet toned down into the thin-lipped, almost monkish-looking king of later pictures. He seems to have retained a love of this psalm to the end of his life.

Liturgical use.—Introit to 3rd Sunday in Lent (e).
Latins.—Tuesday at Lauds.
Greeks.—Monday evening.

PSALM XLIV. *Deus, auribus.*

WE have heard with our ears, O God, our fathers have told us : what thou hast done in their time of old;

2 How thou hast driven out the heathen with thy

hand, and planted them in : how thou hast destroyed the nations, and cast them out.

3 For they gat not the land in possession through their own sword : neither was it their own arm that helped them ;

4 But thy right hand, and thine arm, and the light of thy countenance : because thou hadst a favour unto them.

5 Thou art my King, O God : send help unto Jacob.

6 Through thee will we overthrow our enemies : and in thy Name will we tread them under, that rise up against us.

7 For I will not trust in my bow : it is not my sword that shall help me ;

8 But it is thou that savest us from our enemies : and puttest them to confusion that hate us.

9 We make our boast of God all day long : and will praise thy Name for ever.

10 But now thou art far off, and puttest us to confusion : and goest not forth with our armies.

11 Thou makest us to turn our backs upon our enemies : so that they which hate us spoil our goods.

12 Thou lettest us be eaten up like sheep : and hast scattered us among the heathen.

13 Thou sellest thy people for nought : and takest no money for them.

14 Thou makest us to be rebuked of our neighbours : to be laughed to scorn, and had in derision of them that are round about us.

15 Thou makest us to be a by-word among the heathen : and that the people shake their heads at us.

16 My confusion is daily before me : and the shame of my face hath covered me ;

17 For the voice of the slanderer and blasphemer : for the enemy and avenger.

18 And though all this be come upon us, yet do we not forget thee : nor behave ourselves frowardly in thy covenant.

19 Our heart is not turned back : neither our steps gone out of thy way ;

20 No, not when thou hast smitten us into the place of dragons : and covered us with the shadow of death.

21 If we have forgotten the Name of our God, and holden up our hands to any strange god : shall not God search it out ? for he knoweth the very secrets of the heart.

22 For thy sake also are we killed all the day long : and are counted as sheep appointed to be slain.

23 Up, Lord, why sleepest thou : awake, and be not absent from us for ever.

24 Wherefore hidest thou thy face : and forgettest our misery and trouble ?

25 For our soul is brought low, even unto the dust : our belly cleaveth unto the ground.

26 Arise, and help us : and deliver us for thy mercy's sake.

Verse 1. In 1544 Cranmer added the opening words of this psalm to our Litany : "O God, we have heard with our ears, and our fathers have declared unto us, the noble works that thou didst in their days, and in the old time before them." He took them from the lesser Litany of Salisbury, and the words are a translation of the Vulgate, and from none of our versions, which, it is needless to say, caused some offence to the severer critics of the Prayer-book.

Verse 22. Quoted by St. Paul, to show how the Catholic Faith brings light out of the darkest things of life—" God's throne from man's grave " (Rom. viii. 36).

Verse 23. St. Ambrose of Milan died as he was dictating a commentary. He had just reached this verse.

Latins.—Tuesday Matins.
Greeks.—Monday evening.

PSALM XLV. *Eructavit cor meum.*

MY heart is inditing of a good matter : I speak of the things which I have made unto the King.

2 My tongue is the pen : of a ready writer.

3 Thou art fairer than the children of men : full of grace are thy lips, because God hath blessed thee for ever.

4 Gird thee with thy sword upon thy thigh, O thou most Mighty : according to thy worship and renown.

5 Good luck have thou with thine honour : ride on, because of the word of truth, of meekness, and righteousness ; and thy right hand shall teach thee terrible things.

6 Thy arrows are very sharp, and the people shall be subdued unto thee : even in the midst among the King's enemies.

7 Thy seat, O God, endureth for ever : the sceptre of thy kingdom is a right sceptre.

8 Thou hast loved righteousness, and hated iniquity : wherefore God, even thy God, hath anointed thee with the oil of gladness above thy fellows.

9 All thy garments smell of myrrh, aloes, and cassia : out of the ivory palaces, whereby they have made thee glad.

10 Kings' daughters were among thy honourable women : upon thy right hand did stand the queen in a vesture of gold, wrought about with divers colours.

11 Hearken, O daughter, and consider, incline thine ear : forget also thine own people, and thy father's house.

12 So shall the King have pleasure in thy beauty : for he is thy Lord God, and worship thou him.

13 And the daughter of Tyre shall be there with a gift : like as the rich also among the people shall make their supplication before thee.

14 The King's daughter is all glorious within : her clothing is of wrought gold.

15 She shall be brought unto the King in raiment of needlework : the virgins that be her fellows shall bear her company, and shall be brought unto thee.

16 With joy and gladness shall they be brought : and shall enter into the King's palace.

17 Instead of thy fathers thou shalt have children : whom thou mayest make princes in all lands.

18 I will remember thy name from one generation to another : therefore shall the people give thanks unto thee, world without end.

St. Columba with his tremendous voice chanted this psalm so loud, when a body of Picts interrupted his evening devotions, near the mouth of the river Ness, that they fled in fear and amazement. He was remarkable for his power of voice.

Verse 1. *Eructavit cor meum, verbum bonum.* This was a verse often quoted against the Arians. St. Athanasius, for instance, says, "Let the Son of God be always and everywhere acknowledged to be what He is, the living Counsel, the genuine and co-essential Offspring of the Father, just as the brightness is of the light; for thus the Father Himself hath spoken: 'My heart hath given forth a good Word.'"

Verse 7. The Arian leaders, Arius and Eusebius, on the other hand, "were always talking about this verse in streets, shops, and market-places." It was their stronghold.

Verse 8. "I have loved righteousness, and hated iniquity, and therefore I die in exile," were the last words of the fierce and masterful Hildebrand, who did so much to enlarge and consolidate the power of the Papacy.

Verse 11. Capgrave's comment upon the baptism of baby Henry VI. applies this verse to those "regenerate in baptism, who are to forget the House of Wrath."

Liturgical use.—Christmas morning.
Latins.—Matins on Tuesday; Christmas Day; Circumcision; Festivals of Our Lady; Apostles and Evangelists.
Greeks.—Monday evening.

PSALM XLVI. *Deus noster refugium.*

GOD is our hope and strength : a very present help in trouble.

2 Therefore will we not fear, though the earth be moved : and though the hills be carried into the midst of the sea.

3 Though the waters thereof rage and swell : and though the mountains shake at the tempest of the same.

4 The rivers of the flood thereof shall make glad the city of God : the holy place of the tabernacle of the most Highest.

5 God is in the midst of her, therefore shall she not be removed : God shall help her, and that right early.

6 The heathen make much ado, and the kingdoms are moved : but God hath showed his voice, and the earth shall melt away.

7 The Lord of hosts is with us : the God of Jacob is our refuge.

8 O come hither, and behold the works of the Lord : what destruction he hath brought upon the earth.

9 He maketh wars to cease in all the world : he breaketh the bow, and knappeth the spear in sunder, and burneth the chariots in the fire.

10 "Be still then, and know that I am God : I will be exalted among the heathen, and I will be exalted in the earth."

11 The Lord of hosts is with us : the God of Jacob is our refuge.

This psalm is the foundation of Luther's hymn, *Ein' feste Burg ist unser Gott*, which has played such a prominent part in German history, and was the "Marseillaise of the Reformation."

On June 19, 1645, after the battle of Naseby, both Houses of Parliament attended a thanksgiving service in the Grey Friars' Church, and dined together in the Grocers' Hall, Poultry. After dinner they sang together their favourite Ps. xlvi.

Verse 7. "God was our refuge and strength : the Lord of armies was with us : the God of Jacob was our Protector." These words are the epitaph of brave Blanche Lady Arundel, who defended Wardour Castle with a handful of men, and held it for the king against Hungerford, Ludlow, and an army. She obtained at last honourable terms, not very honourably kept. Her husband was killed fighting for the king at Oxford. She was a large-eyed lady, with a flexible, humorous mouth, whose picture still survives at Arundel Castle.

Verse 10. Vincent of Lerins (*ob.* 450 A.D.) chose the quiet abbey in the island off Cannes as his lot in life, that he might without great distraction practise that psalm-song, *Vacate et videte quoniam ego sum Deus;* and so, after divers and sad storms in the wars of the world, he sheltered himself in "the most certain port of the religious life."

Latins.—Matins on Tuesday ; Epiphany ; Dedication festivals ; Our Lady.
Greeks.—Monday evening ; Mesorion of first hour.

PSALM XLVII. *Omnes gentes, plaudite.*

O CLAP your hands together, all ye people : O sing unto God with the voice of melody.

2 For the Lord is high, and to be feared : he is the great King upon all the earth.

3 He shall subdue the people under us : and the nations under our feet.

4 He shall choose out an heritage for us : even the worship of Jacob, whom he loved.

5 God is gone up with a merry noise : and the Lord with the sound of the trump.

6 O sing praises, sing praises unto our God : O sing praises, sing praises unto our King.

7 For God is the King of all the earth : sing ye praises with understanding.

8 God reigneth over the heathen : God sitteth upon his holy seat.

9 The princes of the people are joined unto the people of the God of Abraham : for God, which is very high exalted, doth defend the earth, as it were with a shield.

Verse 7. The motto Archbishop Parker chose for his metrical Psalms, which were his "exercise in his religious exile," A.D. 1557. Since then the same motto has served for many Psalters, *e.g.*, Hellmore's.

Liturgical use.—Ascension Day evening ; Introit on Ascension Day (e).
Latins.—Matins on Tuesday ; Epiphany ; Trinity Sunday ; Apostles and Evangelists.
Greeks.—Tuesday morning.

PSALM XLVIII. *Magnus Dominus.*

GREAT is the Lord, and highly to be praised : in the city of our God, even upon his holy hill.

2 The hill of Sion is a fair place, and the joy of the whole earth : upon the north side lieth the city of the great King ; God is well known in her palaces as a sure refuge.

3 For lo, the kings of the earth : are gathered, and gone by together.

4 They marvelled to see such things : they were astonished, and suddenly cast down.

5 Fear came there upon them, and sorrow : as upon a woman in her travail.

6 Thou shalt break the ships of the sea : through the east wind.

7 Like as we have heard, so have we seen in the city of the Lord of Hosts, in the city of our God : God upholdeth the same for ever.

8 We wait for thy loving-kindness, O God : in the midst of thy temple.

9 O God, according to thy Name, so is thy praise unto the world's end : thy right hand is full of righteousness.

10 Let the mount Sion rejoice, and the daughter of Judah be glad : because of thy judgements.

11 Walk about Sion, and go round about her : and tell the towers thereof.

12 Mark well her bulwarks, set up her houses : that ye may tell them that come after.

13 For this God is our God for ever and ever : he shall be our guide unto death.

This is the psalm in which the Church celebrates her victories over the World, that is to say, over the unchristian arrangements of Society. It commemorated the triumph of St. Athanasius, Constantine, St. Bernard, St. Thomas of Canterbury, and many more.

Verse 7. When this was applied to Christ, it "made the Arians frenzied with rage," that He should be regarded as the God who upholds the world.

Liturgical use.—Whit Sunday morning.
Latins.—Matins on Tuesday ; Christmas Day ; Whitsunday ; Trinity Sunday ; Dedication feast.
Greeks.—Tuesday morning.

PSALM XLIX. *Audite hæc, omnes.*

O HEAR ye this, all ye people : ponder it with your ears, all ye that dwell in the world ;

2 High and low, rich and poor : one with another.

3 My mouth shall speak of wisdom : and my heart shall muse of understanding.

4 I will incline mine ear to the parable : and show my dark speech upon the harp.

5 Wherefore should I fear in the days of wickedness : and when the wickedness of my heels compasseth me round about?

6 There be some that put their trust in their goods : and boast themselves in the multitude of their riches.

7 But no man may deliver his brother : nor make agreement unto God for him ;

8 For it cost more to redeem their souls : so that he must let that alone for ever ;

9 Yea, though he live long : and see not the grave.

10 For he seeth that wise men also die, and perish together : as well as the ignorant and foolish, and leave their riches for other.

11 And yet they think that their houses shall continue for ever : and that their dwelling-places shall endure from one generation to another ; and call the lands after their own names.

12 Nevertheless, man will not abide in honour : see-

ing he may be compared unto the beasts that perish; this is the way of them.

13 This is their foolishness : and their posterity praise their saying.

14 They lie in the hell like sheep, death gnaweth upon them, and the righteous shall have domination over them in the morning : their beauty shall consume in the sepulchre out of their dwelling.

15 But God hath delivered my soul from the place of hell : for he shall receive me.

16 Be not thou afraid, though one be made rich : or if the glory of his house be increased;

17 For he shall carry nothing away with him when he dieth : neither shall his pomp follow him.

18 For while he lived, he counted himself an happy man : and so long as thou doest well unto thyself, men will speak good of thee.

19 He shall follow the generation of his fathers : and shall never see light.

20 Man being in honour hath no understanding : but is compared unto the beasts that perish.

This is the psalm which contained for Matthew Arnold's "Obermann once more" the whole message of David's land. He says of Christ :

"While we believed, on earth He went
And open stood His grave;
Men call'd from chamber, church, and tent,
And Christ was by to save.

"Now He is dead ! Far hence He lies
In the lorn Syrian town,
And on His grave, with shining eyes,
The Syrian stars look down.

"In vain men still, with hoping new,
Regard His death-place dumb,
And say the stone is not yet to,
And wait for words to come.

"Ah, from that silent sacred land
Of sun and arid stone,
And crumbling wall, and sultry sand,
Comes now one word alone !

"From David's lips this word did roll,
'Tis true and living yet :
*No man can save his brother's soul,
Nor pay his brother's debt.*

"Alone, self-poised, henceforward man
Must labour ! must resign
His all too human creeds, and scan
Simply the way Divine."

Henry Lok, an Elizabethan courtier, translated this psalm with some others into English verse, and thought the Book of Ecclesiastes was a commentary

Day 10   PSALM L   *Morning Prayer*

upon it, a conclusion which seems parallel to that of the nineteenth century poet.

Verse 1 opens St. Gregory Nazianzen's first great polemic against Julian the Apostate.

Latins.—Matins on Tuesday.
Greeks.—Tuesday morning.

PSALM L. *Deus deorum.*

THE Lord, even the most mighty God, hath spoken : and called the world, from the rising up of the sun, unto the going down thereof.

2 Out of Sion hath God appeared : in perfect beauty.

3 Our God shall come, and shall not keep silence : there shall go before him a consuming fire, and a mighty tempest shall be stirred up round about him.

4 He shall call the heaven from above : and the earth, that he may judge his people.

5 "Gather my saints together unto me : those that have made a covenant with me with sacrifice."

6 And the heaven shall declare his righteousness : for God is Judge himself.

7 "Hear, O my people, and I will speak : I myself will testify against thee, O Israel; for I am God, even thy God.

8 "I will not reprove thee because of thy sacrifices, or for thy burnt-offerings : because they were not alway before me.

9 "I will take no bullock out of thine house : nor he-goat out of thy folds.

10 "For all the beasts of the forest are mine : and so are the cattle upon a thousand hills.

11 "I know all the fowls upon the mountains : and the wild beasts of the field are in my sight.

12 "If I be hungry, I will not tell thee : for the whole world is mine, and all that is therein.

13 "Thinkest thou that I will eat bulls' flesh : and drink the blood of goats ?

14 "Offer unto God thanksgiving : and pay thy vows unto the most Highest.

15 "And call upon me in the time of trouble : so will I hear thee, and thou shalt praise me."

16 But unto the ungodly said God : "Why dost thou preach my laws, and takest my covenant in thy mouth ;

17 " Whereas thou hatest to be reformed : and hast cast my words behind thee ?

18 " When thou sawest a thief, thou consentedst unto him : and hast been partaker with the adulterers.

19 " Thou hast let thy mouth speak wickedness : and with thy tongue thou hast set forth deceit.

20 " Thou satest, and spakest against thy brother : yea, and hast slandered thine own mother's son.

21 " These things hast thou done, and I held my tongue, and thou thoughtest wickedly, that I am even such a one as thyself : but I will reprove thee, and set before thee the things that thou hast done.

22 " O consider this, ye that forget God : lest I pluck you away, and there be none to deliver you.

23 " Whoso offereth me thanks and praise, he honoureth me : and to him that ordereth his conversation right will I shew the salvation of God."

Verse 16. Origen was threatened, says Suidas, with an abuse and shame worse than torture, if he did not sacrifice to Cæsar. In a moment of fear he consented, and they filled his hand with incense, and thrust it over the altar. He thus escaped martyrdom, and fled from Alexandria to Judæa, where he was entreated to preach. He took the Psalter, prayed, and opened at this verse, read it : shut the book, sat down, and burst into tears, in which all the audience joined. "The prophet David himself shut the door of my lips," as he wrote in his bitter lament, which is one of the most tragic passages in literature.

Verse 18. This was once much used in magic for thief-finding. A number of suspected names or letters were put into a key, and the key was laid and turned over the verse *Si videbas furem currebas cum eo*, and the name which leaped out showed the thief. So with adultery, slander, back-biting, etc., the psalm always consulted was *Deus deorum*, " whose title implies that He is God over evil spirits and imps of mischief."

Latins.—Matins on Tuesday.
Greeks.—Tuesday morning.

PSALM LI. *Miserere mei, Deus.*

HAVE mercy upon me, O God, after thy great goodness : according to the multitude of thy mercies do away mine offences.

2 Wash me throughly from my wickedness : and cleanse me from my sin.

3 For I acknowledge my faults : and my sin is ever before me.

4 Against thee only have I sinned, and done this evil in thy sight : that thou mightest be justified in thy saying, and clear when thou art judged.

5 Behold, I was shapen in wickedness : and in sin hath my mother conceived me.

6 But lo, thou requirest truth in the inward parts : and shalt make me to understand wisdom secretly.

7 Thou shalt purge me with hyssop, and I shall be clean : thou shalt wash me, and I shall be whiter than snow.

8 Thou shalt make me hear of joy and gladness : that the bones which thou hast broken may rejoice.

9 Turn thy face from my sins : and put out all my misdeeds.

10 Make me a clean heart, O God : and renew a right spirit within me.

11 Cast me not away from thy presence : and take not thy holy Spirit from me.

12 O give me the comfort of thy help again : and stablish me with thy free Spirit.

13 Then shall I teach thy ways unto the wicked : and sinners shall be converted unto thee.

14 Deliver me from blood-guiltiness, O God, thou that art the God of my health : and my tongue shall sing of thy righteousness.

15 Thou shalt open my lips, O Lord : and my mouth shall shew thy praise.

16 For thou desirest no sacrifice, else would I give it thee : but thou delightest not in burnt-offerings.

17 The sacrifice of God is a troubled spirit : a broken and contrite heart, O God, shalt thou not despise.

18 O be favourable and gracious unto Sion : build thou the walls of Jerusalem.

19 Then shalt thou be pleased with the sacrifice of righteousness, with the burnt-offerings and oblations : then shall they offer young bullocks upon thine altar.

This is the fourth penitential psalm. The others are vi., xxxii., xxxviii., cii., cxxx., and cxliii. It is an antidote to the deadly sin of lechery (*contra luxuriam*).

None of the other psalms have had half the effect upon

men's minds that this one has exercised. It has a library of its own. "The more one meditates upon it, the richer it seems, and that unendingly," is most folk's comment.

The earliest English version of the Psalms begins with this one: for it, more than any other, inspired Adhelm in the eighth century, and was his favourite, as it was Keble's in this age. St. Dunstan's canons so highly esteemed it that a sick man who said fifteen *Misereres* and *Pater nosters* redeemed a day's fasting. In Theodulf's Capitula it is given for private daily prayers; and Archbishop Ælfric, in 995, ordered his clergy so to use it (with xxv. and xxvi.). It has been *the* psalm to many of the sternest and most active-minded men; for instance, St. Bernard, who heard its cadences as the first prelude to his monastic life, and loved it best. Indeed, when Dante saw the heavenly rose of saints round God's throne, St. Bernard pointed out Ruth to him as "the ancestress of him who wrote the *Miserere*." The same Dante heard it in purgatory, chanted by the spirits of those who had delayed repentance till their violent deaths. It was sung at great humiliations and repentances: by those, for instance, who were absolved from excommunication; by King John at Winchester, in 1213 A.D. Hardly any holy men died on a death-bed, or at a scaffold, or at a stake, without breathing out the unworn passion of this great prayer.

Savonarola, just before his death, with his hand trembling from the torture, wrote upon it a wonderful commentary, which some influential people—probably inspired by Colet—tried to have inserted in our Prayerbook as a Passion meditation in the Reformation times. The opening sentences of this meditation Cranmer repeated on his knees in St. Mary's, Oxford, before he was burnt. Sir Thomas More repeated the psalm on the scaffold; Lady Jane Grey at her execution (1554); Rowland Taylor, while he was burning (1555), said it, and was struck in the mouth for not saying it in Latin; just as Alexander Brian, Robert Johnson, and William Filbie, Romanists, who would not betray Parsons the Jesuit, at their execution, were ill-treated for not saying it in English. When Dr. Arnold knew he was dying, and was asked what should be read to him, he answered instantly, "The fifty-first psalm."

Verse 7. Dr. Ker says that in the northernmost grave in the world, near Cape Beechy, in the white Polar regions, is buried a sailor who went exploring with Sir George Nares. Above it there is a copper tablet, with the words, "Thou shalt wash me, and I shall be whiter than snow."

This is the verse used in the *Asperges*, when the holy-water is sprinkled.

Verse 17. Bernabo Visconti (1385), who was dying in filth and neglect in Trezzo prison, where so many of his victims had died, used to drag himself to the grating, and repeat without ceasing, again and again, *Cor contritum et humiliatum*,

Deus non despicies. The very term "contrition" comes from this verse, just as the *Kyrie Eleison* does from the opening words.

Verse 18. When Henry V. heard this on his death-bed, he raised himself up, and said that the great ambition of his life had been to lead a crusade to restore Jerusalem.

"The souls of the faithful pilgrims plead ever to God for us in these words," says Capgrave.

Liturgical use.—Commination service.
Latins.—On all weekdays at Lauds ; Communion of the Sick ; Burial of the Dead, in procession from the house ; Preces, etc.
Greeks.—Tuesday morning ; daily Nocturns ; Saturday ; Third Hour ; late Evensong ; Visitation of the Sick ; Confession ; Office for the Dying ; burial of laymen, monks, infants, and of priests.

PSALM LII. *Quid gloriaris?*

WHY boastest thou thyself, thou tyrant : that thou canst do mischief ;

2 Whereas the goodness of God : endureth yet daily?

3 Thy tongue imagineth wickedness : and with lies thou cuttest like a sharp razor.

4 Thou hast loved unrighteousness more than goodness : and to talk of lies more than righteousness.

5 Thou hast loved to speak all words that may do hurt : O thou false tongue.

6 Therefore shall God destroy thee for ever : he shall take thee, and pluck thee out of thy dwelling, and root thee out of the land of the living.

7 The righteous also shall see this, and fear : and shall laugh him to scorn ;

8 "Lo, this is the man that took not God for his strength : but trusted unto the multitude of his riches, and strengthened himself in his wickedness."

9 As for me, I am like a green olive-tree in the house of God : my trust is in the tender mercy of God for ever and ever.

10 I will always give thanks unto thee for that thou hast done : and I will hope in thy Name, for thy saints like it well.

When Charles I. came to the Scotch camp at Newark, though the generals affected to treat him respectfully, the ministers knew no check, and often insulted the unhappy king to his face. One of them, after a railing sermon, ordered Ps. lii. to be sung:

> "Why doest thou, tyrant, boast abroad,
> Thy wicked works to praise?
> Dost thou not know there is a God
> Whose mercies last always?"

Then the king stood up, and, with a meekness and dignity that touched even those rigid enthusiasts, called for Ps. lvi. instead:

> "Have mercy, Lord, on me, I pray,
> For man would me devour;
> He fighteth with me day by day,
> And troubleth me each hour."

This version is Sternhold and Hopkins', of whom Fuller says "that they had drunk more of Jordan than of Helicon," and who "have in many verses such poor rhyme that two hammers on a smith's anvil would make better music." It is said (falsely said, Fuller declares) that Queen Elizabeth called these versions "Geneva Gigs." "Some have made libellous verses in abuse of them; and no wonder if songs were made on the translators of the Psalms, seeing drunkards made them on David, the author thereof." "Such as sing them must endeavour to amend them, by singing them with understanding heads and gracious hearts, whereby that which is but bad *matter* on earth will be made good *music* in heaven."

In the life of St. Porphyrius, Bishop of Gaza, it is told that the great idol temple there took fire, and burnt for many days. The Christians gathered round and chanted this psalm, esteeming this fire the work of God; and, indeed, not a few heathen were thus converted.

Verse 8. In reference to this verse, and its warning against trusting in riches, King Edward VI. put on the English groats, *Posui Deum aiutorem meum* —"I have taken God for my strength," and Queen Elizabeth had the same words engraved upon her household silver.

Liturgical use.—Introit for St. Stephen's Mass (e).
Latins.—Tuesday Matins.
Greeks.—Tuesday morning.

PSALM LIII. *Dixit insipiens.*

1 THE foolish body hath said in his heart: There is no God.

2 Corrupt are they, and become abominable in their wickedness: there is none that doeth good.

3 God looked down from heaven upon the children of men: to see if there were any that would understand, and seek after God.

4 But they are all gone out of the way, they are altogether become abominable : there is also none that doeth good, no not one.

5 Are not they without understanding that work wickedness : eating up my people as if they would eat bread? they have not called upon God.

6 They were afraid where no fear was : for God hath broken the bones of him that besieged thee ; thou hast put them to confusion, because God hath despised them.

7 Oh, that the salvation were given unto Israel out of Sion : Oh, that the Lord would deliver his people out of captivity!

8 Then should Jacob rejoice : and Israel should be right glad.

This psalm, which is the Elohist version of Ps. xiv., is one of the bones of contention among modern critics.

Verse 1. The discourses upon this verse opened the wide field of controversy upon the ontological argument for the existence of God; St. Anselm, Duns Scotus, and Descartes, being among the defenders of that argument. St. Thomas Aquinas and Kant rejected it, and most modern philosophers have practically abandoned it. The argument is briefly this, Can we suppose that the mind fashioned and invented a thought so great that it fills all thought? Prof. Caird sums up and approves the meaning which underlies this " proof " : " As spiritual beings, our whole conscious life is based on a universal self-consciousness, an absolute spiritual life, which is not a mere subjective notion or conception, but which carries with it the proof of its necessary existence or reality."

Latins.—On Wednesday at Matins.
Greeks.—On Tuesday morning.

PSALM LIV. *Deus, in nomine.*

SAVE me, O God, for thy Name's sake : and avenge me in thy strength.

2 Hear my prayer, O God : and hearken unto the words of my mouth.

3 For strangers are risen up against me : and tyrants, which have not God before their eyes, seek after my soul.

4 Behold, God is my helper : the Lord is with them that uphold my soul.

5 He shall reward evil unto mine enemies : destroy thou them in thy truth.

6 An offering of a free heart will I give thee, and praise thy Name, O Lord : because it is so comfortable.

7 For he hath delivered me out of all my trouble : and mine eye hath seen his desire upon mine enemies.

Verse 6. These words decided both popes and councils to make it illegal to devote children of a tender age to the monkish life, until they could give "a free heart." Unfortunately, they could not control the inside of the monasteries, and hence many a Filippo Lippi was forced to take vows for which he had no call.

Liturgical use.—Good Friday morning.
Latins.—Daily at Prime ; Easter Eve.
Greeks.—On Tuesday morning, at sixth hour.

PSALM LV. *Exaudi, Deus.*

HEAR my prayer, O God : and hide not thyself from my petition.

2 Take heed unto me, and hear me : how I mourn in my prayer, and am vexed.

3 The enemy crieth so, and the ungodly cometh on so fast : for they are minded to do me some mischief ; so maliciously are they set against me.

4 My heart is disquieted within me : and the fear of death is fallen upon me.

5 Fearfulness and trembling are come upon me : and an horrible dread hath overwhelmed me.

6 And I said, O that I had wings like a dove : for then would I flee away, and be at rest.

7 Lo, then would I get me away far off : and remain in the wilderness.

8 I would make haste to escape : because of the stormy wind and tempest.

9 Destroy their tongues, O Lord, and divide them : for I have spied unrighteousness and strife in the city.

10 Day and night they go about within the walls thereof : mischief also and sorrow are in the midst of it.

11 Wickedness is therein : deceit and guile go not out of their streets.

12 For it is not an open enemy, that hath done me this dishonour : for then I could have borne it.

13 Neither was it mine adversary, that did magnify himself against me : for then peradventure I would have hid myself from him.

14 But it was even thou, my companion : my guide, and mine own familiar friend.

15 We took sweet counsel together : and walked in the house of God as friends.

16 Let death come hastily upon them, and let them go down quick into hell : for wickedness is in their dwellings, and among them.

17 As for me, I will call upon God : and the Lord shall save me.

18 In the evening, and morning, and at noonday will I pray, and that instantly : and he shall hear my voice.

19 It is he that hath delivered my soul in peace from the battle that was against me : for there were many with me.

20 Yea, even God, that endureth for ever, shall hear me, and bring them down : for they will not turn, nor fear God.

21 He laid his hands upon such as be at peace with him : and he brake his covenant.

22 The words of his mouth were softer than butter, having war in his heart : his words were smoother than oil, and yet be they very swords.

23 O cast thy burden upon the Lord, and he shall nourish thee : and shall not suffer the righteous to fall for ever.

24 And as for them : thou, O God, shalt bring them into the pit of destruction.

25 The blood-thirsty and deceitful men shall not live out half their days : nevertheless, my trust shall be in thee, O Lord.

This was the last psalm (his favourite) read by the wretched Darnley, the night he was blown up at Kirk-o'-Field, February, 1567.

Verse 1, first part, is the motto carved on the Jacobæan reading-pew in Newport Church, Isle of Wight.

Verse 6. St. Jerome says that this motto was constantly in the mouths of the peaceful and pious Egyptian Cœnobites while they listened to the words of their "Father," whose praise as a speaker was in the weeping of his hearers. Their holy, obedient, and disciplined life was the loveliest contrast to the fierce anarchy and lust about them. The verse was, at any rate, one which St. Jerome himself repeats again and again. It has also played no small part in literature and art, *e.g.*, Mendelssohn's well known musical setting; Browning's "Pompilia," iii. 991-997, etc.

Verse 15. Hooker deduced from this that it is reasonable to think, that if walking as friends in the house of God made the bond of men's love insoluble, that all piety will be witnessed to and kindled by the use of psalms between clergy, and those "between whom there daily and interchangeably pass in the hearing of God Himself and in the presence of His holy angels, so many heavenly acclamations, exultations, provocations, petitions, songs of comfort, psalms of praise and thanksgiving."

Verse 25. Giraldus Cambrensis' comment upon the death of King John, and a very apposite one, too. The same words formed the fierce retort of old Cecil, Lord Burleigh, to the Earl of Essex, when the latter vehemently opposed the policy of peace with Spain.

Latins.—Matins on Wednesday.
Greeks.—On Tuesday morning; Sixth hour; Visitation of the Sick.

PSALM LVI. *Miserere mei, Deus.*

BE merciful unto me, O God, for man goeth about to devour me : he is daily fighting, and troubling me.

2 Mine enemies are daily in hand to swallow me up : for they be many that fight against me, O thou most Highest.

3 Nevertheless, though I am sometime afraid : yet put I my trust in thee.

4 I will praise God, because of his word : I have put my trust in God, and will not fear what flesh can do unto me.

5 They daily mistake my words : all that they imagine is to do me evil.

6 They hold all together, and keep themselves close : and mark my steps, when they lay wait for my soul.

7 Shall they escape for their wickedness : thou, O God, in thy displeasure shalt cast them down.

8 Thou tellest my flittings; put my tears into thy bottle : are not these things noted in thy book?

9 Whensoever I call upon thee, then shall mine enemies be put to flight : this I know; for God is on my side.

10 In God's word will I rejoice : in the Lord's word will I comfort me.

11 Yea, in God have I put my trust : I will not be afraid what man can do unto me.

12 Unto thee, O God, will I pay my vows : unto thee will I give thanks.

13 For thou hast delivered my soul from death, and my feet from falling : that I may walk before God in the light of the living.

In the Middle Ages this psalm was usually said by the sick, before they took their physic.

Charles I.'s choice (*vide* Ps. lii.) when insulted by the Presbyterian ministers. There was a picture of this king at St. John's College, Oxford, which the *Spectator* noticed. It had the whole Book of Psalms written in the lines of the face ; no doubt because of the king's love for them. Charles II. begged it of the college, and it was given him with so strong a hint of the loss to the society that he felt obliged to restore it.

Verse 8. These words were a favourite saying of holy Archbishop Usher (1580-1655).

Latins.—Wednesday morning.
Greeks.—Tuesday morning ; Mesorion of sixth hour.

PSALM LVII. *Miserere mei, Deus.*

BE merciful unto me, O God, be merciful unto me, for my soul trusteth in thee : and under the shadow of thy wings shall be my refuge, until this tyranny be over-past.

2 I will call unto the most high God : even unto the God that shall perform the cause which I have in hand.

3 He shall send from heaven : and save me from the reproof of him that would eat me up.

4 God shall send forth his mercy and truth : my soul is among lions.

5 And I lie even among the children of men, that are set on fire : whose teeth are spears and arrows, and their tongue a sharp sword.

6 Set up thyself, O God, above the heavens : and thy glory above all the earth.

7 They have laid a net for my feet, and pressed down my soul : they have digged a pit before me, and are fallen into the midst of it themselves.

8 My heart is fixed, O God, my heart is fixed : I will sing and give praise.

9 Awake up, my glory ; awake, lute and harp : I myself will awake right early.

10 I will give thanks unto thee, O Lord, among the people : and I will sing unto thee among the nations.

11 For the greatness of thy mercy reacheth unto the heavens : and thy truth unto the clouds.

12 Set up thyself, O God, above the heavens : and thy glory above all the earth.

Verse 1. *Miserere mei, Domine, miserere mei,* was the motto of Pope Nicholas III. (1277-1279), the great opponent of Charles of Anjou.

The last words were in constant use in reference to the enforced signing of the Covenant, January 29, 1643.

Verse 5. This verse was not without reason applied by St. Athanasius to the fiery and persecuting Arians, whose arguments frequently did take sword form.

Verse 8. These words were among the last of Dr. Robert Sanderson, as Walton tells us in his Lives. This learned and pious man commended to Walton and everyone else the frequent use of the Psalms of David, saying "that they were the treasury of Christian comfort, fitted for all persons and necessities : able to raise the soul from dejection by the frequent mention of God's mercies to repentant sinners; to stir up holy desires ; to increase joy : to moderate sorrow ; to nourish hope and teach us patience by waiting God's leisure ; to beget a trust in the mercy, power, and providence of the Creator ; and to cause a resignation of ourselves to His will ; and then, and not till then, to believe ourselves happy."

Liturgical use.—Easter morning.
Latins.—Wednesday morning.
Greeks.—Tuesday morning ; Mesorion of sixth hour.

PSALM LVIII. *Si vere utique.*

ARE your minds set upon righteousness, O ye congregation : and do ye judge the thing that is right, O ye sons of men ?

2 Yea, ye imagine mischief in your heart upon the earth : and your hands deal with wickedness.

3 The ungodly are froward, even from their mother's womb : as soon as they are born, they go astray, and speak lies.

4 They are as venomous as the poison of a serpent : even like the deaf adder that stoppeth her ears ;

5 Which refuseth to hear the voice of the charmer : charm he never so wisely.

6 Break their teeth, O God, in their mouths ; smite the jawbones of the lions, O Lord : let them fall away like water that runneth apace ; and when they shoot their arrows let them be rooted out.

7 Let them consume away like a snail, and be like the untimely fruit of a woman : and let them not see the sun.

8 Or ever your pots be made hot with thorns : so let indignation vex him, even as a thing that is raw.

9 The righteous shall rejoice when he seeth the vengeance : he shall wash his footsteps in the blood of the ungodly.

10 So that a man shall say, Verily there is a reward for the righteous : doubtless there is a God that judgeth the earth.

This psalm was much used by St. Bernard in his Crusade sermons.

Verse 7. A queer piece of natural history came from the Jews with this verse, that the snail (the waster) was born big, and crawled until it had worn itself away into slime. By Albertus Magnus' time, however, snails had been observed more carefully, for he says the verse refers to snails when salted.

Verse 9. St. Hugh of Lincoln, one of the bravest, wisest, and most lovable of all English saints and bishops, used to justify himself by this verse for his tremendous severity of rebuke and fierce indignation against the proud evil-doers of his day. Though he was the great idol of children, the gentlest nurse of lepers, the friend of birds and beasts, and one so careful of the dead that to bury a dead tramp he would keep the king waiting for dinner, yet his rebukes were so severe they seemed almost unmeasured.

Latins.—Wednesday morning.
Greeks.—On Tuesday morning.

PSALM LIX. *Eripe me de inimicis.*

DELIVER me from mine enemies, O God : defend me from them that rise up against me.

2 O deliver me from the wicked doers : and save me from the blood-thirsty men.

3 For lo, they lie waiting for my soul : the mighty men are gathered against me, without any offence or fault of me, O Lord.

4 They run and prepare themselves without my fault : arise thou therefore to help me, and behold.

5 Stand up, O Lord God of hosts, thou God of Israel, to visit all the heathen : and be not merciful unto them that offend of malicious wickedness.

6 They go to and fro in the evening : they grin like a dog, and run about through the city.

7 Behold, they speak with their mouth, and swords are in their lips : for " who doth hear ?"

8 But thou, O Lord, shalt have them in derision : and thou shalt laugh all the heathen to scorn.

9 My strength will I ascribe unto thee : for thou art the God of my refuge.

10 God sheweth me his goodness plenteously : and God shall let me see my desire upon mine enemies.

11 Slay them not, lest my people forget it : but scatter them abroad among the people, and put them down, O Lord, our defence.

12 For the sin of their mouth, and for the words of their lips, they shall be taken in their pride : and why : their preaching is of cursing and lies.

13 Consume them in thy wrath, consume them, that they may perish ; and know that it is God that ruleth in Jacob, and unto the ends of the world.

14 And in the evening they will return : grin like a dog, and will go about the city.

15 They will run here and there for meat : and grudge if they be not satisfied.

16 As for me, I will sing of thy power, and will praise thy mercy betimes in the morning : for thou hast been my defence and refuge in the day of my trouble.

17 Unto thee, O my strength, will I sing : for thou, O God, art my refuge, and my merciful God.

In the time of Henry VIII. this psalm was used as a Passion psalm.

This is one of the vindictive psalms, as they are called, the others being lxix., lxxix., and cix., and they have caused no little controversy in every age, especially among us since the English Church has familiarized people with them by using them on Sundays. The word "vindictive" has only lately acquired the meaning of studied malice. "Vindication" is a special virtue in the eyes of St. Thomas Aquinas, opposed to savagery and cruelty on the one hand, and carelessness about evil on the other. He insists, of course, that it must not spring from hate, but from a good motive, charity to the evil-doer (his amendment or restraint), or for the general peace and welfare. If any defence is made of these psalms, it usually goes on these lines. But if the New Testament were merely a repetition of the Old, it would be unnecessary. These psalms show how widely the two differ in places, even when the words of the Old are weighed impartially, and without modern misconceptions.

Latins.—Matins on Wednesday.
Greeks.—Tuesday morning.

PSALM LX. *Deus, repulisti nos.*

O GOD, thou hast cast us out, and scattered us abroad : thou hast also been displeased ; O turn thee unto us again.

2 Thou hast moved the land, and divided it : heal the sores thereof, for it shaketh.

3 Thou hast shewed thy people heavy things : thou hast given us a drink of deadly wine.

4 Thou hast given a token for such as fear thee : that they may triumph because of the truth.

5 Therefore were thy beloved delivered : help me with thy right hand, and hear me.

6 God hath spoken in his holiness, I will rejoice, and divide Sichem : and mete out the valley of Succoth.

7 Gilead is mine, and Manasses is mine : Ephraim also is the strength of my head ; Judah is my lawgiver ;

8 Moab is my wash-pot ; over Edom will I cast out my shoe : Philistia, be thou glad of me.

9 Who will lead me into the strong city : who will bring me into Edom?

10 Hast not thou cast us out, O God : wilt not thou. O God, go out with our hosts ?

11 O be thou our help in trouble : for vain is the help of man.

12 Through God will we do great acts : for it is he that shall tread down our enemies.

When St. Cuthbert drew near his end he was in his cell off Lindisfarne, alone with his eider ducks. Herefrid and certain monks landed to give him the last Sacrament. At midnight he raised his hands and sped forth his spirit. When Herefrid told the brethren outside they were just beginning the midnight psalm, *Deus quare repulisti nos*, and a brother went to the higher ground and raised two torches, as a signal to Lindisfarne. The brethren there were chanting the same psalm when the signal was spied, and they knew that their chief was gone. So this psalm has been called the Dirge of St. Cuthbert, and was the dirge also of Celtic Christianity, which died with him.

Verse 2. The text of the Bishop of Exeter, Joseph Hall's magnificent and brave plea for peace, which he preached to Charles I. at Whitehall, on the 2nd Sunday in Lent, 1641, "On the Mischiefe of Faction and the Remedie of it." He was translated to Norwich; but his advice was left to lie where it fell.

Latins.—Wednesday morning.
Greeks.—Tuesday morning.

PSALM LXI. *Exaudi, Deus.*

HEAR my crying, O God : give ear unto my prayer.

2 From the ends of the earth will I call upon thee : when my heart is in heaviness.

3 O set me up upon the rock that is higher than I : for thou hast been my hope, and a strong tower for me against the enemy.

4 I will dwell in thy tabernacle for ever : and my trust shall be under the covering of thy wings.

5 For thou, O Lord, hast heard my desires : and hast given an heritage unto those that fear thy Name.

6 Thou shalt grant the King a long life : that his years may endure throughout all generations.

7 He shall dwell before God for ever : O prepare thy loving mercy and faithfulness, that they may preserve him.

8 So will I alway sing praise unto thy Name : that I may daily perform thy vows.

Verse 5. St. Chrysostom's comment on this is that the "heritage" is Christ Himself. "A thousand hells are nothing to the evil of being shut out from this heavenly heritage, of being eternally repelled from Christ, and hearing from His mouth, 'I never knew you.'"

Latins.—Wednesday morning; Apostles and Evangelists; All Saints'.
Greeks.— Tuesday morning ; Visitation of the Sick.

PSALM LXII. *Nonne Deo?*

MY soul truly waiteth still upon God : for of him cometh my salvation.

2 He verily is my strength and my salvation : he is my defence, so that I shall not greatly fall.

3 How long will ye imagine mischief against every man : ye shall be slain all the sort of you; yea, as a tottering wall shall ye be, and like a broken hedge.

4 Their device is only how to put him out whom God will exalt : their delight is in lies; they give good words with their mouth, but curse with their heart.

5 Nevertheless, my soul, wait thou still upon God : for my hope is in him.

6 He truly is my strength and my salvation : he is my defence, so that I shall not fall.

7 In God is my health, and my glory : the rock of my might, and in God is my trust.

8 O put your trust in him alway, ye people : pour out your hearts before him, for God is our hope.

9 As for the children of men, they are but vanity : the children of men are deceitful upon the weights, they are altogether lighter than vanity itself.

10 O trust not in wrong and robbery, give not yourselves unto vanity : if riches increase, set not your heart upon them.

11 God spake once, and twice I have also heard the same : that power belongeth unto God;

12 And that thou, Lord, art merciful : for thou rewardest every man according to his work.

St. Athanasius's favourite psalm. "Against all attempts upon thy body, thy state, thy soul, thy fame, temptations, tribulations, machinations, defamations, say this psalm." He probably learnt his great love for it in the desert with St. Anthony. There he had time to meditate upon the corruptions of Alexandria, where he was born, and where he died (373).

Verse 1. Allan Gardiner painted these words in red over the cave in which he was starved to death (*vide* xvii.).

Liturgical use.—Introit for Mass on Easter morning (e).
Latins.—Wednesday Matins.
Greeks.—Tuesday morning.

PSALM LXIII. *Deus, Deus meus.*

O GOD, thou art my God : early will I seek thee.

2 My soul thirsteth for thee, my flesh also longeth after thee : in a barren and dry land where no water is.

3 Thus have I looked for thee in holiness : that I might behold thy power and glory.

4 For thy loving-kindness is better than the life itself : my lips shall praise thee.

5 As long as I live will I magnify thee on this manner : and lift up my hands in thy Name.

6 My soul shall be satisfied, even as it were with marrow and fatness : when my mouth praiseth thee with joyful lips.

7 Have I not remembered thee in my bed : and thought upon thee when I was waking?

8 Because thou hast been my helper : therefore under the shadow of thy wings will I rejoice.

9 My soul hangeth upon thee : thy right hand hath upholden me.

10 These also that seek the hurt of my soul : they shall go under the earth.

11 Let them fall upon the edge of the sword : that they may be a portion for foxes.

12 But the King shall rejoice in God; all they also that swear by him shall be commended : for the mouth of them that speak lies shall be stopped.

The African Church used this as the morning psalm, and in the Apostolic constitutions it begins the day's devotions. It has been called the morning hymn of the Early Church. It was also called the psalm of the Three Kings.

It was St. Chrysostom's favourite psalm, and he thought that the spirit of the whole book was compressed into it.

Theodore Beza (after whom the rhymed psalms were called "Beza's Ballets") said that this was the psalm he always said over and over to himself on his sleepless nights.

Verse 8. The last words of "Blessed" John Forrest, who was burnt at Smithfield (May 22, 1538), with the approval of Bishop Latimer.

Latins.—Lauds daily.
Greeks.—On Tuesday morning.

PSALM LXIV. *Exaudi, Deus.*

HEAR my voice, O God, in my prayer : preserve my life from fear of the enemy.

2 Hide me from the gathering together of the froward : and from the insurrection of wicked doers ;

3 Who have whet their tongue like a sword : and shoot out their arrows, even bitter words ;

4 That they may privily shoot at him that is perfect : suddenly do they hit him, and fear not.

5 They encourage themselves in mischief : and commune among themselves how they may lay snares, and say, that no man shall see them.

6 They imagine wickedness, and practise it : that they keep secret among themselves, every man in the deep of his heart.

7 But God shall suddenly shoot at them with a swift arrow : that they shall be wounded.

8 Yea, their own tongues shall make them fall : insomuch that whoso seeth them shall laugh them to scorn.

9 And all men that see it shall say, "This hath God done" : for they shall perceive that it is his work.

10 The righteous shall rejoice in the Lord, and put his trust in him : and all they that are true of heart shall be glad.

The proper psalms once appointed to be said on Gunpowder Treason Day were lxiv., cxxiv., and cxxv.

John Holland, in his "Psalmists of Britain," numbers 173 authors of metrical translations from the sixteenth century. Up to the year 1720, Le Long numbers 1,120 editions of the Old Testament made since the year 1475, and counts 500 commentators on the Psalms ; but Calmet, not long afterwards, asserted that there were close upon a thousand known.

Among the much-wronged minor authors, who out of love for the Psalter published metrical editions, were Vicars the Presbyterian, lampooned in "Hudibras," and Blackmore, William III.'s physician, whom Pope called "the godless author, who burlesqued a psalm." These poor fellows must have understood this psalm, at any rate.

Verse 7. This verse (which in the Vulgate ends, *sagitta parvulorum facta sunt plagæ eorum*, their blows are turned into children's arrows) was accepted by St. Ambrose, as a promise of deliverance, when he was threatened with fire, sword, and banishment.

Latins.—Wednesday at Matins ; Apostles and Evangelists.
Greeks.—Tuesday morning.

PSALM LXV. *Te decet hymnus.*

THOU, O God, art praised in Sion : and unto thee shall the vow be performed in Jerusalem.

2 Thou that hearest the prayer : unto thee shall all flesh come.

3 My misdeeds prevail against me : O be thou merciful unto our sins.

4 Blessed is the man, whom thou choosest, and receivest unto thee : he shall dwell in thy court, and shall be satisfied with the pleasures of thy house, even of thy holy temple.

5 Thou shalt show us wonderful things in thy righteousness. O God of our salvation : thou that art the hope of all the ends of the earth, and of them that remain in the broad sea.

6 Who in his strength setteth fast the mountains : and is girded about with power.

7 Who stilleth the raging of the sea : and the noise of his waves, and the madness of the people.

8 They also that dwell in the uttermost parts of the earth shall be afraid at thy tokens : thou that makest the outgoings of the morning and evening to praise thee.

9 Thou visitest the earth, and blessest it : thou makest it very plenteous.

10 The river of God is full of water : thou preparest their corn, for so thou providest for the earth.

11 Thou waterest her furrows, thou sendest rain into the little valleys thereof : thou makest it soft with the drops of rain, and blessest the increase of it.

12 Thou crownest the year with thy goodness : and thy clouds drop fatness.

13 They shall drop upon the dwellings of the wilderness : and the little hills shall rejoice on every side.

14 The folds shall be full of sheep : the valleys also shall stand so thick with corn, that they shall laugh and sing.

This is the basis of Origen's prayer for the Alexandrine Church.

This (with Psalms civ. and cxxi.) was a favourite with Henry Vaughan, the Wordsworth of the seventeenth century, whose intense delight in nature gives his sacred poems some of the freshness of the Psalms themselves.

"Thou waterest every ridge of land,
And settlest with Thy secret hand
The furrows of it ; then Thy warm
And opening showers, restrain'd from harm,
Soften the mould, while all unseen
The blade grows up alive and green."

Verse 11. *In stillicidiis ejus lætabitur germinans benedices coronæ.* Out of these words a prophecy of the birth of Charles VIII. was extracted by forming the date mccclxxv., *i.e.* 1470. It was a curious instance of ingenuity, and celebrated because it succeeded.

Latins.—Wednesday Lauds.
Greeks.—Tuesday evening ; Saturday evening.

PSALM LXVI. *Jubilate Deo.*

O BE joyful in God, all ye lands : sing praises unto the honour of his Name, make his praise to be glorious.

2 Say unto God, "O how wonderful art thou in thy works : through the greatness of thy power shall thine enemies be found liars unto thee.

3 "For all the world shall worship thee : sing of thee, and praise thy Name."

4 O come hither, and behold the works of God : how wonderful he is in his doing toward the children of men.

5 He turned the sea into dry land : so that they went through the water on foot ; there did we rejoice thereof.

6 He ruleth with his power for ever ; his eyes behold the people : and such as will not believe shall not be able to exalt themselves.

7 O praise our God, ye people : and make the voice of his praise to be heard ;

8 Who holdeth our soul in life : and suffereth not our feet to slip.

9 For thou, O God, hast proved us : thou also hast tried us, like as silver is tried.

10 Thou broughtest us into the snare : and laidest trouble upon our loins.

11 Thou sufferedst men to ride over our heads : we went through fire and water, and thou broughtest us out into a wealthy place.

12 I will go into thine house with burnt-offerings : and will pay thee my vows, which I promised with my lips, and spake with my mouth, when I was in trouble.

13 " I will offer unto thee fat burnt-sacrifices, with the incense of rams : I will offer bullocks and goats."

14 O come hither, and hearken, all ye that fear God : and I will tell you what he hath done for my soul.

15 I called unto him with my mouth ; and gave him praises with my tongue.

16 If I incline unto wickedness with mine heart : the Lord will not hear me.

17 But God hath heard me : and considered the voice of my prayer.

18 Praised be God who hath not cast out my prayer : nor turned his mercy from me.

Verse 11. Transivimus per ignem et aquam et eduxisti nos in refrigerium. This is the motto Savonarola's Venetian editors chose for his sermons (1543, etc.). It was also St. Basil's text for the forty martyrs, who were exposed to the cold and frozen to death.

Verses 16, 17 and 18. This syllogism, without a conclusion in logical form, caused no little debate among the schoolmen, and no less comment. Fuller's note upon it perhaps settled the question of its " bad logic."

" Lord, I find David making a syllogism, in mood and figure, two propositions he perfected.

" ' If I regard wickedness in my heart, the Lord will not hear me.

" But verily God hath heard me, He hath attended to the voice of my prayer.'

" Now, I expected that David should have concluded thus : ' Therefore I regard not wickedness in my heart.' But, far otherwise, he concludes : ' Blessed be God, who hath not turned away my prayer, nor His mercy from me.' Thus David hath deceived, but not wronged me. I looked that he should have clapped the crown on his own, and he puts it on God's head. I will learn this excellent logic ; for I like David's better than Aristotle's syllogisms, that, whatsoever the premises be, I make God's glory the conclusion."

Liturgical use.—Thanksgiving after a storm at sea.
Latins.—Wednesday Matins ; Epiphany.
Greeks.—Tuesday night ; Saturday night.

PSALM LXVII. *Deus misereatur.*

GOD be merciful unto us, and bless us : and shew us the light of his countenance, and be merciful unto us.

2 That thy way may be known upon earth : thy saving health among all nations.

3 Let the people praise thee, O God : yea, let all the people praise thee.

4 O let the nations rejoice and be glad : for thou shalt judge the folk righteously, and govern the nations upon earth.

5 Let the people praise thee, O God : let all the people praise thee.

6 Then shall the earth bring forth her increase : and God, even our own God, shall give us his blessing.

7 God shall bless us : and all the ends of the world shall fear him.

Verse 3. These words decided Pope John VIII., in the ninth century, to allow Methodius to evangelize the Bulgarians, who knew neither Latin, Greek, nor Hebrew, and he thus opened the door to foreign missions. This Pope carried the papal claims to their greatest height, anticipating Gregory VII. by two centuries, and even going beyond him in claims, for he declared that the election of the emperor rested with him. This mission is all the more important from the fact that Methodius and his brother Cyrillus were the first to invent an alphabet and reduce the Slavonian language to writing.

Liturgical use.—Marriage psalm ; Evensong psalm, alternative to *Nunc Dimittis ;* Introit to Mass on Trinity Sunday (e).
Latins.—Daily at Lauds.
Greeks.—Tuesday evening ; Saturday evening.

PSALM LXVIII. *Exurgat Deus.*

LET God arise, and let his enemies be scattered : let them also that hate him flee before him.

2 Like as the smoke vanisheth, so shalt thou drive them away : and like as wax melteth at the fire, so let the ungodly perish at the presence of God.

3 But let the righteous be glad and rejoice before God : let them also be merry and joyful.

4 O sing unto God, and sing praises unto his Name :

magnify him that rideth upon the heavens, as it were upon an horse; praise him in his Name JAH, and rejoice before him.

5 He is a Father of the fatherless, and defendeth the cause of the widows : even God in his holy habitation.

6 He is the God that maketh men to be of one mind in an house, and bringeth the prisoners out of captivity : but letteth the runagates continue in scarceness.

7 O God, when thou wentest forth before the people : when thou wentest through the wilderness,

8 The earth shook, and the heavens dropped at the presence of God : even as Sinai also was moved at the presence of God, who is the God of Israel.

9 Thou, O God, sentest a gracious rain upon thine inheritance : and refreshedst it when it was weary.

10 Thy congregation shall dwell therein : for thou, O God, hast of thy goodness prepared for the poor.

11 The Lord gave the word : great was the company of the preachers.

12 " Kings with their armies did flee, and were discomfited : and they of the household divided the spoil."

13 Though ye have lien among the pots, yet shall ye be as the wings of a dove : that is covered with silver wings, and her feathers like gold.

14 When the Almighty scattered kings for their sake : then were they as white as snow in Salmon.

15 As the hill of Basan, so is God's hill : even an high hill, as the hill of Basan.

16 Why hop ye so, ye high hills ? this is God's hill, in the which it pleaseth him to dwell : yea, the Lord will abide in it for ever.

17 The chariots of God are twenty thousand, even thousands of angels : and the Lord is among them, as in the holy place of Sinai.

18 Thou art gone up on high, thou hast led captivity captive, and received gifts for men : yea, even for thine enemies, that the Lord God might dwell among them.

19 Praised be the Lord daily : even the God who helpeth us, and poureth his benefits upon us.

20 He is our God, even the God of whom cometh salvation : God is the Lord, by whom we escape death.

21 God shall wound the head of his enemies : and

Day 13   PSALM LXVIII   *Morning Prayer*

the hairy scalp of such a one as goeth on still in his wickedness.

22 The Lord hath said, I will bring my people again, as I did from Basan : mine own will I bring again, as I did sometime from the deep of the sea.

23 That thy foot may be dipped in the blood of thine enemies : and that the tongue of thy dogs may be red through the same.

24 It is well seen, O God, how thou goest : how thou, my God and King, goest in the sanctuary.

25 The singers go before, the minstrels follow after : in the midst are the damsels playing with the timbrels.

26 Give thanks, O Israel, unto God the Lord in the congregations : from the ground of the heart.

27 There is little Benjamin their ruler, and the princes of Judah their counsel : the princes of Zabulon, and the princes of Nephthali.

28 Thy God hath sent forth strength for thee : stablish the thing, O God, that thou hast wrought in us ;

29 For thy temple's sake at Jerusalem : so shall kings bring presents unto thee.

30 When the company of the spearmen, and multitude of the mighty are scattered abroad among the beasts of the people, so that they humbly bring pieces of silver : and when he hath scattered the people that delight in war ;

31 Then shall the princes come out of Egypt : the Morians' land shall soon stretch out her hands unto God.

32 Sing unto God, O ye kingdoms of the earth : O sing praises unto the Lord ;

33 Who sitteth in the heavens over all from the beginning : lo, he doth send out his voice, yea, and that a mighty voice.

34 Ascribe ye the power to God over Israel : his worship and strength is in the clouds.

35 O God, wonderful art thou in thy holy places : even the God of Israel ; he will give strength and power unto his people ; blessed be God.

This warrior psalm, as Adhelm names it (*psalmum sacri certaminis*), has chiefly been used at times of conflict. Whitsuntide has always been regarded in the Church as a time of strength for battle, and the Comforter cheers men, as a trumpet comforts them. The great warriors, who often had a special devotion to the Holy Ghost, found particular delight in this psalm. It was Charlemagne's favourite; and he is said to have written the prayer for purity in the Eucharistic Office for the "inspiration of the Holy Spirit" and the *Veni Creator Spiritus* (Come, Holy Ghost), both of which contain echoes of it.

It was sung by the Christian women under old Publia in defiance of Julian the Apostate (362). They selected all the psalms most likely to goad that Emperor into acts of tyranny. The guard by his orders seized Publia and brought her to the Emperor, still singing this psalm, and he disappointed her, for, instead of a worse punishment, he ordered her ears to be boxed until they were red.

When St. Anthony was thirty-five years old, he lived in a ruined castle. One day the monks heard so fierce an altercation going on that they feared the people of the country had broken in upon the hermit; but they found no one, and presently they heard the song of triumph ("Let God arise") resound from the castle, and knew that Anthony had overcome his ghostly foes.

St. Dunstan, while he was praying before St. George's altar at Glastonbury, fell into a light sleep, and saw in a vision a huge bear rushing upon him. He seized a staff and smote it, but his staff passed through the vision and struck the walls of the church. In despair he recollected the psalm of holy battle and chanted it loudly. This put the enemy to flight, and he found that it was just here his devotions had been interrupted by sleep.

Perhaps Browning alludes to these and similar uses in his quotations of it, "Ring and the Book," ii., 1302.

Savonarola, on his way to the ordeal by fire in the Piazza in 1497, chanted this psalm. The enemy were in this case the Franciscan monks, who disputed his mission, and were the allies of the Pope, the Medici, and the Compagnacci, for the destruction of the great leader.

On September 3, 1650, Oliver Cromwell and his army raised this psalm as they fell upon the Scotch at the battle of Dunbar.

An old West-Country recipe for charming a snake is to draw a circle round the reptile, sign the cross, and repeat the first two verses of this psalm.

Verse 1. When James I. came to the throne, he was asked to choose a motto for the coins of the realm. He chose *Exurgat Deus et dissipentur inimici.*

Verse 20. Dr. Donne preached from this verse his last sermon, his own funeral sermon (1631), looking the image of death, and speaking in a faint sepulchral voice.

Verse 35. A voice from heaven chanted this to St. Hugh, the valorous Bishop of Lincoln, and cheered him when he was in low spirits at the disturbed state of England.

Liturgical use.—Whit-Sunday Matins.
Latins.—Wednesday Matins; Whit-Sunday.
Greeks.—Tuesday night; Saturday Nocturns.

PSALM LXIX. *Salvum me fac.*

SAVE me, O God : for the waters are come in, even unto my soul.

2 I stick fast in the deep mire, where no ground is : I am come into deep waters, so that the floods run over me.

3 I am weary of crying; my throat is dry : my sight faileth me for waiting so long upon my God.

4 They that hate me without a cause are more than the hairs of my head : they that are mine enemies, and would destroy me guiltless, are mighty.

5 I paid them the things that I never took : God, thou knowest my simpleness, and my faults are not hid from thee.

6 Let not them that trust in thee, O Lord God of hosts, be ashamed for my cause : let not those that seek thee be confounded through me, O Lord God of Israel.

7 And why? for thy sake have I suffered reproof : shame hath covered my face.

8 I am become a stranger unto my brethren : even an alien unto my mother's children.

9 For the zeal of thine house hath even eaten me : and the rebukes of them that rebuked thee are fallen upon me.

10 I wept, and chastened myself with fasting : and that was turned to my reproof.

11 I put on sackcloth also : and they jested upon me.

12 They that sit in the gate speak against me : and the drunkards make songs upon me.

13 But, Lord, I make my prayer unto thee : in an acceptable time.

14 Hear me, O God, in the multitude of thy mercy : even in the truth of thy salvation.

15 Take me out of the mire, that I sink not : O let me be delivered from them that hate me, and out of the deep waters.

16 Let not the water-flood drown me, neither let the deep swallow me up : and let not the pit shut her mouth upon me.

17 Hear me, O Lord, for thy loving-kindness is comfortable : turn thee unto me according to the multitude of thy mercies.

18 And hide not thy face from thy servant, for I am in trouble : O haste thee, and hear me.

19 Draw nigh unto my soul, and save it : O deliver me, because of mine enemies.

20 Thou hast known my reproof, my shame, and my dishonour : mine adversaries are all in thy sight.

21 Thy rebuke hath broken my heart; I am full of heaviness : I looked for some to have pity on me, but there was no man, neither found I any to comfort me.

22 They gave me gall to eat : and when I was thirsty they gave me vinegar to drink.

23 Let their table be made a snare to take themselves withal : and let the things that should have been for their wealth be unto them an occasion of falling.

24 Let their eyes be blinded, that they see not : and ever bow thou down their backs.

25 Pour out thine indignation upon them : and let thy wrathful displeasure take hold of them.

26 Let their habitation be void : and no man to dwell in their tents.

27 For they persecute him whom thou hast smitten : and they talk how they may vex them whom thou hast wounded.

28 Let them fall from one wickedness to another : and not come into thy righteousness.

29 Let them be wiped out of the book of the living : and not be written among the righteous.

30 As for me, when I am poor and in heaviness : thy help, O God, shall lift me up.

31 I will praise the Name of God with a song : and magnify it with thanksgiving.

32 This also shall please the Lord : better than a bullock that hath horns and hoofs.

33 The humble shall consider this, and be glad : seek ye after God, and your soul shall live.

34 For the Lord heareth the poor : and despiseth not his prisoners.

35 Let heaven and earth praise him : the sea, and all that moveth therein.

36 For God will save Sion, and build the cities of Judah : that men may dwell there, and have it in possession.

37 The posterity also of his servants shall inherit it : and they that love his Name shall dwell therein.

This psalm was used for meditations upon the Passion in the primer of Henry VIII. It was a medicine psalm in the fourteenth and fifteenth centuries.

Verse 2. St. Gregory the Great lamented that he was so buffeted by the waves of business and sunk by fortune, that he could say of himself: "I am come into deep waters, so that the floods run over me."

Verse 9. St. John relates ii. 17) that the disciples applied this verse to Christ, when He had cleansed the Temple.

Verse 19. St. Boniface quoted this verse in his farewell speech to his friends. He was waiting for a number of confirmation candidates, and instead a band of armed heathen appeared, brandishing their weapons, and threatening the missionaries with death. St. Boniface laid his head upon the Gospel book and was thus slain. This was in Friesland, at a place called Dockum (A.D. 755).

Liturgical use.—Good Friday evening.
Latins.—Thursday Matins ; Maundy Thursday.
Greeks.—Tuesday night ; Nocturns for Saturday.

PSALM LXX. *Deus in adjutorium.*

HASTE thee, O God, to deliver me : make haste to help me, O Lord.

2 Let them be ashamed and confounded that seek after my soul : let them be turned backward and put to confusion that wish me evil.

3 Let them for their reward be soon brought to shame : that cry over me, There, there.

4 But let all those that seek thee be joyful and glad in thee : and let all such as delight in thy salvation say alway, the Lord be praised.

5 As for me, I am poor and in misery : haste thee unto me, O God.

6 Thou art my helper and my redeemer : O Lord, make no long tarrying.

Among the once famous writers on the Psalms was William Nicholson, author of "David's Harp strung and tuned" (1662). He was a Magdalen choir-boy, Croydon schoolmaster, Archdeacon of Brecknock, a refugee, a friend of Clarendon's, and at last Bishop of Gloucester. He was "a person of great erudition, prudence, modesty, and of a moderate mind," says Wood, meaning by the last term that he was just and fair. He maintained that the older a man gets the more he loves the Psalms. "The best of expositors have presented their thoughts on the Psalms in their riper years, and made them one of their last works."

Liturgical use.—Introit for Mass 2nd Sunday after Easter (e).
Latins.—Matins on Thursday; Maundy Thursday.
Greeks.—Tuesday night; Saturday Nocturns; Mesorion of sixth hour; late Evensong in Lent; Office for the Dying.

PSALM LXXI. *In te, Domine, speravi.*

IN thee, O Lord, have I put my trust; let me never be put to confusion : but rid me, and deliver me, in thy righteousness; incline thine ear unto me, and save me.

2 Be thou my stronghold, whereunto I may alway resort : thou hast promised to help me; for thou art my house of defence, and my castle.

3 Deliver me, O my God, out of the hand of the ungodly : out of the hand of the unrighteous and cruel man.

4 For thou, O Lord God, art the thing that I long for : thou art my hope, even from my youth.

5 Through thee have I been holden up ever since I was born : thou art he that took me out of my mother's womb; my praise shall alway be of thee.

6 I am become as it were a monster unto many : but my sure trust is in thee.

7 O let my mouth be filled with thy praise : that I may sing of thy glory and honour all the day long.

8 Cast me not away in the time of age : forsake me not when my strength faileth me.

9 For mine enemies speak against me, and they that lay wait for my soul take their counsel together, saying : God hath forsaken him, persecute him, and take him; for there is none to deliver him.

10 Go not far from me, O God : my God, haste thee to help me.

11 Let them be confounded and perish that are

against my soul : let them be covered with shame and dishonour that seek to do me evil.

12 As for me, I will patiently abide alway : and will praise thee more and more.

13 My mouth shall daily speak of thy righteousness and salvation : for I know no end thereof.

14 I will go forth in the strength of the Lord God : and will make mention of thy righteousness only.

15 Thou, O God, hast taught me from my youth up until now : therefore will I tell of thy wondrous works.

16 Forsake me not, O God, in mine old age, when I am gray-headed : until I have shewed thy strength unto this generation, and thy power to all them that are yet for to come.

17 Thy righteousness, O God, is very high, and great things are they that thou hast done : O God, who is like unto thee ?

18 O what great troubles and adversities hast thou shewed me ! and yet didst thou turn and refresh me : yea, and broughtest me from the deep of the earth again.

19 Thou hast brought me to great honour : and comforted me on every side.

20 Therefore will I praise thee and thy faithfulness, O God, playing upon an instrument of musick : unto thee will I sing upon the harp, O thou Holy One of Israel.

21 My lips will be fain when I sing unto thee ; and so will my soul whom thou hast delivered.

22 My tongue also shall talk of thy righteousness all the day long : for they are confounded and brought unto shame that seek to do me evil.

This is one of the Dirge psalms (see note on Psalm v.) in the English Dirge for the Dead.

This psalm, though it is one made up out of texts from other psalms, has been much used by Christians in their last hours. Its leading thoughts were embodied by Mary Queen of Scots, in a passionate Latin hymn she wrote before her execution : *O Domine Jesu, speravi in te.*

Bishop Fisher recited it on his way to the scaffold from the Tower ; and the blessed Thomas Cottam on the scaffold in 1568. It was sung to Bishop Jewel on his death-bed, and he joined in as well as his feeble strength would allow him. Kirke White alludes to it in his prayer found on the fly-leaf in his memorandum book.

It is this "composition psalm" which determined the compilers of our Prayer-book to compose psalms, in the same way, for the King's Accession and for Thanksgiving after a Victory at Sea.

Verse 7. This was used in the Anglo-Saxon office of Prime, very early translated into the English tongue.

Verse 8. When George Herbert was dying he quoted these words, "Lord, forsake me not when my strength faileth; but grant me mercy for the merits of my Jesus. And now, Lord —Lord, now receive my soul."

Liturgical use.—Visitation of the sick.
Latins.—Thursday morning ; Maundy Thursday.
Greeks.—Wednesday morning.

PSALM LXXII. *Deus judicium.*

GIVE the King thy judgements, O God : and thy righteousness unto the King's son.

2 Then shall he judge thy people according unto right : and defend the poor.

3 The mountains also shall bring peace : and the little hills righteousness unto the people.

4 He shall keep the simple folk by their right : defend the children of the poor, and punish the wrong doer.

5 They shall fear thee, as long as the sun and moon endureth : from one generation to another.

6 He shall come down like the rain into a fleece of wool : even as the drops that water the earth.

7 In his time shall the righteous flourish : yea, and abundance of peace, so long as the moon endureth.

8 His dominion shall be also from the one sea to the other : and from the flood unto the world's end.

9 They that dwell in the wilderness shall kneel before him : his enemies shall lick the dust.

10 The kings of Tharsis and of the isles shall give presents : the kings of Arabia and Saba shall bring gifts.

11 All kings shall fall down before him : all nations shall do him service.

12 For he shall deliver the poor when he crieth : the needy also, and him that hath no helper.

13 He shall be favourable to the simple and needy : and shall preserve the souls of the poor.

14 He shall deliver their souls from falsehood and wrong : and dear shall their blood be in his sight.

15 He shall live, and unto him shall be given of the gold of Arabia : prayer shall be made ever unto him, and daily shall he be praised.

16 There shall be an heap of corn in the earth, high upon the hills : his fruit shall shake like Libanus, and shall be green in the city like grass upon the earth.

17 His name shall endure for ever; his name shall remain under the sun among the posterities : which shall be blessed through him; and all the heathen shall praise him.

18 Blessed be the Lord God, even the God of Israel : which only doeth wondrous things;

19 And blessed be the Name of his Majesty for ever : and all the earth shall be filled with his Majesty. Amen, Amen.

This noble ideal of kingship has moulded the lives of many devout sovereigns, among them King Alfred, and Edmund of Thetford, the martyr and St. Sebastian of England. Of the latter Carlyle says, "How then, may it be asked, did this Edmund rise into favour? Really, except it were by doing justly and loving mercy to an unprecedented extent, we do not know. The man, it would seem, 'had walked,' as they say, 'humbly with God'—humbly and valiantly with God, struggling to make the earth heavenly, as he could, instead of walking sumptuously and pridefully with Mammon, leaving the earth to grow hellish as it liked, seen and felt by all men to have done a man's part in this life-pilgrimage of his; and benedictions and overflowing love and admiration from the universal heart were his meed. 'Well done! well done!' cried the hearts of all men."

Verses 10 *and* 11. These verses have caused the wise men from the East to be represented in Art as three kings.

Latins.—Thursday Matins ; Christmas; Epiphany ; Maundy Thursday ; Trinity Sunday.
Greeks.—Wednesday morning.

PSALM LXXIII. *Quam bonus Israel!*

TRULY God is loving unto Israel : even unto such as are of a clean heart.

2 Nevertheless, my feet were almost gone : my treadings had well-nigh slipt.

3 And why? I was grieved at the wicked : I do also see the ungodly in such **prosperity.**

4 For they are in no peril of death : but are lusty and strong.

5 They come in no misfortune like other folk : neither are they plagued like other men.

6 And this is the cause that they are so holden with pride ; and overwhelmed with cruelty.

7 Their eyes swell with fatness : and they do even what they lust.

8 They corrupt other, and speak of wicked blasphemy : their talking is against the most High.

9 For they stretch forth their mouth unto the heaven : and their tongue goeth through the world.

10 Therefore fall the people unto them : and thereout suck they no small advantage.

11 "Tush," say they, "how should God perceive it : is there knowledge in the most High?"

12 Lo, these are the ungodly, these prosper in the world, and these have riches in possession : and I said. "Then have I cleansed my heart in vain, and washed mine hands in innocency.

13 "All the day long have I been punished : and chastened every morning."

14 Yea, and I had almost said "even as they" : but lo, then I should have condemned the generation of thy children.

15 Then thought I to understand this : but it was too hard for me,

16 Until I went into the sanctuary of God : then understood I the end of these men ;

17 Namely, how thou dost set them in slippery places : and castest them down, and destroyest them.

18 Oh, how suddenly do they consume : perish, and come to a fearful end !

19 Yea, even like as a dream when one awaketh : so shalt thou make their image to vanish out of the city.

20 Thus my heart was grieved : and it went even through my reins.

21 So foolish was I, and ignorant : even as it were a beast before thee.

22 Nevertheless, I am alway by thee : for thou hast holden me by my right hand.

23 Thou shalt guide me with thy counsel : and after that receive me with glory.

24 Whom have I in heaven but thee : and there is none upon earth that I desire in comparison of thee.

25 My flesh and my heart faileth : but God is the strength of my heart, and my portion for ever.

26 For lo, they that forsake thee shall perish : thou hast destroyed all them that commit fornication against thee.

27 But it is good for me to hold me fast by God, to put my trust in the Lord God : and to speak of all thy works in the gates of the daughter of Sion.

Verse 17. St. Gregory the Great pathetically applies these words to his own great busy life, amid the earthly cares of which he was prevented " from thinking, much more from preaching publicly, of the miraculous works of the Lord." " Overwhelmed by the tumult of secular affairs, I am one of those," he says, " of whom it is written, ' Thou dost set them in slippery places : and castest them down.' "

Verse 17. Strafford's successor, Lord Leicester, thus comments upon the executions of the Duke of Hamilton, Lord Capel, and Lord Holland " on a cold March morning, 1650." " So the glory of the world passes away, and those that think themselves to be great and happy and safe are sette in slippery places, perish, and come to a fearfull end."

Verse 25. Charles Wesley, when dying, wrote a hymn from these words.

Latins.—Thursday Matins ; Maundy Thursday (the eve of the Passion).
Greeks.—Wednesday morning.

PSALM LXXIV. *Ut quid, Deus ?*

O GOD, wherefore art thou absent from us so long : why is thy wrath so hot against the sheep of thy pasture ?

2 O think upon thy congregation : whom thou hast purchased, and redeemed of old.

3 Think upon the tribe of thine inheritance : and mount Sion, wherein thou hast dwelt.

4 Lift up thy feet, that thou mayest utterly destroy every enemy : which hath done evil in thy sanctuary.

5 Thine adversaries roar in the midst of thy congregations : and set up their banners for tokens.

6 He that hewed timber afore out of the thick trees : was known to bring it to an excellent work.

7 But now they break down all the carved work thereof : with axes and hammers.

8 They have set fire upon thy holy places : and have defiled the dwelling-place of thy Name, even unto the ground.

9 Yea, they said in their hearts, " Let us make havock of them altogether " : thus have they burnt up all the houses of God in the land.

10 We see not our tokens, there is not one prophet more : no, not one is there among us, that understandeth any more.

11 O God, how long shall the adversary do this dishonour : how long shall the enemy blaspheme thy Name, for ever ?

12 Why withdrawest thou thy hand : why pluckest thou not thy right hand out of thy bosom to consume the enemy ?

13 For God is my King of old : the help that is done upon earth he doeth it himself.

14 Thou didst divide the sea through thy power : thou brakest the heads of the dragons in the waters.

15 Thou smotest the heads of Leviathan in pieces : and gavest him to be meat for the people in the wilderness.

16 Thou broughtest out fountains and waters out of the hard rocks : thou driedest up mighty waters.

17 The day is thine, and the night is thine : thou hast prepared the light and the sun.

18 Thou hast set all the borders of the earth : thou hast made summer and winter.

19 Remember this, O Lord, how the enemy hath rebuked : and how the foolish people hath blasphemed thy Name.

20 O deliver not the soul of thy turtle-dove unto the multitude of the enemies : and forget not the congregation of the poor for ever.

21 Look upon the covenant : for all the earth is full of darkness, and cruel habitations.

22 O let not the simple go away ashamed : but let the poor and needy give praise unto thy Name.

23 Arise, O God, maintain thine own cause : remember how the foolish man blasphemeth thee daily.

24 Forget not the voice of thine enemies : the presumption of them that hate thee increaseth ever more and more.

This psalm was much used in the great northern rebellion, the Pilgrimage of Grace, 1537, which followed the suppression of the abbeys. Robert Aske, the leader, accounts for the revolt, saying that in the North "the abbeys gave great alms to poor men, and laudably served God. In which parts, of late days, they had but small comfort of ghostly teaching ; and by occasion of the said suppression the divine service of Almighty God is much diminished, great numbers of Masses unsaid, and the blessed consecration of the Sacrament now not used and showed in those places, to the distress of the faith and spiritual comfort to man's soul. The temple of God (is now) razed and pulled down ; the ornaments and relics of the Church of God unreverently used ; the tombs and sepulchres of honourable and noble men pulled down and sold."

Emanuel Swedenborg — beloved of Coleridge — concluded from the same psalm that "The Church, with all things belonging thereto, has been entirely destroyed and its holy things profaned," and that he was commissioned to refound and reconsecrate it (1688-1772).

Verse 17. *Tuus est dies et tua est nox: tu fabricatus es auroram et solem.* This is the dial motto at Maxey Vicarage, Northampton.

Verse 24. *Ne obliviscaris* is the old motto of the Dukes of Argyle.

Latins.—Thursday Matins ; Maundy Thursday (eve of the Passion).
Greeks.—Wednesday morning.

PSALM LXXV. *Confitebimur tibi.*

UNTO thee, O God, do we give thanks : yea, unto thee do we give thanks.

2 Thy Name also is so nigh : and that do thy wondrous works declare.

3 "When I receive the congregation : I shall judge according unto right.

4 "The earth is weak, and all the inhabiters thereof : I bear up the pillars of it.

5 "I said unto the fools, Deal not so madly : and to the ungodly, Set not up your horn."

6 Set not up your horn on high : and speak not with a stiff neck.

7 For promotion cometh neither from the east, nor from the west : nor yet from the south.

8 And why? God is the Judge : he putteth down one, and setteth up another.

9 For in the hand of the Lord there is a cup, and the wine is red : it is full mixed, and he poureth out of the same.

10 As for the dregs thereof : all the ungodly of the earth shall drink them, and suck them out.

11 But I will talk of the God of Jacob : and praise him for ever.

12 All the horns of the ungodly also will I break : and the horns of the righteous shall be exalted.

Sir Walter Raleigh, in his "History of the World" (a book which Cromwell loved and studied), has an interesting note on the Psalter. "For his internal gifts and graces David so far exceeded all other men, as, putting his human frailty apart, he was said by God Himself to be a man according to His own heart. The psalms which he wrote instance his piety and his *excellent learning*, of whom Jerome to Paulinus : 'David,' saith he, 'our Simonides, Pindarus, and Alcæus, Horatius Catullus and Serenus, playeth Christ on his harp, and on a ten-stringed lute raiseth Him up rising from the dead. And being both a king and prophet, he foretelleth Christ more lightsomely and lively than all the rest.'"

Liturgical use.—Introit for the Mass 3rd Sunday after Easter (e).

Latins.—Thursday Matins ; Maundy Thursday ; Apostles and Evangelists.

Greeks.—Wednesday morning.

PSALM LXXVI. *Notus in Judæa.*

IN Jewry is God known : his name is great in Israel.

2 At Salem is his tabernacle : and his dwelling in Sion.

3 There brake he the arrows of the bow : the shield, the sword, and the battle.

4 Thou art of more honour and might : than the hills of the robbers.

5 The proud are robbed, they have slept their sleep :

and all the men whose hands were mighty have found nothing.

6 At thy rebuke, O God of Jacob : both the chariot and horse are fallen.

7 Thou, even thou art to be feared : and who may stand in thy sight when thou art angry ?

8 Thou didst cause thy judgement to be heard from heaven : the earth trembled, and was still,

9 When God arose to judgement : and to help all the meek upon earth.

10 The fierceness of man shall turn to thy praise : and the fierceness of them shalt thou refrain.

11 Promise unto the Lord your God, and keep it, all ye that are round about him : bring presents unto him that ought to be feared.

12 He shall refrain the spirit of princes : and is wonderful among the kings of the earth.

This psalm was Charles Kingsley's favourite : he called it "my psalm."

The rebel covenanters at Drumclog (in 1649), so vividly described by Scott in "Old Mortality," sang this psalm. It had been sung in Edinburgh at the defeat of the Armada, and in many of the London churches at the same news.

Verse 11. When St. Bonaventura (the Seraphic doctor) was twenty-two years old, he was meditating upon this verse, he remembered that when he was a child, and near death with sickness, his mother had promised him to St. Francis. He then joined that order.

Latins.—Thursday morning ; Maundy Thursday ; Easter Eve.
Greeks.—Wednesday morning.

PSALM LXXVII. *Voce mea ad Dominum.*

"I WILL cry unto God with my voice : even unto God will I cry with my voice, and he shall hearken unto me."

2 In the time of my trouble I sought the Lord : my sore ran, and ceased not in the night-season ; my soul refused comfort.

3 "When I am in heaviness, I will think upon God : when my heart is vexed, I will complain."

4 Thou holdest mine eyes waking : I am so feeble, that I cannot speak.

5 I have considered the days of old : and the years that are past.

6 I call to remembrance my song : and in the night I commune with mine own heart, and search out my spirits.

7 " Will the Lord absent himself for ever : and will he be no more intreated ?

8 " Is his mercy clean gone for ever : and is his promise come utterly to an end for evermore ?

9 " Hath God forgotten to be gracious : and will he shut up his loving-kindness in displeasure ?"

10 And I said, " It is mine own infirmity : but I will remember the years of the right hand of the most Highest.

11 " I will remember the works of the Lord : and call to mind thy wonders of old time.

12 " I will think also of all thy works : and my talking shall be of thy doings."

13 Thy way, O God, is holy : who is so great a God as our God ?

14 Thou art the God that doeth wonders : and hast declared thy power among the people.

15 Thou hast mightily delivered thy people : even the sons of Jacob and Joseph.

16 The waters saw thee, O God, the waters saw thee, and were afraid : the depths also were troubled.

17 The clouds poured out water, the air thundered : and thine arrows went abroad.

18 The voice of thy thunder was heard round about : the lightnings shone upon the ground ; the earth was moved, and shook withal.

19 Thy way is in the sea, and thy paths in the great waters : and thy footsteps are not known.

20 Thou leddest thy people like sheep : by the hand of Moses and Aaron.

This is the psalm Bishop Hooper recommended to his wife " when you find yourself too much oppressed." He had just been condemned to be burned.

Verse 5. " Not pathetic only, but profound also, and of the most solid substance, was that reply made by the old Carthusian monk to the trifler who asked him how he managed to get through his life. *Cogitavi dies antiquos et annos æternos in mente habui*" (M. Arnold, on the study of history).

Latins.—Matins on Thursday ; Maundy Thursday.
Greeks.—Wednesday morning.

PSALM LXXVIII. *Attendite, popule.*

HEAR my law, O my people : incline your ears unto the words of my mouth.

2 I will open my mouth in a parable : I will declare hard sentences of old;

3 Which we have heard and known : and such as our fathers have told us;

4 That we should not hide them from the children of the generations to come : but to shew the honour of the Lord, his mighty and wonderful works that he hath done.

5 He made a covenant with Jacob, and gave Israel a law : which he commanded our forefathers to teach their children;

6 That their posterity might know it : and the children which were yet unborn;

7 To the intent that when they came up : they might shew their children the same;

8 That they might put their trust in God : and not to forget the works of God, but to keep his commandments;

9 And not to be as their forefathers, a faithless and stubborn generation : a generation that set not their heart aright, and whose spirit cleaveth not stedfastly unto God;

10 Like as the children of Ephraim : who being harnessed, and carrying bows, turned themselves back in the day of battle.

11 They kept not the covenant of God : and would not walk in his law;

12 But forgat what he had done : and the wonderful works that he had shewed for them.

13 Marvellous things did he in the sight of our forefathers, in the land of Egypt : even in the field of Zoan.

14 He divided the sea, and let them go through : he made the waters to stand on an heap.

15 In the day-time also he led them with a cloud : and all the night through with a light of fire.

16 He clave the hard rocks in the wilderness : and

gave them drink thereof, as it had been out of the great depth.

17 He brought waters out of the stony rock : so that it gushed out like the rivers.

18 Yet for all this they sinned more against him : and provoked the most Highest in the wilderness.

19 They tempted God in their hearts : and required meat for their lust.

20 They spake against God also, saying : Shall God prepare a table in the wilderness?

21 He smote the stony rock indeed, that the water gushed out, and the streams flowed withal : but can he give bread also, or provide flesh for his people?

22 When the Lord heard this, he was wroth : so the fire was kindled in Jacob, and there came up heavy displeasure against Israel;

23 Because they believed not in God : and put not their trust in his help.

24 So he commanded the clouds above : and opened the doors of heaven.

25 He rained down manna also upon them for to eat : and gave them food from heaven.

26 So man did eat angels' food : for he sent them meat enough.

27 He caused the east wind to blow under heaven : and through his power he brought in the south-west wind.

28 He rained flesh upon them as thick as dust : and feathered fowls like as the sand of the sea.

29 He let it fall among their tents : even round about their habitation.

30 So they did eat, and were well filled; for he gave them their own desire : they were not disappointed of their lust.

31 But while the meat was yet in their mouth, the heavy wrath of God came upon them, and slew the wealthiest of them : yea, and smote down the chosen men that were in Israel.

32 But for all this they sinned yet more : and believed not his wondrous works.

33 Therefore their days did he consume in vanity : and their years in trouble.

34 When he slew them, they sought him : and turned them early, and inquired after God.

35 And they remembered that God was their strength : and that the high God was their redeemer.

36 Nevertheless, they did but flatter him with their mouth : and dissembled with him in their tongue.

37 For their heart was not whole with him : neither continued they stedfast in his covenant.

38 But he was so merciful, that he forgave their misdeeds : and destroyed them not.

39 Yea, many a time turned he his wrath away : and would not suffer his whole displeasure to arise.

40 For he considered that they were but flesh : and that they were even a wind that passeth away, and cometh not again.

41 Many a time did they provoke him in the wilderness : and grieved him in the desert.

42 They turned back, and tempted God : and moved the Holy One in Israel.

43 They thought not of his hand : and of the day when he delivered them from the hand of the enemy;

44 How he had wrought his miracles in Egypt : and his wonders in the field of Zoan.

45 He turned their waters into blood : so that they might not drink of the rivers.

46 He sent lice among them, and devoured them up : and frogs to destroy them.

47 He gave their fruit unto the caterpillar : and their labour unto the grasshopper.

48 He destroyed their vines with hail-stones : and their mulberry-trees with the frost.

49 He smote their cattle also with hail-stones : and their flocks with hot thunderbolts.

50 He cast upon them the furiousness of his wrath, anger, displeasure, and trouble : and sent evil angels among them.

51 He made a way to his indignation, and spared not their soul from death : but gave their life over to the pestilence;

52 And smote all the first-born in Egypt : the most principal and mightiest in the dwellings of Ham.

53 But as for his own people, he led them forth like sheep : and carried them in the wilderness like a flock.

54 He brought them out safely, that they should not fear : and overwhelmed their enemies with the sea.

55 And brought them within the borders of his sanctuary : even to his mountain which he purchased with his right hand.

56 He cast out the heathen also before them : caused their land to be divided among them for an heritage, and made the tribes of Israel to dwell in their tents.

57 So they tempted, and displeased the most high God : and kept not his testimonies;

58 But turned their backs, and fell away like their forefathers : starting aside like a broken bow.

59 For they grieved him with their hill-altars : and provoked him to displeasure with their images.

60 When God heard this, he was wroth : and took sore displeasure at Israel.

61 So that he forsook the tabernacle in Silo : even the tent that he had pitched among men.

62 He delivered their power into captivity : and their beauty into the enemy's hand.

63 He gave his people over also unto the sword : and was wroth with his inheritance.

64 The fire consumed their young men : and their maidens were not given to marriage.

65 Their priests were slain with the sword : and there were no widows to make lamentation.

66 So the Lord awaked as one out of sleep : and like a giant refreshed with wine.

67 He smote his enemies in the hinder parts : and put them to a perpetual shame.

68 He refused the tabernacle of Joseph : and chose not the tribe of Ephraim;

69 But chose the tribe of Judah : even the hill of Sion which he loved.

70 And there he built his temple on high : and laid the foundation of it like the ground which he hath made continually.

71 He chose David also his servant : and took him away from the sheep-folds.

72 As he was following the ewes great with young

ones he took him : that he might feed Jacob his people, and Israel his inheritance.

73 So he fed them with a faithful and true heart : and ruled them prudently with all his power.

Uppingham boys will like to know that this was the last psalm read in the school by Edward Thring, their great head-master, before he died, "weary, ill and battered." Many of those who knew him felt that the last verse was one that exactly summed up his own head-mastership.

"Of the other Scriptures," says Theodore in the fifth century, "the generality of men know next to nothing. But the Psalms you will find again and again repeated in private houses, in market places, in streets, by those who have learned them by heart, and who soothe themselves by their divine melody." "When other parts of Scripture are used," says St. Ambrose, "there is such a noise of talking in the church that you cannot hear what is said. But when the Psalter is read, all are silent." The Psalms were sung by the ploughmen of Palestine in the time of Jerome ; by the boatmen of Gaul in the time of Sidonius Apollinaris. In the most barbarous of churches—the Abyssinian—the Psalter is treated almost as an idol, is the only book allowed to be read by the children of the laity, and is sung through from end to end at every funeral. In the most Protestant of churches—the Presbyterians of Scotland, the Nonconformists of England—"psalm-singing" has almost passed into a familiar description of their ritual. In the churches of Rome and of England they are daily recited, in proportions such as far exceed the reverence shown to any other portion of the Scriptures (*Stanley*).

Verse 2. St. Matthew quotes this of Christ's parables.

Verse 34. St. Porphyry, Bishop of Gaza, used often to point out this verse to his people, to remind them that God's service is purified by a persecution even to the death.

Verse 71. Bishop Lightfoot's motto for St. Columba's window at Bishop Auckland is *Sustulit eum de gregibus ovium*.

Latins.—Thursday Matins.
Greeks.—Wednesday morning.

PSALM LXXIX. *Deus, venerunt.*

O GOD, the heathen are come into thine inheritance : thy holy temple have they defiled, and made Jerusalem an heap of stones.

2 The dead bodies of thy servants have they given to be meat unto the fowls of the air : and the flesh of thy saints unto the beasts of the land.

3 Their blood have they shed like water on every side of Jerusalem : and there was no man to bury them.

4 We are become an open shame to our enemies : a very scorn and derision unto them that are round about us.

5 Lord, how long wilt thou be angry : shall thy jealousy burn like fire for ever ?

6 Pour out thine indignation upon the heathen that have not known thee : and upon the kingdoms that have not called upon thy Name.

7 For they have devoured Jacob : and laid waste his dwelling-place.

8 O remember not our old sins, but have mercy upon us, and that soon : for we are come to great misery.

9 Help us, O God of our salvation, for the glory of thy Name : O deliver us, and be merciful unto our sins, for thy Name's sake.

10 Wherefore do the heathen say : Where is now their God ?

11 O let the vengeance of thy servants' blood that is shed : be openly shewed upon the heathen in our sight.

12 O let the sorrowful sighing of the prisoners come before thee : according to the greatness of thy power, preserve thou those that are appointed to die.

13 And for the blasphemy wherewith our neighbours have blasphemed thee : reward thou them, O Lord, seven-fold into their bosom.

14 So we, that are thy people, and sheep of thy pasture, shall give thee thanks for ever : and will alway be shewing forth thy praise from generation to generation.

This psalm was formerly used in the Evensong of King Charles, the martyr, the proper psalms then being lxxix., xciv., and lxxxv. It was applied as freely to the Puritan excesses as it afterwards was to the profanity of the French Revolutionists ; and who can wonder, when pious Bishop Hall saw Norwich Cathedral filled with "muskatiers drinking and tobacconing freely"? "Lord, what work was here, what clattering of glasses, what beating down of Walls, what tearing up of Monuments, what pulling down of Seates, what wrestling out of Irons and Brass from the Windowes and Graves! What defacing of Armes, what demolishing of curious stonework, that had not any representation in the World, but only of the cost of the Founder and skill of the Mason, what toting and piping upon the destroyed Organ pipe, and what a hideous triumph on the Market-day before all the Countrey, when, in a kind of Sacrilegious and profane procession, all the Organ-pipes, Vestments, both Copes and Surplices, together with the Leaden Crosse which had been newly sawne down from over the Green-Yard Pulpit, and the Service books and singing-books that could be had were carried to the fire in the publick Market-place; A leud wretch walking before the Train, in his Cope trailing in the dirt, with a Service book in his hand, imitating in an impious scorne the tune and usurping the words of the Letany; neer the publick Crosse, all these monuments of Idolatry must be sacrificed to the fire, not without much Ostentation of a zealous joy."

This is a psalm much used by our people during the Indian Mutiny. It was read at Lucknow frequently during the siege; at Cawnpore and in Meerut the Roman Catholics added it to their daily devotions.

Among the other saints who made use of it were the noble brothers SS. Crispin and Crispinian at the martyrdom at Soissons. They had renounced their rank, and for the love of Christ made shoes for the poor, and were slain as traitors to the Empire. Their bodies were cast into the sea, "but the waves, from love of His feet who had walked upon them, carried the holy bodies of the brothers to Romney Marsh, where the inhabitants, weeping for joy, received them and built a church to receive them" at Lydd.

Abbot Hobbs, the last Abbot of Woburn Abbey, in a pathetic last effort to inspire his disordered community with the old Faith and Order, bade each monk to recite this psalm on Fridays, "because of the evil times and his own sorrow, till certain did murmur about the saying of it, and so it was left;" and shortly after the Abbey was secularized and given to the Russells.

Every Friday the Jews use this great lament over the ruins of Jerusalem.

Verse 2. This is the motto which Parsons, the Jesuit, chose for his celebrated book, *De persecutione Anglicana*, 1581.

Verses 5 and 8. These are the words of St. Augustine's great agony under the fig-tree in the garden, when he was tortured by the great struggle which ended in his conversion.

Liturgical use.—Introit for Childermas (e).
Latins.—Thursday Matins (*Sarum*, All Saints').
Greeks.—Wednesday morning.

PSALM LXXX. *Qui regis Israel.*

HEAR, O thou Shepherd of Israel, thou that leadest Joseph like a sheep: shew thyself also, thou that sittest upon the cherubims.

Morning Prayer　　PSALM LXXX　　*Day* 16

2 Before Ephraim, Benjamin, and Manasses : stir up thy strength and come and help us.

3 Turn us again, O God : shew the light of thy countenance, and we shall be whole.

4 O Lord God of hosts : how long wilt thou be angry with thy people that prayeth ?

5 Thou feedest them with the bread of tears : and givest them plenteousness of tears to drink.

6 Thou hast made us a very strife unto our neighbours : and our enemies laugh us to scorn.

7 Turn us again, thou God of hosts : shew the light of thy countenance, and we shall be whole.

8 Thou hast brought a vine out of Egypt : thou hast cast out the heathen, and planted it.

9 Thou madest room for it : and when it had taken root it filled the land.

10 The hills were covered with the shadow of it : and the boughs thereof are like the goodly cedar-trees.

11 She stretched out her branches unto the sea : and her boughs unto the river.

12 Why hast thou then broken down her hedge : that all they that go by pluck off her grapes ?

13 The wild boar out of the wood doth root it up : and the wild beasts of the field devour it.

14 Turn thee again, thou God of hosts, look down from heaven : behold, and visit this vine ;

15 And the place of the vineyard that thy right hand hath planted : and the branch that thou madest so strong for thyself.

16 It is burnt with fire, and cut down : and they shall perish at the rebuke of thy countenance.

17 Let thy hand be upon the man of thy right hand : and upon the son of man, whom thou madest so strong for thine own self.

18 And so will not we go back from thee : O let us live, and we shall call upon thy Name.

19 Turn us again, O Lord God of hosts : show the light of thy countenance, and we shall be whole.

Verse 3. On a sundial in Abbeyfield is written, "Shew me the light of Thy countenance."

Verses 8, 9, *and* 10. Among the numberless versifiers of the Psalms was Walton's friend, Dr. Henry King, Bishop of Chichester, who appeared at the Savoy Conference. He was once disgusted at the wretched expression of a metrical psalm "which quite marred the penman's matter and his own devotion" in the current metrical version, and, thinking George Sandys' version "too eloquent for the vulgar use," composed a version of his own, and dedicated to Archbishop Usher in 1651:

"Thou didst a Vine from Ægypt bring,
  Thy hand which planted made it spring,
  And that it might have room to spred,
  The Heathen were discomfited:

"Its root Thou caused'st fast to stand,
  And with faire branches fill the land;
  The Hills were cover'd with Hir shade,
  Hir boughes like goodly Cedar's made."

Here is Sandys' version of the same verses (1635):

"This vine from Egypt brought (the foe Expeld) was planted by thy hand,
  Thou gav'st it roome and strength to grow
  Until her branches fill'd the Land.

"The Mountaines tooke a shade from these,
  Which like a grove of Cedars stood,
  Extending to the Tyrian seas
  And to Euphrates rowling Flood."

Verse 13. Applied by Origen to himself in the bitter lament he made for his apostasy (*vide* Psalm l.).

Verse 14. Archbishop Thomas de Rotherham refounded Lincoln College, Oxford, owing to a stirring sermon preached from this text by Tristoppe, the Rector in 1478. Bishop Flemmyng had founded it in 1426, but it languished. By the licence of Edward IV. five new fellowships were added. The vines in the college are in allusion to this.

Verse 19. This is used in the Anglo-Saxon vernacular office of Prime, and occurs frequently in a detached form in many services.

Latins.—Matins on Thursday.
Greeks.—Wednesday morning.

PSALM LXXXI. *Exultate Deo.*

SING we merrily unto God our strength : make a cheerful noise unto the God of Jacob.

2 Take the psalm, bring hither the tabret : the merry harp with the lute.

3 Blow up the trumpet in the new-moon : even in the time appointed, and upon our solemn feast-day.

4 For this was made a statute for Israel : and a law of the God of Jacob.

5 This he ordained in Joseph for a testimony : when he came out of the land of Egypt, and had heard a strange language.

6 I eased his shoulder from the burden : and his hands were delivered from making the pots.

7 Thou calledst upon me in troubles, and I delivered thee : and heard thee what time as the storm fell upon thee.

8 I proved thee also : at the waters of strife.

9 Hear, O my people, and I will assure thee, O Israel : if thou wilt hearken unto me,

10 There shall no strange god be in thee : neither shalt thou worship any other god.

11 I am the Lord thy God, who brought thee out of the land of Egypt : open thy mouth wide, and I shall fill it.

12 But my people would not hear my voice : and Israel would not obey me.

13 So I gave them up unto their own hearts' lusts : and let them follow their own imaginations.

14 O that my people would have hearkened unto me : for if Israel had walked in my ways,

15 I should soon have put down their enemies : and turned my hand against their adversaries.

16 The haters of the Lord should have been found liars : but their time should have endured for ever.

17 He should have fed them also with the finest wheat-flour : and with honey out of the stony rock should I have satisfied thee.

To carry a Psalter seemed a necessity to the religious of the Middle Ages. In Chaucer's Romaunt of the Rose, when "Dame Abstinence-Streyned" wishes to dress up as a Beguine, she takes the coverchief of thread, "But she forgate not hir Sawter," which was quite as much part of the costume.

Latins.—Friday Matins.
Greeks.—Wednesday morning.

PSALM LXXXII. *Deus stetit.*

GOD standeth in the congregation of princes : he is a Judge among gods.

2 How long will ye give wrong judgement : and accept the persons of the ungodly?

3 Defend the poor and fatherless: see that such as are in need and necessity have right.

4 Deliver the out-cast and poor : save them from the hand of the ungodly.

5 They will not be learned nor understand, but walk on still in darkness : all the foundations of the earth are out of course.

6 I have said, Ye are gods : and ye are all the children of the most Highest.

7 But ye shall die like men : and fall like one of the princes.

8 Arise, O God, and judge thou the earth : for thou shalt take all heathen to thine inheritance.

Verse 1. This is the thought which decided Constantine not to act as umpire between contending bishops at Nicæa ; for he regarded the "gods" as meaning the clergy. This use of the term, of course, was prominent in the struggles between Popes and Emperors in after-ages.

Bishop Andrewes preached before the House of Lords in Westminster Abbey (Jan. 30, 1621) from this text, and by making no allusion to the critical state of public affairs, made "a tacit protest against the growing tendency of Churchmen to engage in politics and serve in secular affairs."

Verse 6. Our Lord quoted these words to justify His language when He said, "I and My Father are one," after which they were about to stone Him, in Solomon's Porch.

Latins.—Friday Matins.
Greeks.—Wednesday morning.

PSALM LXXXIII. *Deus, quis similis?*

HOLD not thy tongue, O God, keep not still silence : refrain not thyself, O God.

2 For lo, thine enemies make a murmuring : and they that hate thee have lift up their head.

3 They have imagined craftily against thy people : and taken counsel against thy secret ones.

4 They have said, Come, and let us root them out, that they be no more a people : and that the name of Israel may be no more in remembrance.

5 For they have cast their heads together with one consent : and are confederate against thee ;

6 The tabernacles of the Edomites, and the Ismaelites : the Moabites, and Hagarenes ;

7 Gebal, and Ammon, and Amalek : the Philistines, with them that dwell at Tyre.

8 Assur also is joined with them : and have holpen the children of Lot.

9 But do thou to them as unto the Madianites : unto Sisera, and unto Jabin at the brook of Kison;

10 Who perished at Endor : and became as the dung of the earth.

11 Make them and their princes like Oreb and Zeb : yea, make all their princes like as Zeba and Salmana;

12 Who say, " Let us take to ourselves : the houses of God in possession."

13 O my God, make them like unto a wheel : and as the stubble before the wind;

14 Like as the fire that burneth up the wood : and as the flame that consumeth the mountains.

15 Persecute them even so with thy tempest : and make them afraid with thy storm.

16 Make their faces ashamed, O Lord : that they may seek thy Name.

17 Let them be confounded and vexed ever more and more : let them be put to shame, and perish.

18 And they shall know that thou, whose Name is Jehovah : art only the most Highest over all the earth.

The monks at Jarrow were chanting this psalm while St. Benedict Biscop died, and they took it as an omen that the powers of evil could not prevail against his parting soul.

James I. translated the Psalter into metre rather well. Charles I. published his " dear father's " work, and hoped with it to oust Sternhold, but in vain. Here is his version of the close of this psalm. It was printed at the side of our version :

" So with Thy tempest them pursue,
and with Thy storm them fright ;
Their faces fill with shame, that they may seek Thy Name aright.
Let them confounded be, and prove
from trouble never free ;
Yea, let them all be put to shame,
and wholly ruined be.
That men may know that Thou, whose name Jehovah is alone,
Art the most high, the like of whom
o'er all the earth is none."

Bishop Williams declares that the royal author died after he had done only thirty of these psalms ; but Charles's *Imprimatur* gives the whole book to his father.

Liturgical use.—Introit for Mass on IV Sunday after Easter (e).
Latins.—Matins on Friday.
Greeks.—Wednesday morning.

PSALM LXXXIV. *Quam dilecta!*

O HOW amiable are thy dwellings : thou Lord of hosts!

2 My soul hath a desire and longing to enter into the courts of the Lord : my heart and my flesh rejoice in the living God.

3 Yea, the sparrow hath found her an house, and the swallow a nest where she may lay her young : even thy altars, O Lord of hosts, my King and my God.

4 Blessed are they that dwell in thy house : they will be alway praising thee.

5 Blessed is the man whose strength is in thee : in whose heart are thy ways.

6 Who going through the vale of misery use it for a well : and the pools are filled with water.

7 They will go from strength to strength : and unto the God of gods appeareth every one of them in Sion.

8 O Lord God of hosts, hear my prayer : hearken, O God of Jacob.

9 Behold, O God our defender : and look upon the face of thine Anointed.

10 For one day in thy courts : is better than a thousand.

11 I had rather be a door-keeper in the house of my God : than to dwell in the tents of ungodliness.

12 For the Lord God is a light and defence : the Lord will give grace and worship, and no good thing shall he withhold from them that live a godly life.

13 O Lord God of hosts : blessed is the man that putteth his trust in thee.

This is used as a psalm of preparation for the Holy Communion by devout people of all shades of belief. It is recommended, not only by the Pope, but by our own great divines for this use, and even by devout Nonconformists and Separatists.

It is a preparation for Holy Dying as well as for Holy Living. When the aged Paula drew near her end she repeated again and again the opening verses, the tenth verse, and (Psalm xxvi. 8) " Lord, I have loved the habitation of Thy house, and the place where Thine honour dwelleth." St. Jerome had inspired her with this enthusiasm for the Church, and what it represented.

This psalm was a favourite with Rev. F. H. Lyte, the editor of Henry Vaughan's *Silex Scintillans*, and the author of "Abide with me." It is the basis of his hymn, "Pleasant are thy courts above." He translated many of the Psalms into verse.

Verse 2. The monk Jocelyn in his life of England's St. Augustine, tells us how passionate was the saint's longing to depart and be with Christ. "Who will give me wings as of a dove? My soul hath a desire and longing to enter into the courts of the Lord." The saint was "a tall, straight man, kind and dignified in face, with his hair falling on either side of his open countenance. He mostly went barefoot."

Verse 7. St. Columba's motto, when he met in conference with Kentigern (584 A.D.), near where Glasgow stands.

Verse 11. St. Thomas Aquinas's verse, which resolved him to join the Dominican order. He was but thirteen years old when he received this vocation, and had to combat all the wishes of his family to obey the call.

Verse 12. "This, as it was the ancient Psalmist's faith, let it likewise be ours. It is the Alpha and Omega, I reckon, of all possessions that belong to man" (Carlyle to his brother, June 27, 1824).

Liturgical use.—Introit to the Mass for the V Sunday after Easter.
Latins.—Friday Matins; Dedication of a church.
Greeks.—Wednesday morning; Ninth hour; Burial of Priests.

PSALM LXXXV. *Benedixisti, Domine.*

LORD, thou art become gracious unto thy land : thou hast turned away the captivity of Jacob.

2 Thou hast forgiven the offence of thy people : and covered all their sins.

3 Thou hast taken away all thy displeasure : and turned thyself from thy wrathful indignation.

4 Turn us then, O God our Saviour : and let thine anger cease from us.

5 Wilt thou be displeased at us for ever : and wilt thou stretch out thy wrath from one generation to another?

6 Wilt thou not turn again and quicken us : that thy people may rejoice in thee?

7 Shew us thy mercy, O God : and grant us thy salvation.

8 I will hearken what the Lord God will say concerning me : for he shall speak peace unto his people, and to his saints, that they turn not again.

9 For his salvation is nigh them that fear him : that glory may dwell in our land.

10 Mercy and truth are met together : righteousness and peace have kissed each other.

11 Truth shall flourish out of the earth : and righteousness hath looked down from heaven.

12 Yea, the Lord shall shew loving-kindness : and our land shall give her increase.

13 Righteousness shall go before him : and he shall direct his going in the way.

Another preparation psalm, with Psalm lxxxiv., lxxxvi., and cxxx.

Verse 4. This was in the Anglo-Saxon vernacular Prime office, said at six o'clock.

Verse 8. This is the thought which grew into the third book of St. Thomas à Kempis's *De Imitatione Christi*, on Internal Consolation, perhaps the best part of one of the best of books. "The small old-fashioned book, for which you need only pay sixpence on a bookstall, works miracles to this day, turning bitter waters into sweetness; while expensive sermons and treatises, newly issued, leave all things as they were before. It was written down by a hand that waited for the heart's prompting ; it is the chronicle of a solitary hidden anguish, trust and triumph—not written on velvet cushions to teach endurance to those who are treading with bleeding feet on the stones. And so it remains to all time a lasting record of human needs and human consolations ; the voice of a brother who years ago felt and suffered and renounced—in the cloister, perhaps, with serge gown and tonsured head, with much chanting and long fasts, and with a fashion of speech different from ours—but under the same silent far-off heavens, and with the same passionate desires, the same strivings, the same failures, the same weariness' (G. Eliot).

Verse 10. This was the verse chosen by King Henry III. when he preached to the Winchester monks upon their duties to the Crown. He succeeded in his object, which was to get Æthelmar, his nominee, elected abbot, for, as the historian remarks, *Stricto supplicat ense potens !* It was a favourite text in the mouth of Bishop Andrewes, and one much used in mediæval writers for the Incarnation. Blake, from his instinctive sympathy with the Middle Ages, painted his illustration of the text "in two figures, not four. Jesus is the representative of Mercy and Righteousness : Truth and Peace are embodied in a beardless youth. The two are seated, and turn round to kiss and embrace, their arms meeting over a Greek cross. Above, at the summit of some steps, is an aged man with a book, no doubt representing the Deity. He is surrounded by a glory of angels." An interesting work, yellow being the predominant tint !

Liturgical use.—Christmas morning.
Latins.—Friday Matins ; Christmas Day.
Greeks.—Wednesday morning ; Ninth hour.

PSALM LXXXVI. *Inclina, Domine.*

BOW down thine ear, O Lord, and hear me : for I am poor, and in misery.

2 Preserve thou my soul, for I am holy : my God, save thy servant that putteth his trust in thee.

3 Be merciful unto me, O God : for I will call daily upon thee.

4 Comfort the soul of thy servant : for unto thee, O Lord, do I lift up my soul.

5 For thou, Lord, art good and gracious : and of great mercy unto all them that call upon thee.

6 Give ear, Lord, unto my prayer : and ponder the voice of my humble desires.

7 In the time of my trouble I will call upon thee : for thou hearest me.

8 Among the gods there is none like unto thee, O Lord : there is not one that can do as thou doest.

9 All nations whom thou hast made shall come and worship thee, O Lord : and shall glorify thy Name.

10 For thou art great, and doest wondrous things : thou art God alone.

11 Teach me thy way, O Lord, and I will walk in thy truth : O knit my heart unto thee, that I may fear thy Name.

12 I will thank thee, O Lord my God, with all my heart : and will praise thy Name for evermore.

13 For great is thy mercy toward me : and thou hast delivered my soul from the nethermost hell.

14 O God, the proud are risen against me : and the congregations of naughty men have sought after my soul, and have not set thee before their eyes.

15 But thou, O Lord God, art full of compassion and mercy : long-suffering, plenteous in goodness and truth.

16 O turn thee then unto me, and have mercy upon me : give thy strength unto thy servant, and help the son of thine handmaid.

17 Shew some token upon me for good, that they who hate me may see it, and be ashamed : because thou, Lord, hast holpen me, and comforted me.

This psalm is also a devout preparation for the Holy Communion (*vide* Psalm lxxxiv.).

"Men seemingly the most unlikely to express enthusiasm about any such matter," says Trench, speaking of the Psalter, "have been forward as the forwardest to set their seal to this book, have left their confession that it was the voice of their innermost heart, that the spirit of it passed into their spirits, as did the spirit of no other book ; that it found them more often and at greater depths of their being, lifted them to higher heights than did any other — or, as one greatly suffering man, telling of the solace which he found from this Book of Psalms in the hours of a long imprisonment, has expressed it, that it bore him up into the everlasting sunlight, till he saw the world and all its troubles for ever underneath him."

Verse 1. The Oxford Movement supplied a metrical version, of a brighter faith, and in a more melodious fashion than the doggerel of the "New Version." Keble undertook it anonymously, but even then unmistakably :

O Lord, bow down Thine ear and hear,
Poor am I, low and lone.
Preserve my soul, for I am dear
And holy, all Thine own."

Verses 10 *and* 11. When Diocletian was beginning to draw men's attention to the Church by persecuting her, a young man, Luxorius of Sardinia, ran through the Psalter, out of curiosity, wishing to know something of Christian literature. He got as far as these verses, and could contain himself no longer, but rushed to a Christian Church and entered himself as a catechumen. On his way back he heard the words *Retribue servo tuo vivam et custodiam vias tuas* (Ps. cix.), which comforted him in the faith, so that he boldly endured martyrdom with the sword.

Verse 15. This is evidently the verse to which Tennyson's poor old Rizpah appeals, against the callous visiting lady :

" Sin ? O yes—we are sinners, I know—let all that be,
And read me a Bible verse of the Lord's goodwill towards men.
' Full of compassion and mercy, the Lord,' let me hear it again,
' Full of compassion and mercy — long suffering.' Yes, O yes !
For the lawyer is born but to murder, the Saviour lives but to bless.
He'll never put on the black cap, except for the worst of the worst,
And the first may be last—I have heard it in church— and the last may be first."

Latins.—Friday Matins ; Epiphany ; Visitation of the Sick.
Greeks.—Wednesday evening ; Ninth hour.

PSALM LXXXVII. *Fundamenta ejus.*

HER foundations are upon the holy hills : the Lord loveth the gates of Sion more than all the dwellings of Jacob.

2 Very excellent things are spoken of thee : thou city of God.

3 "I will think upon Rahab and Babylon : with them that know me.

4 "Behold ye the Philistines also : and they of Tyre, with the Morians; lo, there was he born."

5 And of Sion it shall be reported that he was born in her : and the most High shall stablish her.

6 The Lord shall rehearse it when he writeth up the people : that he was born there.

7 The singers also and trumpeters shall he rehearse : All my fresh springs shall be in thee.

The favourite psalm of Thomas Pierson, the Puritan, who calls it "The Great Charter of the Church," and "excellent encouragements against afflictions."

Verse 1. The motto chosen by Van Mildert for Durham University in 1832 is *Fundamenta ejus in montibus sanctis.*

Verse 2. *Gloriosa dicta sunt de te Civitas Dei.* This is the verse which gave the title to St. Augustine's great work, "The City of God," in which he draws out the picture of the co-existence of a conflict between the Divine society—the Church—and the disordered political world of the Empire.

Latins.—Friday Matins; Circumcision; Epiphany; Dedication of a Church.

Greeks.—Wednesday evening.

PSALM LXXXVIII. *Domine Deus.*

O LORD God of my salvation, I have cried day and night before thee : O let my prayer enter into thy presence, incline thine ear unto my calling.

2 For my soul is full of trouble : and my life draweth nigh unto hell.

3 I am counted as one of them that go down into the pit : and I have been even as a man that hath no strength.

4 Free among the dead, like unto them that are

wounded, and lie in the grave : who are out of remembrance, and are cut away from thy hand.

5 Thou hast laid me in the lowest pit : in a place of darkness, and in the deep.

6 Thine indignation lieth hard upon me : and thou hast vexed me with all thy storms.

7 Thou hast put away mine acquaintance far from me : and made me to be abhorred of them.

8 I am so fast in prison : that I cannot get forth.

9 My sight faileth for very trouble : Lord, I have called daily upon thee, I have stretched forth my hands unto thee.

10 Dost thou shew wonders among the dead : or shall the dead rise up again, and praise thee ?

11 Shall thy loving-kindness be shewed in the grave : or thy faithfulness in destruction ?

12 Shall thy wondrous work be known in the dark : and thy righteousness in the land where all things are forgotten ?

13 Unto thee have I cried, O Lord : and early shall my prayer come before thee.

14 Lord, why abhorrest thou my soul : and hidest thou thy face from me ?

15 I am in misery, and like unto him that is at the point to die : even from my youth up thy terrors have I suffered with a troubled mind.

16 Thy wrathful displeasure goeth over me : and the fear of thee hath undone me.

17 They came round about me daily like water : and compassed me together on every side.

18 My lovers and friends hast thou put away from me : and hid mine acquaintance out of my sight.

Bishop Hooper (the austere Puritan Bishop of Gloucester, who was burnt before his people, beating upon his breast till his hand fell off), recommended his wife to study this psalm in her misery. He suggested also Psalms vi., xxii., xxx., xxxi., xxxviii., and lxix.

Verse 8. In an early comment on this verse, written by Didymus, is a traditional saying of our Lord's : "The nearer to me, the nearer the fire."

Verse 11. The dirge of the "Solitary" in Wordsworth's "Excursion,"
"And now distinctly could I recognise
These words : ' *Shall in the grave thy love be known, In death thy faithfulness ?* ' "

Verse 13. This was used in the Anglo-Saxon version of Prime.

Liturgical use.—Good Friday; Introit to Easter Eve Mass (e).
Latins.—Friday Matins; Easter Eve; Dedication of a Church.
Greeks.—Wednesday evening; Dawn.

PSALM LXXXIX. *Misericordias Domini.*

MY song shall be alway of the loving-kindness of the Lord : with my mouth will I ever be shewing thy truth from one generation to another.

2 For I have said, " Mercy shall be set up for ever : thy truth shalt thou stablish in the heavens.

3 " I have made a covenant with my chosen : I have sworn unto David my servant;

4 " Thy seed will I stablish for ever : and set up thy throne from one generation to another."

5 O Lord, the very heavens shall praise thy wondrous works : and thy truth in the congregation of the saints.

6 For who is he among the clouds : that shall be compared unto the Lord ?

7 And what is he among the gods : that shall be like unto the Lord ?

8 God is very greatly to be feared in the council of the saints : and to be had in reverence of all them that are round about him.

9 O Lord God of hosts, who is like unto thee : thy truth, most mighty Lord, is on every side.

10 Thou rulest the raging of the sea : thou stillest the waves thereof when they arise.

11 Thou hast subdued Egypt, and destroyed it : thou hast scattered thine enemies abroad with thy mighty arm.

12 The heavens are thine, the earth also is thine : thou hast laid the foundation of the round world, and all that therein is.

13 Thou hast made the north and the south : Tabor and Hermon shall rejoice in thy Name.

14 Thou hast a mighty arm : strong is thy hand, and high is thy right hand.

15 Righteousness and equity are the habitation of thy seat : mercy and truth shall go before thy face.

16 Blessed is the people, O Lord, that can rejoice in thee : they shall walk in the light of thy countenance.

17 Their delight shall be daily in thy Name : and in thy righteousness shall they make their boast.

18 For thou art the glory of their strength : and in thy loving-kindness thou shalt lift up our horns.

19 For the Lord is our defence : the Holy One of Israel is our King.

20 Thou spakest sometime in visions unto thy saints, and saidst : "I have laid help upon one that is mighty; I have exalted one chosen out of the people.

21 "I have found David my servant : with my holy oil have I anointed him.

22 "My hand shall hold him fast : and my arm shall strengthen him.

23 "The enemy shall not be able to do him violence : the son of wickedness shall not hurt him.

24 "I will smite down his foes before his face : and plague them that hate him.

25 "My truth also and my mercy shall be with him : and in my Name shall his horn be exalted.

26 "I will set his dominion also in the sea : and his right hand in the floods.

27 "He shall call me, Thou art my father : my God, and my strong salvation.

28 "And I will make him my first-born : higher than the kings of the earth.

29 "My mercy will I keep for him for evermore : and my covenant shall stand fast with him.

30 "His seed also will I make to endure for ever : and his throne as the days of heaven.

31 "But if his children forsake my law : and walk not in my judgements;

32 "If they break my statutes, and keep not my commandments : I will visit their offences with the rod, and their sin with scourges.

33 "Nevertheless, my loving-kindness will I not utterly take from him : nor suffer my truth to fail.

34 "My covenant will I not break, nor alter the thing that is gone out of my lips : I have sworn once by my holiness, that I will not fail David.

35 " His seed shall endure for ever : and his seat is like as the sun before me.

36 " He shall stand fast for evermore as the moon : and as the faithful witness in heaven."

37 But thou hast abhorred and forsaken thine Anointed : and art displeased at him.

38 Thou hast broken the covenant of thy servant : and cast his crown to the ground.

39 Thou hast overthrown all his hedges : and broken down his strong holds.

40 All they that go by spoil him : and he is become a reproach to his neighbours.

41 Thou hast set up the right hand of his enemies : and made all his adversaries to rejoice.

42 Thou hast taken away the edge of his sword : and givest him not victory in the battle.

43 Thou hast put out his glory : and cast his throne down to the ground.

44 The days of his youth hast thou shortened : and covered him with dishonour.

45 Lord, how long wilt thou hide thyself, for ever : and shall thy wrath burn like fire ?

46 O remember how short my time is : wherefore hast thou made all men for nought ?

47 What man is he that liveth, and shall not see death : and shall he deliver his soul from the hand of hell ?

48 Lord, where are thy old loving-kindnesses : which thou swarest unto David in thy truth ?

49 Remember, Lord, the rebuke that thy servants have : and how I do bear in my bosom the rebukes of many people ;

50 Wherewith thine enemies have blasphemed thee, and slandered the footsteps of thine Anointed : Praised be the Lord for evermore. Amen, and Amen.

St. Athanasius (in the reign of Constantius) was about to preach at a church near Constantinople one day, when a cry was raised by the crowded congregation that the Arians had surrounded the building with 500 soldiers, and meant to slay their great opponent in a trap. The saint was hardly dissuaded from preaching, but bade the deacon strike up this psalm—one much used by the Catholics in this controversy—and while it was being sung he escaped as by a miracle, passing through the soldiers without recognition.

Abraham, in the spirit of prophecy, the Talmudists say, wrote this psalm.

Verse 46. A sundial motto, and one often engraved on old clocks, is, "O remember how short my time is"—*e.g.*, St. Patrick's, Isle of Man.

Verse 47. Is not this the verse which Shakespeare's Justice Shallow has in mind when he assures Silence that "death, as the Psalmist saith, is certain to all"?

Liturgical use.—Christmas evening.
Latins.—Friday Matins; Christmas.
Greeks.—Wednesday evening.

PSALM XC. *Domine, refugium.*

LORD, thou hast been our refuge : from one generation to another.

2 Before the mountains were brought forth, or ever the earth and the world were made : thou art God from everlasting, and world without end.

3 Thou turnest men to destruction : again thou sayest, Come again, ye children of men.

4 For a thousand years in thy sight are but as yesterday : seeing that is past as a watch in the night.

5 As soon as thou scatterest them they are even as a sleep : and fade away suddenly like the grass.

6 In the morning it is green, and groweth up : but in the evening it is cut down, dried up, and withered.

7 For we consume away in thy displeasure : and are afraid at thy wrathful indignation.

8 Thou hast set our misdeeds before thee : and our secret sins in the light of thy countenance.

9 For when thou art angry all our days are gone : we bring our years to an end, as it were a tale that is told.

10 The days of our age are threescore years and ten ; and though men be so strong that they come to fourscore years : yet is their strength then but labour and sorrow ; so soon passeth it away, and we are gone.

11 But who regardeth the power of thy wrath : for even thereafter as a man feareth, so is thy displeasure.

12 So teach us to number our days : that we may apply our hearts unto wisdom.

13 Turn thee again, O Lord, at the last : and be gracious unto thy servants.

14 O satisfy us with thy mercy, and that soon : so shall we rejoice and be glad all the days of our life.

15 Comfort us again now after the time that thou hast plagued us : and for the years wherein we have suffered adversity.

16 Show thy servants thy work : and their children thy glory.

17 And the glorious Majesty of the Lord our God be upon us : prosper thou the work of our hands upon us, O prosper thou our handy-work.

This psalm has a double interest for English folk, apart from all its merits. It has been sung or read since 1662 over the graves of our fathers, and it will be sung or read over our own. But before Edward VI.'s time our funeral psalms were cxvi., cxxxix., and cxlvi. ; and with the Celebration, Psalm xlii. The reason all these burial psalms were abolished by the Reformers of 1552 will be evident to anyone who glances at them. In this connection these taught Mass for the dead and Purgatory. But they gave us none instead. Bishop Cosin supplied this "song of Moses" and xxxix. ; the former to propitiate the Puritans ; the latter because Laud used it for burials.

Dr. Watts's most successful hymn, "O God, our Help in ages past," is a rhymed version of this psalm, and one much delighted in by John Wesley. Contrast his version with the weaker one of the far greater poet Burns, who also delighted in this psalm.

"Thou givest the word, Thy creature man
  Is to existence brought :
Again thou say'st, ' Ye sons of men,
  Return ye into nought.'

Thou layest them with all their cares
  In everlasting sleep,
As with a flood thou tak'st them off
  With overwhelming sweep."

Charles V., the most powerful emperor since Charlemagne's time, who left his throne for the cloister at St. Juste, used to declare that he preferred *Domine, refugium factus es nobis* to all other psalms.

J. H. Newman's Gerontius hears the souls in Purgatory singing this psalm.

Verse 10. "So soon passeth it away"—a common sundial motto—St. Matins', Looe ; St. Matthias', Liskeard ; Biddenden, etc.

"Yet is their strength then but labour and sorrow." Mr. Ruskin thinks that in commentary upon these words Dürer painted his Melancholia, and thus, "Yes," he replies to them, " but labour and sorrow are their strength."

Verse 12. This was the text which Dr. Rudd chose to preach upon before Queen Elizabeth, when he dwelt upon the infirmities of old age, and applied his words to the aged queen. It is needless to say that "he fell out of favour" with her Majesty, who had before resolved to make him an archbishop.

Verses 16 *and* 17 were in the early Prime office in the English tongue; that is to say, they rose to God from English homes at six in the morning, before the people went out to the labour of the day; and not only from the clergy-houses, but from the homes of devout lay-folk also.

Liturgical use.—Burial Service.
Latins.—Thursday at Lauds.
Greeks.—Wednesday night; First hour.

PSALM XCI. *Qui habitat.*

WHOSO dwelleth under the defence of the most High : shall abide under the shadow of the Almighty.

2 I will say unto the Lord, "Thou art my hope, and my strong hold" : my God, in him will I trust.

3 For he shall deliver thee from the snare of the hunter : and from the noisome pestilence.

4 He shall defend thee under his wings, and thou shalt be safe under his feathers : his faithfulness and truth shall be thy shield and buckler.

5 "Thou shalt not be afraid for any terror by night : nor for the arrow that flieth by day;

6 "For the pestilence that walketh in darkness : nor for the sickness that destroyeth in the noon-day.

7 "A thousand shall fall beside thee, and ten thousand at thy right hand : but it shall not come nigh thee.

8 "Yea, with thine eyes shalt thou behold : and see the reward of the ungodly."

9 For thou, Lord, art my hope : thou hast set thine house of defence very high.

10 "There shall no evil happen unto thee : neither shall any plague come nigh thy dwelling.

11 "For he shall give his angels charge over thee : to keep thee in all thy ways.

12 "They shall bear thee in their hands : that thou hurt not thy foot against a stone.

13 "Thou shalt go upon the lion and adder : the young lion and the dragon shalt thou tread under thy feet.

14 "Because he hath set his love upon me, therefore will I deliver him : I will set him up, because he hath known my Name.

15 " He shall call upon me, and I will hear him : yea, I am with him in trouble ; I will deliver him, and bring him to honour.

16 " With long life will I satisfy him : and shew him my salvation."

"My excellent holy mother in law, Mary, widow to my dear father," says Richard Baxter, " was one of the most humble, mortified holy persons that ever I knew, and lived in longing to be with Christ till she was a hundred years old (wanting three or four), in full understanding, and at last rejoicing in the frequent hearing and repeating of Psalm xci."

Verse 7. This was the verse by which the Bishop of Marseilles encouraged his clergy to stick to their duty during the great plague of 1720.

Verse 11. The devil can quote this Scripture for his purpose. But how much of Christian teaching about the angels begins here ! Spenser thus writes:

" How oft do they their silver bowers leave,
   To come to succour us, that succour want !
How oft do they with golden pinions cleave
The flitting skies, like flying pursuivant,
Against fowle fiends to aid us militant !
They for us fight, they watch and duly ward,
And their bright squadrons round about us plant ;
And all for love and nothing for reward :
Oh ! why should heav'nly God to man have such regard?"

Similarly Milton and others, and not least that ancient English prayer still taught by simple folk to their children which quiets them by the promise of " four angels round my bed !"

Verse 13. In the sixth room of the National Gallery is a picture of St. Michael and the dragon, by Fra Carnovale, which gives the Christian comment upon this verse. The spirit of the Church Militant is treading the dragon of sensuality and injustice under his feet.

In Salisbury Cathedral a " boy-bishop," who died during his brief term of office, is carved trampling upon a monster in allusion to the words *Conculcabis leonem et draconem*. The boy-bishop reigned from St. Nicholas Day till Childermas, and preached in the cathedral of his see. Dean Colet ordered all his scholars to attend this sermon without fail.

Latins.—Daily at Compline (*i.e.*, 9 p.m.); Visitation of the Sick (*Sarum* for All Saints') ; Dedication of a Church.

Greeks.—Last psalm for Wednesday evening ; Sixth hour ; Late Evensong in Lent ; Burial of laymen, monks, and infants.

PSALM XCII. *Bonum est confiteri.*

IT is a good thing to give thanks unto the Lord : and to sing praises unto thy Name, O most Highest ;

2 To tell of thy loving-kindness early in the morning : and of thy truth in the night-season ;

3 Upon an instrument of ten strings, and upon the lute : upon a loud instrument, and upon the harp.

4 For thou, Lord, hast made me glad through thy works : and I will rejoice in giving praise for the operations of thy hands.

5 O Lord, how glorious are thy works : thy thoughts are very deep.

6 An unwise man doth not well consider this : and a fool doth not understand it.

7 When the ungodly are green as the grass, and when all the workers of wickedness do flourish : then shall they be destroyed for ever ; but thou, Lord, art the most Highest for evermore.

8 For lo, thine enemies, O Lord, lo, thine enemies shall perish : and all the workers of wickedness shall be destroyed.

9 But mine horn shall be exalted like the horn of an unicorn : for I am anointed with fresh oil.

10 Mine eye also shall see his lust of mine enemies : and mine ear shall hear his desire of the wicked that arise up against me.

11 The righteous shall flourish like a palm-tree : and shall spread abroad like a cedar in Libanus.

12 Such as are planted in the house of the Lord : shall flourish in the courts of the house of our God.

13 They also shall bring forth more fruit in their age : and shall be fat and well-liking.

14 That they may shew how true the Lord my strength is : and that there is no unrighteousness in him.

Dr. George Matheson uses this psalm (with Pss. ii. and lxxii.) to show that the principle of survival is as completely taught by natural religion as it is by modern science.

The Talmudic tradition says that this psalm was written in the morning of the world by Adam, the father of mankind.

Verse 1. Sir Christopher Hatton's motto for his Psalter ; *vide* Ps. cviii.

Verse 4. Dante hears Matilda his guide singing in the terrestrial paradise the psalm *Dele-*

casti (me Domine in factura tua, et in operibus manuum tuarum exultabo), vide Purg., xxviii. 80.

This Matilda, supposed to be the great countess of the eleventh century, "notable equally for her ceaseless activity, her brilliant political genius, her perfect piety, and her deep reverence for the See of Rome," is standing on the other side of Lethe, passing the flowers through her hands. She represents the noblest form of "the active life which forms the felicity of earth, and the spirit of Beatrice the contemplative life, which forms the felicity of Heaven."

Verse 5. Our historian, Matthew Paris, always quotes this verse when he relates some miracle of the saints (of Robert of Lincoln, Thomas of Hertford, etc.). Indeed, it sums up the mediæval view of God's working in the world.

Latins.—Saturday Lauds.
Greeks.—Thursday morning; Mesorion of first hour.

PSALM XCIII. *Dominus regnavit.*

THE Lord is King, and hath put on glorious apparel: the Lord hath put on his apparel, and girded himself with strength.

2 He hath made the round world so sure: that it cannot be moved.

3 Ever since the world began hath thy seat been prepared: thou art from everlasting.

4 The floods are risen, O Lord, the floods have lift up their voice: the floods lift up their waves.

5 The waves of the sea are mighty, and rage horribly: but yet the Lord, who dwelleth on high, is mightier.

6 Thy testimonies, O Lord, are very sure: holiness becometh thine house for ever.

Edward Irving wrote of the Psalter in a way that seems an echo of a time when the world was yet undrowned by floods of watery criticism. "These Psalms," he says, "are to a Christian what the love of parents and the sweet affections of home, and the clinging memories of infant scenes and the generous love of country, are to men of every rank and order and employment, of every kindred and tongue and nation."

Shakespeare has the valiant spirit of the psalm, if not a literal echo, in Queen Margaret's speech:

"We will not from the helm,
   to sit and weep;
But keep our course, though
   the rough wind say no
From shelves and rocks that
   threaten us with wrack."

Liturgical use.—Introit to the Mass on I. Sunday after the Ascension.
Latins.—Sunday at Lauds.
Greeks.—Thursday morning ; Mesorion of first hour.

PSALM XCIV. *Deus ultionum.*

O LORD God, to whom vengeance belongeth : thou God, to whom vengeance belongeth, shew thyself.

2 Arise, thou Judge of the world : and reward the proud after their deserving.

3 Lord, how long shall the ungodly : how long shall the ungodly triumph ?

4 How long shall all wicked doers speak so disdainfully : and make such proud boastings ?

5 They smite down thy people, O Lord : and trouble thine heritage.

6 They murder the widow, and the stranger : and put the fatherless to death.

7 And yet they say, "Tush, the Lord shall not see : neither shall the God of Jacob regard it."

8 Take heed, ye unwise among the people : O ye fools, when will ye understand ?

9 He that planted the ear, shall he not hear : or he that made the eye, shall he not see ?

10 Or he that nurtureth the heathen : it is he that teacheth man knowledge, shall not he punish ?

11 The Lord knoweth the thoughts of man : that they are but vain.

12 Blessed is the man whom thou chastenest, O Lord : and teachest him in thy law ;

13 That thou mayest give him patience in time of adversity : until the pit be digged up for the ungodly.

14 For the Lord will not fail his people : neither will he forsake his inheritance ;

15 Until righteousness turn again unto judgement : all such as are true in heart shall follow it.

16 Who will rise up with me against the wicked : or will take my part against the evil-doers ?

17 If the Lord had not helped me : it had not failed but my soul had been put to silence.

18 But when I said, "My foot hath slipt" : thy mercy, O Lord, held me up.

19 In the multitude of the sorrows that I had in my heart : thy comforts have refreshed my soul.

20 Wilt thou have any thing to do with the stool of wickedness : which imagineth mischief as a law ?

21 They gather them together against the soul of the righteous : and condemn the innocent blood.

22 But the Lord is my refuge : and my God is the strength of my confidence.

23 He shall recompense them their wickedness, and destroy them in their own malice : yea, the Lord our God shall destroy them.

Among the curious misuses of this psalm is one by Sir Henry Parker, Lord Morley, who, in 1534, wrote an "exposition" upon it, and dedicated it to the "kynges highnes." He was one of the peers who sat in the Parliament of 1530, and signed the ultimatum to Pope Clement VII. Full of fury at the Pope, he applies this psalm to the quarrel, blessing "the chastened" Henry, that "perfect arke of all princely goodness and honour," and wishing to his "ennemye the Babylonicall byshoppe of Rome, reproufe, shame, and utter ruine." He was "adorned with all kinds of superficial learning," says Wood, and wrote in a style of refreshing liveliness.

Verse 1. Sir John Oldcastle, when tried before Parliament for levying war upon Henry V., made a defence by appealing to something like the principles which are now called anarchic, for he reminded his judges that, according to this psalm, vengeance being God's, they must not by punishing him intrench upon the prerogative of the Almighty. He then appealed to his "sovereign King Richard," whom he said was alive and in Scotland. He was ordered to be hanged and burnt for treason and heresy.

Verse 17. Basil of Seleucia relates an old Christian tradition that Lazarus came from the tomb with these words (and Ps. xl. 2) on his lips.

Latins.—Friday Matins.
Greeks.—Thursday morning.

PSALM XCV. *Venite exultemus.*

O COME, let us sing unto the Lord : let us heartily rejoice in the strength of our salvation.

2 Let us come before his presence with thanksgiving : and shew ourselves glad in him with psalms.

3 For the Lord is a great God : and a great King above all gods.

4 In his hand are all the corners of the earth : and the strength of the hills is his also.

5 The sea is his, and he made it : and his hands prepared the dry land.

6 O come, let us worship, and fall down : and kneel before the Lord our Maker.

7 For he is the Lord our God : and we are the people of his pasture, and the sheep of his hand.

8 To day if ye will hear his voice, "harden not your hearts : as in the provocation, and as in the day of temptation in the wilderness;

9 "When your fathers tempted me : proved me, and saw my works.

10 "Forty years long was I grieved with this generation, and said : It is a people that do err in their hearts, for they have not known my ways.

11 "Unto whom I sware in my wrath : that they should not enter into my rest."

This was the battle-song of the Knights Templars, for whom war was an act of worship. They had the privilege of asserting and proclaiming that the hotly-debated Holy Land was in "His hand."

It was the first hymn which in summer rose from the 20,000 religious houses of the West.

This psalm has always been among the preludes to worship both in the East and West. In the Middle Ages it used to be "farsed," as it was called—interspersed, as we say—with fragments of other psalms, called "invitatories." In 1549 it was ordered to be sung simply. The Greeks, who seem to like cutting and carving the Psalms, begin their worship with verses 1, 3, and 6.

Liturgical use.—Daily at Matins.
Latins.—Epiphany ; daily at Matins.
Greeks.—Thursday morning.

PSALM XCVI. *Cantate Domino.*

O SING unto the Lord a new song : sing unto the Lord, all the whole earth.

2 Sing unto the Lord, and praise his Name : be telling of his salvation from day to day.

3 Declare his honour unto the heathen : and his wonders unto all people.

4 For the Lord is great, and cannot worthily be praised : he is more to be feared than all gods.

5 As for all the gods of the heathen, they are but idols : but it is the Lord that made the heavens.

6 Glory and worship are before him : power and honour are in his sanctuary.

7 Ascribe unto the Lord, O ye kindreds of the people : ascribe unto the Lord worship and power.

8 Ascribe unto the Lord the honour due unto his Name : bring presents, and come into his courts.

9 O worship the Lord in the beauty of holiness : let the whole earth stand in awe of him.

10 Tell it out among the heathen that the Lord is King : and that it is he who hath made the round world so fast that it cannot be moved ; and how that he shall judge the people righteously.

11 Let the heavens rejoice, and let the earth be glad : let the sea make a noise, and all that therein is.

12 Let the field be joyful, and all that is in it : then shall all the trees of the wood rejoice before the Lord.

13 For he cometh, for he cometh to judge the earth : and with righteousness to judge the world, and the people with his truth.

This psalm and the next were the songs of triumph and defiance used by the Christians, when in Julian's reign they bore away the body of the martyr Babylas from the Orontes.

Verse 10. St. Justin Martyr accuses the Jews of purposely leaving out the words ἀπὸ ξύλου (from the tree) from their manuscripts of the LXX. Bible. These words, or their Latin equivalent (*a ligno*), therefore became a kind of banner motto against Jews, Arians, and other oppugners of our Lord's royalty. This is the meaning of the third verse of that hymn of Fortunatus, *Vexilla Regis prodeunt*, (which Dr. Neale translated " The Royal Banners forward go"), "Our God is reigning from the tree."

Liturgical use.—Introit to the Epiphany Mass (e).
Latins.—Friday Matins ; Christmas ; Circumcision ; Epiphany ; Trinity Sunday ; Dedication of a Church ; Feasts of Our Lady ; St. Michael.
Greeks.—Thursday morning.

PSALM XCVII. *Dominus regnavit.*

THE Lord is King, the earth may be glad thereof : yea, the multitude of the isles may be glad thereof.

2 Clouds and darkness are round about him : righteousness and judgement are the habitation of his seat.

3 There shall go a fire before him : and burn up his enemies on every side.

4 His lightnings gave shine unto the world : the earth saw it, and was afraid.

5 The hills melted like wax at the presence of the Lord : at the presence of the Lord of the whole earth.

6 The heavens have declared his righteousness : and all the people have seen his glory.

7 Confounded be all they that worship carved images, and that delight in vain gods : worship him, all ye gods.

8 Sion heard of it, and rejoiced : and the daughters of Judah were glad, because of thy judgements, O Lord.

9 For thou, Lord, art higher than all that are in the earth : thou art exalted far above all gods.

10 O ye that love the Lord, see that ye hate the thing which is evil : the Lord preserveth the souls of his saints ; he shall deliver them from the hand of the ungodly.

11 There is sprung up a light for the righteous ; and joyful gladness for such as are true-hearted.

12 Rejoice in the Lord, ye righteous : and give thanks for a remembrance of his holiness.

This psalm has been a great favourite with the Calvinist writers, who use it to teach their chief tenets, the Sovereignty of God, the danger of idolatry, Election and Reprobation, and the right of the saints to rule the world. It is no less of a favourite with their greatest opponents, who never suppose that it teaches things inconsistent with the tradition of the Church Catholic.

Verse 3. Perhaps this verse (with Pss. xi. 6 and xcvi. 13) helped to make up the witness of David in the *Dies Iræ* (see Ps. cii. 25 and 26).

Latins.—Friday Matins ; Circumcision ; Epiphany ; Ascensiontide ; Trinity Sunday ; Apostles and Evangelists ; Festivals of Our Lady ; St. Michael ; All Saints.

Greeks.—Thursday morning.

PSALM XCVIII. *Cantate Domino.*

O SING unto the Lord a new song : for he hath done marvellous things.

2 With his own right hand, and with his holy arm : hath he gotten himself the victory.

3 The Lord declared his salvation : his righteousness hath he openly showed in the sight of the heathen.

4 He hath remembered his mercy and truth toward the house of Israel : and all the ends of the world have seen the salvation of our God.

5 Shew yourselves joyful unto the Lord, all ye lands : sing, rejoice, and give thanks.

6 Praise the Lord upon the harp : sing to the harp with a psalm of thanksgiving.

7 With trumpets also, and shawms : O shew yourselves joyful before the Lord the King.

8 Let the sea make a noise, and all that therein is : the round world, and they that dwell therein.

9 Let the floods clap their hands, and let the hills be joyful together before the Lord : for he is come to judge the earth.

10 With righteousness shall he judge the world : and the people with equity.

This psalm was allowed at Evensong as an alternative to the Magnificat in 1552, in order that the extreme Protestants should not be forced to use the triumph song of the Blessed Virgin Mary. This was a kindly act of inclusion.

"The Psalms have dwelt in the Christian heart and in the centre of that heart : and wherever the pursuits of the inner life have been most largely conceived and cultivated, there, and in the same proportion, the Psalms have towered over every other vehicle of general devotion." "We have a conspicuous illustration of their office in the fact that, of two hundred and forty-three citations from the Old Testament found in the pages of the New, no less than one hundred and sixteen are from the single Book of Psalms, and that a similar proportion holds with most of the early Fathers" (*Mr. Gladstone*).

Liturgical use.—Introit for the Christ Mass (e) ; alternative to the Magnificat in the daily Evensong.

Latins.—Saturday Matins ; Christmas ; Circumcision ; Trinity Sunday ; Feasts of Our Lady.

Greeks.—Thursday morning.

PSALM XCIX. *Dominus regnavit.*

THE Lord is King, be the people never so impatient : he sitteth between the cherubims, be the earth never so unquiet.

2 The Lord is great in Sion : and high above all people.

3 They shall give thanks unto thy Name : which is great, wonderful, and holy.

4 The King's power loveth judgement; thou hast prepared equity : thou hast executed judgement and righteousness in Jacob.

5 O magnify the Lord our God : and fall down before his footstool, for he is holy.

6 Moses and Aaron among his priests, and Samuel among such as call upon his Name : these called upon the Lord, and he heard them.

7 He spake unto them out of the cloudy pillar : for they kept his testimonies, and the law that he gave them.

8 Thou heardest them, O Lord our Lord : thou forgavest them, O God, and punishedst their own inventions.

9 O magnify the Lord our God, and worship him upon his holy hill : for the Lord our God is holy.

This psalm was much used by the Puritan party in the Civil Wars, and by the Covenanters. The version authorized by the Kirk of Scotland in 1641 thus paraphrases the original :

"The Lord doth reigne, although at it
The people rage full sore
Yea, He on Cherubins doth sit,
Though all the world doth roar.

The Lord that doth in Sion dwell
Is high and wondrous great :
Above all folk He doth excell,
And He aloft is set."

Southey tells us that the change from the Old Version to the New Version created a great bitterness and outcry in Northern parishes, possibly as great as when the colour of the gowns is changed, or stoles are used instead of scarves.

Latins.—Saturday Matins; Circumcision; Ascension-tide; Apostles and Evangelists; Dedication Feast.
Greeks.—Thursday morning.

PSALM C. *Jubilate Deo.*

O BE joyful in the Lord, all ye lands : serve the Lord with gladness, and come before his presence with a song.

2 Be ye sure that the Lord he is God : it is he that hath made us, and not we ourselves; we are his people, and the sheep of his pasture.

3 O go your way into his gates with thanksgiving, and into his courts with praise : be thankful unto him, and speak good of his name.

4 For the Lord is gracious, his mercy is everlasting : and his truth endureth from generation to generation.

This psalm was placed in our daily Morning office to satisfy objections in 1552, and to avoid repetition. It is not, of course, used unless the *Benedictus* comes in other parts of the service.

The hymn "All people that on earth do dwell," was by William Kethe, a Puritan friend of Knox's, and the "Old Hundredth" tune is from the Psalter of 1580 A.D.—a traditional chorale, some say, by Luther. It is probably this version Mrs. Ford (in "Merry Wives") has in mind when she says the hundredth psalm will not keep place together with the tune of "Green sleeves"; and Longfellow alludes to the same version in his hexameter—

"Singing the hundredth psalm, that grand old Puritan anthem."

The Talmud says that Psalms xc. to c., except Ps. xcii., were composed by Moses.

Liturgical use.—At the daily Matins, if *Benedictus* comes in the Gospel or Lesson ; Introit to Mass on Whit Monday (e).
Latins.—Sunday Lauds.
Greeks.—Thursday morning.

PSALM CI. *Misericordiam et judicium.*

MY song shall be of mercy and judgement : unto thee, O Lord, will I sing.

2 O let me have understanding : in the way of godliness.

3 When wilt thou come unto me : I will walk in my house with a perfect heart.

4 I will take no wicked thing in hand; I hate the sins of unfaithfulness : there shall no such cleave unto me.

5 A froward heart shall depart from me : I will not know a wicked person.

6 Whoso privily slandereth his neighbour : him will I destroy.

7 Whoso hath also a proud look and high stomach : I will not suffer him.

8 Mine eyes look upon such as are faithful in the land : that they may dwell with me.

9 Whoso leadeth a godly life : he shall be my servant.

10 There shall no deceitful person dwell in my house : he that telleth lies shall not tarry in my sight.

11 I shall soon destroy all the ungodly that are in the land : that I may root all the wicked doers from the city of the Lord.

This psalm and the next were sung at the death of Monica by St. Augustine and his son Adeodatus, with Euodius, and the household.

Bacon recommended George Villiers to make a study of this psalm, and to be ruled by it when he promoted the courtiers.

Verse 1. The opening words of this psalm were the expression of poor Cowper's joy, on his recovery from the deep melancholy which caused him to be put under the care of Dr. Cotton. When at last the light broke in upon him, he "felt it almost waste of time to sleep, he was so happy." Then he wrote the song of Mercy and Judgment which begins, "Lord, I love the habitation."

" Me through waves of deep affliction,
Dearest Saviour, Thou hast brought ;
Fiery deeps of sharp conviction,
Hard to bear and passing thought.
Sweet the sound of grace Divine,
Sweet the grace which makes me Thine."

Liturgical use.—Introit for Mass on Whit Tuesday (e) ; Queen's Accession.
Latins.—Saturday Matins.
Greeks.—Thursday morning ; First hour.

PSALM CII. *Domine, exaudi.*

HEAR my prayer, O Lord : and let my crying come unto thee.

2 Hide not thy face from me in the time of my trouble : incline thine ear unto me when I call ; O hear me, and that right soon.

3 For my days are consumed away like smoke : and my bones are burnt up as it were a fire-brand.

4 My heart is smitten down, and withered like grass : so that I forget to eat my bread.

5 For the voice of my groaning : my bones will scarce cleave to my flesh.

6 I am become like a pelican in the wilderness : and like an owl that is in the desert.

7 I have watched, and am even as it were a sparrow : that sitteth alone upon the house-top.

8 Mine enemies revile me all the day long : and they that are mad upon me are sworn together against me.

9 For I have eaten ashes as it were bread : and mingled my drink with weeping;

10 And that because of thine indignation and wrath : for thou hast taken me up, and cast me down.

11 My days are gone like a shadow : and I am withered like grass.

12 But, thou, O Lord, shalt endure for ever : and thy remembrance throughout all generations.

13 Thou shalt arise, and have mercy upon Sion : for it is time that thou have mercy upon her, yea, the time is come.

14 And why? thy servants think upon her stones : and it pitieth them to see her in the dust.

15 The heathen shall fear thy Name, O Lord : and all the kings of the earth thy Majesty;

16 When the Lord shall build up Sion : and when his glory shall appear ;

17 When he turneth him unto the prayer of the poor destitute : and despiseth not their desire.

18 This shall be written for those that come after : and the people which shall be born shall praise the Lord.

19 For he hath looked down from his sanctuary : out of the heaven did the Lord behold the earth ;

20 That he might hear the mournings of such as are in captivity : and deliver the children appointed unto death ;

21 That they may declare the Name of the Lord in Sion : and his worship at Jerusalem ;

22 When the people are gathered together : and the kingdoms also, to serve the Lord.

23 He brought down my strength in my journey : and shortened my days.

24 But I said, O my God, take me not away in the midst of mine age : as for thy years, they endure throughout all generations.

25 Thou, Lord, in the beginning hast laid the foundation of the earth : and the heavens are the work of thy hands.

26 They shall perish, but thou shalt endure : they all shall wax old as doth a garment ;

27 And as a vesture shalt thou change them, and they shall be changed : but thou art the same, and thy years shall not fail.

28 The children of thy servants shall continue : and their seed shall stand fast in thy sight.

This is the fifth penitential psalm. These are Pss. vi., xxx., xxxviii., li., cii., cxxx., cxliii. (*vide* Ps. vi.) It is the antidote to Avarice.

The Emperor Charles V. had these seven psalms read again and again to him in his last sickness at St. Juste (Sept., 1568).

Verse 1. These are the words which in so many services usher in the Collect or Summary of all that is prayed for. They are used thus not only in our Litany, for instance, but in that ancient service at which, from Edward the Confessor's time onwards, English monarchs have touched for the King's Evil.

Verse 5. William Hunnis, Queen Elizabeth's choirmaster at the Chapel Royal, was among the earlier authors who "reduced into meeter" the seven psalms. His book is rather a commentary upon than a translation of the original (1583). It is exquisitely bound, and has tunes to it. It is called "Seven sobs of a sorrowfull soule for sinne." This is his comment to this verse :

"Age overtaketh youth, I see,
   and youth by stealth dooth flie,
As dooth the smoke vanish awaie
   aloft vnder the skie.   [so
Yea, manie times it chanceth
   ere age come us upon,
That death by stroke such wound doth make,
   that life with speed is gone.
Thus passeth foorth my time of life
   more swifter, I may saie,
Than is the ship good under saile,
   or eagle after praie."

Verse 6. This gave to Christian art the pelican as the symbol of our Lord, as in St. Thomas Aquinas' hymn "Adoro te" (312 A. and M.) :

"*Pie Pellicane, Jesu Domine !
Me immundum munda Tuo
   sanguine.*"

Verse 10. Quoted by Origen in his bitter lament for his apostasy (*vide* Ps. l.).

Verse 11. "My days are gone like a shadow that declineth" is the Arbroath dial motto. *Dies mei sicut umbra declinaverunt*, is the dial motto of St. Michele, near Venice.

Verses 25 *and* 26. St. Augustine assigns these verses as the witness of David to the Doomsday alluded to in the "anvil hymn" of the *Dies Iræ*, see xcvii. 3.

Liturgical use.—Ash Wednesday evening.
Latins.—Saturday Matins.
Greeks.—Thursday morning ; late Evensong in Lent ; Visitation of the Sick ; Confession ; For the dying.

PSALM CIII. *Benedic, anima mea.*

PRAISE the Lord, O my soul : and all that is within me praise his holy Name.

2 Praise the Lord, O my soul : and forget not all his benefits ;

3 Who forgiveth all thy sins : and healeth all thine infirmities ;

4 Who saveth thy life from destruction : and crowneth thee with mercy and loving-kindness ;

5 Who satisfieth thy mouth with good things : making thee young and lusty as an eagle.

6 The Lord executeth righteousness and judgement : for all them that are oppressed with wrong.

7 He shewed his ways unto Moses : his works unto the children of Israel.

8 The Lord is full of compassion and mercy : long-suffering, and of great goodness.

9 He will not alway be chiding : neither keepeth he his anger for ever.

10 He hath not dealt with us after our sins : nor rewarded us according to our wickednesses.

11 For look how high the heaven is in comparison of the earth ; so great is his mercy also toward them that fear him.

12 Look how wide also the east is from the west : so far hath he set our sins from us.

13 Yea, like as a father pitieth his own children : even so is the Lord merciful unto them that fear him.

14 For he knoweth whereof we are made : he remembereth that we are but dust.

15 The days of man are but as grass : for he flourisheth as a flower of the field.

16 For as soon as the wind goeth over it, it is gone : and the place thereof shall know it no more.

17 But the merciful goodness of the Lord endureth for ever and ever upon them that fear him : and his righteousness upon children's children.

18 Even upon such as keep his covenant : and think upon his commandments to do them.

19 The Lord hath prepared his seat in heaven : and his kingdom ruleth over all.

20 O praise the Lord, ye angels of his, ye that excel in strength : ye that fulfil his commandment, and hearken unto the voice of his words.

21 O praise the Lord, all ye his hosts : ye servants of his that do his pleasure.

22 O speak good of the Lord, all ye works of his, in all places of his dominion : praise thou the Lord, O my soul.

The followers of John Knox sang this as a Eucharistic psalm.

Dr. Robert Saunderson, in his last sickness, always repeated, as he was wont, the psalms for the day both morning and evening. As he drew near his end "he did often say the 103rd psalm to himself, and 'My heart is fixed' (Ps. lvii. 8)."

The first five verses of this psalm were said in the Anglo-Saxon vernacular Prime.

Liturgical use.—Rogation psalm.
Latins.—Saturday Matins ; Ascension-tide ; St. Michael (*Sarum*, All Saints).
Greeks.—Thursday morning ; Dawn.

PSALM CIV. *Benedic, anima mea.*

PRAISE the Lord, O my soul : O Lord my God, thou art become exceeding glorious ; thou art clothed with majesty and honour.

2 Thou deckest thyself with light as it were with a garment : and spreadest out the heavens like a curtain.

3 Who layeth the beams of his chambers in the waters : and maketh the clouds his chariot, and walketh upon the wings of the wind.

4 He maketh his angels spirits : and his ministers a flaming fire.

5 He laid the foundations of the earth : that it never should move at any time.

6 Thou coveredst it with the deep like as with a garment : the waters stand in the hills.

7 At thy rebuke they flee : at the voice of thy thunder they are afraid.

8 They go up as high as the hills, and down to the valleys beneath : even unto the place which thou hast appointed for them.

9 Thou hast set them their bounds which they shall not pass : neither turn again to cover the earth.

10 He sendeth the springs into the rivers : which run among the hills.

11 All beasts of the field drink thereof : and the wild asses quench their thirst.

12 Beside them shall the fowls of the air have their habitation : and sing among the branches.

13 He watereth the hills from above : the earth is filled with the fruit of thy works.

14 He bringeth forth grass for the cattle : and green herb for the service of men ;

15 That he may bring food out of the earth, and wine that maketh glad the heart of man : and oil to make him a cheerful countenance, and bread to strengthen man's heart.

16 The trees of the Lord also are full of sap : even the cedars of Libanus which he hath planted;

17 Wherein the birds make their nests : and the fir-trees are a dwelling for the stork.

18 The high hills are a refuge for the wild goats : and so are the stony rocks for the conies.

19 He appointed the moon for certain seasons : and the sun knoweth his going down.

20 Thou makest darkness that it may be night : wherein all the beasts of the forest do move.

21 The lions roaring after their pray : do seek their meat from God.

22 The sun ariseth, and they get them away together : and lay them down in their dens.

23 Man goeth forth to his work and to his labour : until the evening.

24 O Lord, how manifold are thy works : in wisdom hast thou made them all ; the earth is full of thy riches.

25 So is the great and wide sea also : wherein are things creeping innumerable, both small and great beasts.

26 There go the ships, and there is that Leviathan : whom thou hast made to take his pastime therein.

27 These wait all upon thee : that thou mayest give them meat in due season.

28 When thou givest it them they gather it : and when thou openest thy hand they are filled with good.

29 When thou hidest thy face they are troubled : when thou takest away their breath they die, and are turned again to their dust.

30 When thou lettest thy breath go forth they shall be made : and thou shalt renew the face of the earth.

31 The glorious Majesty of the Lord shall endure for ever : the Lord shall rejoice in his works.

32 The earth shall tremble at the look of him : if he do but touch the hills, they shall smoke.

33 I will sing unto the Lord as long as I live : I will praise my God while I have my being.

34 And so shall my words please him : my joy shall be in the Lord.

35 As for sinners, they shall be consumed out of the earth, and the ungodly shall come to an end : praise thou the Lord, O my soul, praise the Lord.

On the Monday, Tuesday, and Wednesday before Ascension day (Rogation days) the parish bounds were beaten (called "ganging" in the North), and Litanies were chanted to entreat for the kindly fruits of the earth in due season. The psalms used then were ciii. and civ.

This psalm was a favourite with Henry Vaughan, Bacon, and Alexander von Humboldt. Bacon translated it into metre, and showed thereby that his description of himself as a "concealed poet" was not quite an empty boast.

His book is *Certaine Psalmes written by him in sickness*, 1624, and dedicated to his very good friend George Herbert.

"The sappy cedars tall like stately tow'rs
High flying birds do harbour in their bow'rs,
The holy storks, that are the travellers,
Choose for to dwell and build within the firs ;
The climbing goats hang on steep mountain side,
The digging conies in the rocks do bide."

Verse 23. This was the text of John Henry Newman's first sermon, and also of his last sermon as an English priest, September 25th, 1843.

Verse 24. St. Athanasius may almost be said to have composed his great orations against the Arians as sermons upon this verse, so often does he quote it.

Bauhinus the botanist (1541-1613) chose it as a motto for his *Historia Plantarum*.

Verse 30. St. Wilfrid of York, in 709 A.D., died at St. Andrew's, Oundle, leaning back his head upon the pillow, without groan or murmur, just as from the minster choir rose the chant of *Emitte spiritum tuum et renovabis faciem terræ*. And " he happily resigned his soul into the hands of his Creator, and thus entered into the everlasting banquet of God's Lamb."

Liturgical use.—Whit-Sunday evening ; Rogation psalm.
Latins.—Saturday Matins ; Whitsuntide.
Greeks.—Thursday morning ; Preface to Evensong.

PSALM CV. *Confitemini Domino.*

O GIVE thanks unto the Lord, and call upon his Name : tell the people what things he hath done.

2 O let your songs be of him, and praise him : and let your talking be of all his wondrous works.

3 Rejoice in his holy Name : let the heart of them rejoice that seek the Lord.

4 Seek the Lord and his strength : seek his face evermore.

5 Remember the marvellous works that he hath done : his wonders, and the judgements of his mouth,

6 O ye seed of Abraham his servant : ye children of Jacob his chosen.

7 He is the Lord our God : his judgements are in all the world.

8 He hath been alway mindful of his covenant and promise : that he made to a thousand generations ;

9 Even the covenant that he made with Abraham : and the oath that he sware unto Isaac ;

10 And appointed the same unto Jacob for a law : and to Israel for an everlasting testament ;

11 Saying, " Unto thee will I give the land of Canaan : the lot of your inheritance ;"

12 When there were yet but a few of them : and they strangers in the land ;

13 What time as they went from one nation to another : from one kingdom to another people ;

14 He suffered no man to do them wrong : but reproved even kings for their sakes ;

15 "Touch not mine Anointed : and do my prophets no harm."

16 Moreover, he called for a dearth upon the land : and destroyed all the provision of bread.

17 But he had sent a man before them : even Joseph, who was sold to be a bond-servant;

18 Whose feet they hurt in the stocks : the iron entered into his soul;

19 Until the time came that his cause was known : the word of the Lord tried him.

20 The king sent, and delivered him : the prince of the people let him go free.

21 He made him lord also of his house : and ruler of all his substance;

22 That he might inform his princes after his will : and teach his senators wisdom.

23 Israel also came into Egypt : and Jacob was a stranger in the land of Ham.

24 And he increased his people exceedingly : and made them stronger than their enemies;

25 Whose heart turned so that they hated his people : and dealt untruly with his servants.

26 Then sent he Moses his servant : and Aaron whom he had chosen.

27 And these shewed his tokens among them : and wonders in the land of Ham.

28 He sent darkness, and it was dark : and they were not obedient unto his word.

29 He turned their waters into blood : and slew their fish.

30 Their land brought forth frogs : yea, even in their kings' chambers.

31 He spake the word, and there came all manner of flies : and lice in all their quarters.

32 He gave them hail-stones for rain : and flames of fire in their land.

33 He smote their vines also and fig-trees : and destroyed the trees that were in their coasts.

34 He spake the word, and the grasshoppers came, and caterpillars innumerable : and did eat up all the grass in their land, and devoured the fruit of their ground.

35 He smote all the first-born in their land : even the chief of all their strength.

36 He brought them forth also with silver and gold : there was not one feeble person among their tribes.

37 Egypt was glad at their departing : for they were afraid of them.

38 He spread out a cloud to be a covering : and fire to give light in the night-season.

39 At their desire he brought quails : and he filled them with the bread of heaven.

40 He opened the rock of stone, and the waters flowed out : so that rivers ran in the dry places.

41 For why? he remembered his holy promise : and Abraham his servant.

42 And he brought forth his people with joy : and his chosen with gladness.

43 And gave them the lands of the heathen : and they took the labours of the people in possession ;

44 That they might keep his statutes : and observe his laws.

Verse 14. The first Papal legates, who came over to England to claim Papal supremacy (from Pope Adrian, A.D. 785), used this verse as an instance of the superiority of the ecclesiastical over the civil jurisdiction. It has often done duty for the same purpose since.

Verse 15. It is needless to say that this was constantly in the mouths of loyal Churchmen during the civil wars, plots, and revolutions of the seventeenth century ; and the application was nothing new then, for Thomas Merks, the Bishop of Carlisle, pointed it out to Henry IV., in a vigorous and manful speech he made in defence of Richard II. The bishop was promptly lodged in the dungeon of St. Albans Abbey for his boldness of utterance.

In the letter of Edmund Verney to his brother Ralph (they were both sons of Charles I.'s standard-bearer) we find this remonstrance : " It greeves my hearte to think that my father already and I who soe dearly love and esteeme you should be bound in consequence (because of our duty to our King) to be your enemy. I heare tis a great greefe to my father. I beseech you consider that majesty is sacred ; God sayth Touch not myne anointed ; it troubled Davyd that he cutt but the lapp of Saul's garment."

Verse 28. Dr. Reynolds, at the Hampton Court Conference, proposed that "disobedient" be put for "obedient," as the Nonconformists felt this mistranslation to be a stumbling-block. The Revisers, both then and of our time, followed the Nonconformists here without dispute, and translate, " And they rebelled not against his words."

Dr. Sparks had a controversy with Whitgift on this very verse in 1589, from which armoury the weapons for the later dispute were mostly drawn.

Day 21   PSALM CVI   *Evening Prayer*

Latins.—Saturday Matins.
Greeks.—Last psalm for Thursday Matins.

PSALM CVI.   *Confitemini Domino.*

O GIVE thanks unto the Lord, for he is gracious : and his mercy endureth for ever.

2 Who can express the noble acts of the Lord : or shew forth all his praise ?

3 Blessed are they that alway keep judgement : and do righteousness.

4 Remember me, O Lord, according to the favour that thou bearest unto thy people : O visit me with thy salvation.

5 That I may see the felicity of thy chosen : and rejoice in the gladness of thy people, and give thanks with thine inheritance.

6 We have sinned with our fathers : we have done amiss, and dealt wickedly.

7 Our fathers regarded not thy wonders in Egypt, neither kept they thy great goodness in remembrance : but were disobedient at the sea, even at the Red sea.

8 Nevertheless, he helped them for his Name's sake : that he might make his power to be known.

9 He rebuked the Red sea also, and it was dried up : so he led them through the deep, as through a wilderness.

10 And he saved them from the adversary's hand : and delivered them from the hand of the enemy.

11 As for those that troubled them, the waters overwhelmed them : there was not one of them left.

12 Then believed they his words : and sang praise unto him.

13 But within a while they forgat his works : and would not abide his counsel.

14 But lust came upon them in the wilderness : and they tempted God in the desert.

15 And he gave them their desire : and sent leanness withal into their soul.

16 They angered Moses also in the tents : and Aaron the saint of the Lord.

17 So the earth opened, and swallowed up Dathan : and covered the congregation of Abiram.

18 And the fire was kindled in their company : the flame burnt up the ungodly.

19 They made a calf in Horeb : and worshipped the molten image.

20 Thus they turned their glory : into the similitude of a calf that eateth hay.

21 And they forgat God their Saviour : who had done so great things in Egypt;

22 Wondrous works in the land of Ham : and fearful things by the Red sea.

23 So he said, he would have destroyed them, had not Moses his chosen stood before him in the gap : to turn away his wrathful indignation, lest he should destroy them.

24 Yea, they thought scorn of that pleasant land : and gave no credence unto his word ;

25 But murmured in their tents : and hearkened not unto the voice of the Lord.

26 Then lift he up his hand against them : to overthrow them in the wilderness ;

27 To cast out their seed among the nations : and to scatter them in the lands.

28 They joined themselves unto Baal-peor : and ate the offerings of the dead.

29 Thus they provoked him to anger with their own inventions : and the plague was great among them.

30 Then stood up Phinees and prayed : and so the plague ceased.

31 And that was counted unto him for righteousness : among all posterities for evermore.

32 They angered him also at the waters of strife : so that he punished Moses for their sakes ;

33 Because they provoked his spirit : so that he spake unadvisedly with his lips.

34 Neither destroyed they the heathen : as the Lord commanded them ;

35 But were mingled among the heathen : and learned their works.

36 Insomuch that they worshipped their idols, which turned to their own decay : yea, they offered their sons and their daughters unto devils ;

37 And shed innocent blood, even the blood of their sons and of their daughters : whom they offered unto the idols of Canaan; and the land was defiled with blood.

38 Thus were they stained with their own works : and went a whoring with their own inventions.

39 Therefore was the wrath of the Lord kindled against his people : insomuch that he abhorred his own inheritance.

40 And he gave them over into the hand of the heathen : and they that hated them were lords over them.

41 Their enemies oppressed them : and had them in subjection.

42 Many a time did he deliver them : but they rebelled against him with their own inventions, and were brought down in their wickedness.

43 Nevertheless, when he saw their adversity : he heard their complaint.

44 He thought upon his covenant, and pitied them, according unto the multitude of his mercies : yea, he made all those that led them away captive to pity them.

45 Deliver us, O Lord our God, and gather us from among the heathen : that we may give thanks unto thy holy Name, and make our boast of thy praise.

46 Blessed be the Lord God of Israel from everlasting, and world without end : and let all the people say, Amen.

Fox tells us that William Wolsey, a constable, and Robert Pygot, a painter, were burnt at Ely (October, 1555) for Protestantism. They died reciting Psalm cvi., and clasping New Testaments to their breasts.

It is a curious thing to notice how many commentators there were on the Psalter in the eighteenth century. Zachary Mudge (Dr. Johnson's friend and Reynolds' admired "study") was the first leader; but Bishop Hare, Theocritean Thomas Edwards, George Fenwick, and Bishop George Horne of Norwich, were among the chief. Doddridge gives the palm of metrical translations to James Merrick, Fellow of Trinity College, Oxford—a man very hard to admire.

Verse 11. The Utrecht Psalter, that most interesting and puzzling manuscript, which the critics assign alternately to each of the centuries from the fourth to the ninth, has spirited illustrations of this verse, and some others in this psalm and the next one. The Red Sea is overwhelming the Egyptians; there are ploughmen at work, felons in the stocks, vinedressers and planters, men going down to the sea in the queerest ships, and others building cities. There are also, among other delights, two great chairs which are the seats of the elders (Ps. cvii. verse 32).

Verse 30. This was one of the translations which the Puritans so inveighed against at the Hampton Court Conference. Dr. Reynolds proposed "executed judgement," but the words were retained in the Prayer-Book, though altered in the Bible.

Verse 38. This is the second motto of Father Parsons' work on the English persecution, and summed up the Romanist charge against our people of "will-worship."

Latins.—Saturday Matins.
Greeks.—Thursday evening.

PSALM CVII. *Confitemini Domino.*

O GIVE thanks unto the Lord, for he is gracious : and his mercy endureth for ever.

2 Let them give thanks whom the Lord hath redeemed : and delivered from the hand of the enemy ;

3 And gathered them out of the lands, from the east, and from the west : from the north, and from the south.

4 They went astray in the wilderness out of the way : and found no city to dwell in ;

5 Hungry and thirsty : their soul fainted in them.

6 So they cried unto the Lord in their trouble : and he delivered them from their distress.

7 He led them forth by the right way : that they might go to the city where they dwelt.

8 O that men would therefore praise the Lord for his goodness : and declare the wonders that he doeth for the children of men.

9 For he satisfieth the empty soul : and filleth the hungry soul with goodness.

10 Such as sit in darkness, and in the shadow of death : being fast bound in misery and iron ;

11 Because they rebelled against the words of the Lord : and lightly regarded the counsel of the most Highest ;

12 He also brought down their heart through heaviness : they fell down, and there was none to help them.

13 So when they cried unto the Lord in their trouble : he delivered them out of their distress.

14 For he brought them out of darkness, and out of the shadow of death : and brake their bonds in sunder.

15 O that men would therefore praise the Lord for his goodness : and declare the wonders that he doeth for the children of men!

16 For he hath broken the gates of brass : and smitten the bars of iron in sunder.

17 Foolish men are plagued for their offence : and because of their wickedness.

18 Their soul abhorred all manner of meat : and they were even hard at death's door.

19 So when they cried unto the Lord in their trouble : he delivered them out of their distress.

20 He sent his word, and healed them : and they were saved from their destruction.

21 O that men would therefore praise the Lord for his goodness : and declare the wonders that he doeth for the children of men!

22 That they would offer unto him the sacrifice of thanksgiving : and tell out his works with gladness!

23 They that go down to the sea in ships : and occupy their business in great waters;

24 These men see the works of the Lord : and his wonders in the deep.

25 For at his word the stormy wind ariseth : which lifteth up the waves thereof.

26 They are carried up to the heaven, and down again to the deep : their soul melteth away because of the trouble.

27 They reel to and fro, and stagger like a drunken man : and are at their wit's end.

28 So when they cry unto the Lord in their trouble : he delivereth them out of their distress.

29 For he maketh the storm to cease : so that the waves thereof are still.

30 Then are they glad, because they are at rest : and so he bringeth them unto the haven where they would be.

31 O that men would therefore praise the Lord for his goodness : and declare the wonders that he doeth for the children of men !

32 That they would exalt him also in the congregation of the people : and praise him in the seat of the elders !

33 Who turneth the floods into a wilderness : and drieth up the water-springs.

34 A fruitful land maketh he barren : for the wickedness of them that dwell therein.

35 Again, he maketh the wilderness a standing water : and water-springs of a dry ground.

36 And there he setteth the hungry : that they may build them a city to dwell in ;

37 That they may sow their land, and plant vineyards : to yield them fruits of increase.

38 He blesseth them, so that they multiply exceedingly : and suffereth not their cattle to decrease.

39 And again, when they are minished, and brought low : through oppression, through any plague or trouble ;

40 Though he suffer them to be evil treated through tyrants : and let them wander out of the way in the wilderness ;

41 Yet helpeth he the poor out of misery : and maketh him households like a flock of sheep.

42 The righteous will consider this, and rejoice : and the mouth of all wickedness shall be stopped.

43 Whoso is wise will ponder these things : and they shall understand the loving-kindness of the Lord.

This was the favourite psalm of William Romaine, the Rector of St. Ann's, Blackfriars, and of his friend (and Dr. Johnson's acquaintance), Dr. Benjamin Wheeler, the professor of poetry at Oxford.

Verses 15 *and* 16. In the harrowing of Hell (*vide* Ps. xxiv.), the divine prophet David cries aloud in the darkness, " Did not I truly prophesy, while I was on earth, saying, O that men would praise the Lord for His goodness !" Thus, these verses may be said to be what was regarded in the ages of sorrow as the epitome of the whole Psalter, viz., its tone of triumph and thanksgiving.

Verse 30. This was quoted by "Little Bilney," Latimer's teacher, on his way to the stake. It is the epitaph set up in Beechey Island for Sir John Franklin and his companions.

Verse 42. Gaufridus, St. Bernard's secretary, and the author of that saint's life, with these words sums up his master's earthly life: " For he was both the glory of all the good and the awe of the wicked, that this verse seemed aptly made for him, for in his presence holiness wholly rejoiced, frowardness was curbed, and hardness grew penitent."

Liturgical use.—Thanksgiving after a Storm at Sea.
Latins.—Saturday Matins.
Greeks.—Thursday morning.

PSALM CVIII. *Paratum cor meum.*

O GOD, my heart is ready, my heart is ready : I will sing and give praise with the best member that I have.

2 Awake, thou lute, and harp : I myself will awake right early.

3 I will give thanks unto thee, O Lord, among the people : I will sing praises unto thee among the nations.

4 For thy mercy is greater than the heavens : and thy truth reacheth unto the clouds.

5 Set up thyself, O God, above the heavens : and thy glory above all the earth.

6 That thy beloved may be delivered : let thy right hand save them, and hear thou me.

7 God hath spoken in his holiness : I will rejoice therefore, and divide Sichem, and mete out the valley of Succoth.

8 Gilead is mine, and Manasses is mine : Ephraim also is the strength of my head.

9 Judah is my law-giver, Moab is my wash-pot : over Edom will I cast out my shoe; over Philistia will I triumph.

10 Who will lead me into the strong city : and who will bring me into Edom ?

11 Hast not thou forsaken us, O God : and wilt not thou, O God, go forth with our hosts ?

12 O help us against the enemy : for vain is the help of man.

13 Through God we shall do great acts : and it is he that shall tread down our enemies.

This psalm was a favourite with that "person highly affected to antiquities," Sir Christopher Hatton, the good friend both to Dugdale and to Jeremy Taylor. He calls it in his Psalter "A prayer for victory against our Enemies." He was controller of Charles I.'s household, "being then accounted a friend of all that loved the King and Church of England, for which he suffered in a high degree." Charles II., "in consideration of his vast sufferings and eminent Loyalty," made him Privy Councillor and Governour of Guernsey.

Liturgical use.—Ascension Day evening.
Latins.—Saturday Matins.
Greeks.—Thursday evening.

PSALM CIX. *Deus laudum.*

HOLD not thy tongue, O God of my praise : for the mouth of the ungodly, yea, the mouth of the deceitful is opened upon me.

2 And they have spoken against me with false tongues : they compassed me about also with words of hatred, and fought against me without a cause.

3 For the love that I had unto them, lo, they take now my contrary part : but I give myself unto prayer.

4 Thus have they rewarded me evil for good : and hatred for my good will.

5 " Set thou an ungodly man to be ruler over him : and let Satan stand at his right hand.

6 " When sentence is given upon him, let him be condemned : and let his prayer be turned into sin.

7 " Let his days be few : and let another take his office.

8 " Let his children be fatherless : and his wife a widow.

9 " Let his children be vagabonds, and beg their bread : let them seek it also out of desolate places.

10 " Let the extortioner consume all that he hath : and let the stranger spoil his labour.

11 " Let there be no man to pity him : nor to have compassion upon his fatherless children.

12 " Let his posterity be destroyed : and in the next generation let his name be clean put out.

13 " Let the wickedness of his fathers be had in remembrance in the sight of the Lord : and let not the sin of his mother be done away.

14 " Let them alway be before the Lord : that he may root out the memorial of them from off the earth ;

15 "And that, because his mind was not to do good : but persecuted the poor helpless man, that he might slay him that was vexed at the heart.

16 "His delight was in cursing, and it shall happen unto him : he loved not blessing, therefore shall it be far from him.

17 "He clothed himself with cursing, like as with a raiment : and it shall come into his bowels like water, and like oil into his bones.

18 "Let it be unto him as the cloke that he hath upon him : and as the girdle that he is alway girded withal."

19 Let it thus happen from the Lord unto mine enemies : and to those that speak evil against my soul.

20 But deal thou with me, O Lord God, according unto thy Name : for sweet is thy mercy.

21 O deliver me, for I am helpless and poor : and my heart is wounded within me.

22 I go hence like the shadow that departeth : and am driven away as the grasshopper.

23 My knees are weak through fasting : my flesh is dried up for want of fatness.

24 I became also a reproach unto them : they that looked upon me shaked their heads.

25 Help me, O Lord my God : save me, according to thy mercy;

26 And they shall know, how that this is thy hand : and that thou, Lord, hast done it.

27 Though they curse, yet bless thou : and let them be confounded that rise up against me; but let thy servant rejoice.

28 Let mine adversaries be clothed with shame : and let them cover themselves with their own confusion, as with a cloke.

29 As for me, I will give great thanks unto the Lord with my mouth : and praise him among the multitude;

30 For he shall stand at the right hand of the poor : to save his soul from unrighteous judges.

Fuller quaintly glances at the seventeenth-century uses of this psalm, and at those who cited it copiously to justify their own deeds and spirit (cf. Milton's "Reformation in England"). "Lord, when in my daily service I read David's psalms, give me to alter the accent of my soul according to their several subjects. In such psalms, wherein he confesseth his sins or requesteth thy pardon, or praiseth for former, or prayeth for future favours, in all these give me to raise my soul to as high a pitch as may be. But when I come to such psalms wherein he curseth his enemies, O there let me bring down my soul to a lower note. For those words were made only to fit David's mouth. I have the like breath, but not the same spirit to pronounce them. Nor let me flatter myself that it is lawful for me, with David, to curse thine enemies, lest my deceitful heart entitle all mine enemies to be thine, and so what was religion in David prove malice in me, whilst I act revenge under pretence of piety."

Verse 19. The Hebrew, Greek and Latin all give a better sense to this verse. "This is the reward." The LXX. and Vulgate say, "This is the work of those who slander me to the Lord," which alters the whole character of the psalm.

Latins.—Saturday Matins.
Greeks.—Last psalm on Thursday evening.

PSALM CX. *Dixit Dominus.*

THE Lord said unto my Lord : "Sit thou on my right hand, until I make thine enemies thy footstool."

2 The Lord shall send the rod of thy power out of Sion : "be thou ruler, even in the midst among thine enemies."

3 In the day of thy power shall the people offer thee free-will offerings with an holy worship : the dew of thy birth is of the womb of the morning.

4 The Lord sware, and will not repent : "Thou art a Priest for ever after the order of Melchisedech."

5 The Lord upon thy right hand : shall wound even kings in the day of his wrath.

6 He shall judge among the heathen ; he shall fill the places with the dead bodies : and smite in sunder the heads over divers countries.

7 He shall drink of the brook in the way : therefore shall he lift up his head.

This is one of the psalms quoted by Christ Himself (St. Matt. xxii. 43). The Talmudists assign the psalm to Melchizedeck.

This psalm has been a great favourite always in the Western Church. It is an introit for St. Agnes, and she was perhaps the best-loved Virgin Martyr. It was also popular with the Arians, who used it against St. Athanasius. The storm which arose lately, about *Lux Mundi* raged most fiercely in controversies connected with its origin.

Verse 5. This, perhaps, is one of the passages alluded to in that most wonderful of hymns, *Dies iræ*, by Thomas of Celano, of which some hundred and eight translations into English are recorded. The line *Teste David et Sibilla* perhaps refers to this verse.

Verse 7. A common Easter Day text in mediæval sermons, the brook being the River of Death.

Liturgical use.—Christmas Day evening.
Latins.—Sunday Vespers; Christmas; Circumcision; Epiphany; Easter Day; Apostles and Evangelists; Martyrs; Dedication of a church; Feasts of Our Lady; St. Michael and All Angels; All Saints.
Greeks.—Saturday Matins.

PSALM CXI. *Confitebor tibi.*

I WILL give thanks unto the Lord with my whole heart : secretly among the faithful, and in the congregation.

2 The works of the Lord are great : sought out of all them that have pleasure therein.

3 His work is worthy to be praised, and had in honour : and his righteousness endureth for ever.

4 The merciful and gracious Lord hath so done his marvellous works : that they ought to be had in remembrance.

5 He hath given meat unto them that fear him : he shall ever be mindful of his covenant.

6 He hath shewed his people the power of his works : that he may give them the heritage of the heathen.

7 The works of his hands are verity and judgement : all his commandments are true.

8 They stand fast for ever and ever : and are done in truth and equity.

9 He sent redemption unto his people : he hath commanded his covenant for ever; holy and reverend is his Name.

10 The fear of the Lord is the beginning of wisdom : a good understanding have all they that do thereafter; the praise of it endureth for ever.

This psalm is one of the great Eucharistic psalms of the Western Church. The others are Pss. cx., cxvi. from verse 10, cxxviii., and cxlvii.

Verses 4 and 5. The dauntless statesman and devout monk, St. Dunstan, not least among the makers of England, died with these words on his lips in A.D. 989. When St. Dunstan's strong force was withdrawn, a deluge of misery fell upon England. Ethelred's weakness and the Danish invasions seemed for a time to undo all the good that had ever been accomplished by her wiser rulers.

Verse 10. In the Beauchamp Tower is written this legend, by a "naked and torn" prisoner who was once emissary of the Queen of Scots : *Principium sapientiæ timor Domini* I. H. S. X. P. S. Be frend to one, be ennemye to none. Anno D. 1571."

Liturgical use.—Easter Matins.
Latins.—Sunday Vespers ; Christmas ; Epiphany ; Easter ; Corpus Christi ; Martyrs ; Dedication Feast ; St. Michael ; All Saints.
Greeks.—Saturday Matins.

PSALM CXII. *Beatus vir.*

BLESSED is the man that feareth the Lord : he hath great delight in his commandments.

2 His seed shall be mighty upon earth : the generation of the faithful shall be blessed.

3 Riches and plenteousness shall be in his house : and his righteousness endureth for ever.

4 Unto the godly there ariseth up light in the darkness : he is merciful, loving, and righteous.

5 A good man is merciful, and lendeth : and will guide his words with discretion.

6 For he shall never be moved : and the righteous shall be had in everlasting remembrance.

7 He will not be afraid of any evil tidings : for his heart standeth fast, and believeth in the Lord.

8 His heart is established, and will not shrink : until he see his desire upon his enemies.

9 He hath dispersed abroad, and given to the poor : and his righteousness remaineth for ever; his horn shall be exalted with honour.

10 The ungodly shall see it, and it shall grieve him : he shall gnash with his teeth, and consume away ; the desire of the ungodly shall perish.

Piers Ploughman tells us that Sloth knows better how to find a hare in the furrow than to recite his *Beatus vir*. The fifth verse is his antidote to avarice.

Verse 4. The motto in *Lyra*

Apostolica chosen by John Henry Newman for "Lead, kindly Light."

Verse 6. "The just shall be had in everlasting remembrance." This was the motto Dean Stanley chose for his funeral sermon on George Grote, whom he praised as the most impartial among historians.

Verse 9. St. Anno, an eleventh century Bishop of Cologne, like many others before and since, was so impressed with the force of this verse that he gave away everything he possessed to the poor, so that when he died he left not a halfpenny behind him. It is a verse often used on saints' days, but to none does it better apply than to St. Anno.

King Edward III. put the last words of this verse on the English half-florin, *Exaltabitur in gloria*, thus recalling the whole verse to men as they moved "through busiest mart."

Liturgical use.—Introit to the Mass I. Sunday after Easter, Low Sunday (e).
Latins.—Sunday Vespers; Christmas; Epiphany; Easter; Martyrs; Dedication Feast; St. Michael; All Saints.
Greeks.—Saturday Matins.

PSALM CXIII. *Laudate, pueri.*

PRAISE the Lord, ye servants : O praise the Name of the Lord.

2 Blessed be the Name of the Lord : from this time forth for evermore.

3 The Lord's Name is praised : from the rising up of the sun unto the going down of the same.

4 The Lord is high above all heathen : and his glory above the heavens.

5 Who is like unto the Lord our God, that hath his dwelling so high : and yet humbleth himself to behold the things that are in heaven and earth?

6 He taketh up the simple out of the dust : and lifteth the poor out of the mire;

7 That he may set him with the princes : even with the princes of his people.

8 He maketh the barren woman to keep house : and to be a joyful mother of children.

This psalm begins the Hallel, sung at the Jewish Passover. This and the next were sung before the discourse. Then the cup was blessed, and Psalms cxv., cxvi., and cxvii., were sung, and Ps. cxviii at the end of the rite.

A favourite psalm of the Ven. Bede, whose version of it, *Laudate Altithronum*, was sung for many ages.

This was the last psalm read to Wordsworth the poet, who used to hear or read regularly the daily psalms. He died on October 23, 1850.

In the persecution of the Church in Western Japan, 1624, four martyrs were being burned —three men and a woman. They were concealed by the smoke, when "out of the midst of the fire rose that psalm *Laudate, pueri,* the watchword, as it were, and rallying cry of so many Japanese martyrs"; but the singer's voice "faltered in the mediation of that verse, 'That He may set him with princes,' and the last clause was sung, if sung at all, among the true ' Princes of the People' in Heaven."

Verse 3. *A solis ortu usque ad occasum* — the graveyard dial motto on the wall of St. Gervais, Savoy.

Liturgical use.—Easter Day evening; Introit to the Easter Tuesday Mass, and of St. Michael and all Angels (e).

Latins.—Sunday Vespers; Christmas; Circumcision; Epiphany; Easter; Apostles and Evangelists; Martyrs; Dedication Festival; Feast of Our Lady; St. Michael; All Saints; Burial of Children.

Greeks.—Saturday morning; Mesorion of Ninth hour.

PSALM CXIV. *In exitu Israel.*

WHEN Israel came out of Egypt : and the house of Jacob from among the strange people,

2 Judah was his sanctuary : and Israel his dominion.

3 The sea saw that, and fled : Jordan was driven back.

4 The mountains skipped like rams : and the little hills like young sheep.

5 What aileth thee, O thou sea, that thou fleddest : and thou Jordan, that thou wast driven back?

6 Ye mountains, that ye skipped like rams : and ye little hills, like young sheep?

7 Tremble, thou earth, at the presence of the Lord : at the presence of the God of Jacob;

8 Who turned the hard rock into a standing water : and the flint-stone into a springing well.

This psalm and the next form one in the Vulgate.

This is in the Paschal Hallel, and was therefore sung at the Last Supper.

In the reign of Julian the Apostate, a certain young Christian named Theodotus was racked for the faith and defied his tormentors. He chanted, the whole time, this psalm, as if he felt no pain.

When the torture was over he told his friends that as he was being racked he beheld a man in white sprinkling him with water from a vessel, which eased his torments.

This is the psalm which Dante heard the souls singing as they were wafted into Purgatory in the angels' boat (*Purg.* II.).

It was the chant of triumph of the victors at Bannockburn (1314).

It was sung upon the field of Agincourt (1415), by order of Henry V., when the victory was won. When they reached the verse *Non nobis* (Ps. cxv. in our translation) the whole host fell upon their knees in the mud, and the wounded joined the song. The Tonus Peregrinus was probably the tune used.

St. Francis Xavier travelled through the long desert of Amanguchi to the Japanese city of Meaco, and found the city in a state of siege. He turned back again into the dreadful desert, singing, *In exitu.*

The Duke of Gandia, when he joined the early Jesuits, left all his state and his great castle of Gandia, singing the same psalm, adding, "Our bonds are broken and we are delivered!"

Milton, at fifteen years of age, turned this psalm into rhymed verse (1624).

It was a favourite of Sir Walter Scott, who also versified it.

Liturgical use.—Easter Day Evening.
Latins.—Sunday Vespers; Easter.
Greeks.—Saturday morning.

PSALM CXV. *Non nobis, Domine.*

NOT unto us, O Lord, not unto us, but unto thy Name give the praise : for thy loving mercy, and for thy truth's sake.

2 Wherefore shall the heathen say : Where is now their God?

3 As for our God, he is in heaven : he hath done whatsoever pleased him.

4 Their idols are silver and gold : even the work of men's hands.

5 They have mouths, and speak not : eyes have they, and see not.

6 They have ears, and hear not : noses have they, and smell not.

7 They have hands, and handle not; feet have they, and walk not : neither speak they through their throat.

8 They that make them are like unto them : and so are all such as put their trust in them.

9 But thou, house of Israel, trust thou in the Lord : he is their succour and defence.

10 Ye house of Aaron, put your trust in the Lord : he is their helper and defender.

11 Ye that fear the Lord, put your trust in the Lord : he is their helper and defender.

12 The Lord hath been mindful of us, and he shall bless us : even he shall bless the house of Israel, he shall bless the house of Aaron.

13 He shall bless them that fear the Lord : both small and great.

14 The Lord shall increase you more and more : you and your children.

15 Ye are the blessed of the Lord : who made heaven and earth.

16 All the whole heavens are the Lord's : the earth hath he given to the children of men.

17 The dead praise not thee, O Lord : neither all they that go down into silence.

18 But we will praise the Lord : from this time forth for evermore. Praise the Lord.

Part of the Hallel of the Passover, and therefore sung by our Lord at the Last Supper. At the siege of Oran in Africa, Cardinal Ximenes, in his pontificals, led the troops. He rode on a war-horse, and his crosier was carried before him by a monk. As the town was taken he advanced singing *Non nobis, Domine.*

Verse 1. Henry IV. gave this motto to his son, when he elevated him to a share in the government.

Verse 3 played an important part in converting men from Paganism. Pontius, the Roman senator's son (257 A.D.), is one instance out of many. He embraced the Christian Faith, because of the spiritual conception of God here revealed to him.

Verses 4 and 5 were used by Publia against Julian the Apostate (*vide* Ps. lxviii.). They seem to have been part of the recognised defiance of the early Christian Martyrs, when ordered to sacrifice to Cæsar (*i.e.*, to swear allegiance to society). Almost wherever one turns one finds them thus used. Ruinart's *Acta Sincera* notes many such instances, Petrus Balsamus (311 A.D.) for example.

Verse 16. On Easter Tuesday, 1517, Dr. Bell preached from this a Spital sermon against foreigners in London, and said, "That as birds defend their nestes so ought Englishmen to maintaine themselves and to hurt and grieue alians for respect of their commonwealth." The result was a serious riot : and Bell was lodged in the Tower.

Liturgical use.—Introit for Mass of St. Bartholomew (e).
Latins.—As part of Psalm cxiv. (*q. v.*).
Greeks.—Saturday morning.

PSALM CXVI. *Dilexi, quoniam.*

I AM well pleased : that the Lord hath heard the voice of my prayer;

2 That he hath inclined his ear unto me : therefore will I call upon him as long as I live.

3 The snares of death compassed me round about : and the pains of hell gat hold upon me.

4 I shall find trouble and heaviness, and I will call upon the name of the Lord : " O Lord, I beseech thee, deliver my soul."

5 Gracious is the Lord, and righteous : yea, our God is merciful.

6 The Lord preserveth the simple : I was in misery, and he helped me.

7 Turn again then unto thy rest, O my soul : for the Lord hath rewarded thee.

8 And why? thou hast delivered my soul from death : mine eyes from tears, and my feet from falling.

9 I will walk before the Lord : in the land of the living.

10 I believed, and therefore will I speak ; but I was sore troubled : I said in my haste, "All men are liars."

11 What reward shall I give unto the Lord : for all the benefits that he hath done unto me?

12 I will receive the cup of salvation : and call upon the Name of the Lord.

13 I will pay my vows now in the presence of all his people : right dear in the sight of the Lord is the death of his saints.

14 Behold, O Lord, how that I am thy servant : I am thy servant, and the son of thine handmaid ; thou hast broken my bonds in sunder.

15 I will offer to thee the sacrifice of thanksgiving : and will call upon the name of the Lord.

16 I will pay my vows unto the Lord, in the sight of

all his people : in the courts of the Lord's house, even in the midst of thee, O Jerusalem. Praise the Lord.

This is the first psalm in the Dirge (*vide* Ps. v.).

Our Lord and His Apostles sang this before they went to the Mount of Olives. It was in the second part of the Paschal Hallel, Psalms cxvi. and cxvii.

On May 10, 1509, John, Bishop of Rochester, preached a most notable sermon at the funeral of Henry VII., and "perused the psalme (*dilexi*) in the persone of this noble man." By order of the king's granddame it was printed by Wynkyn de Worde.

In 1625-31 William Gouge, the Blackfriars minister, wishing to give God thanks for the abatement of the plague, whereof 54,265 persons had died in London and the nine suburbs, wrote a book on this psalm called the "Saint's Sacrifice." He added, as additional reasons for praise, that Charles (II.) was born, the Huguenots were tolerated, the Dutch Protestants had triumphed, Gustavus Adolphus had won Leipsic, and Protestantism was triumphant in Germany.

Verse 7. St. Chrysostom says it was an old custom among Christians to repeat this verse over their dead, at funerals.

Verse 8. This is what the biographer of the learned Dr. Thomas Jackson quaintly calls his "cygnean cantion." He was a friend of Laud, and the president of Corpus Christi College, Oxford, till 1640, and died so poor that he left nothing but his papers.

Verse 9. *Placebo Domino in regione vivorum* was and is the Latin antiphon for the funeral psalms : and this is why so many Jesuits and others recited it at their death sentences, during the Protestant counter-persecutions.

Verse 11. It is significant of the mediæval reverence with which men undertook their work, that when Richard de Bury finished his book *Philobiblon* (January 24, 1345), he wrote on the MSS., *Quid retribuam Domino pro omnibus quæ retribuit mihi ?*

Verses 11 *and* 12. These are the words the priest says to himself before he receives the sacrament of Our Lord's Blood.

Verse 12. *Calicem salutis accipiam.* This is a usual motto for the Communion chalice. It was engraved, for instance, upon John Paston's gold chalice of 1464.

Verse 13, *second part.* The Church's comment upon many of her saints. These words were in the Anglo-Saxon Prime, and our fathers thus faced each of the days of their life with them. St. Bernard exhorted the Knights Templars to the Crusade with the same.

Verses 14 *to* 16. With these words St. Augustine resolved upon the new life : and not a few of God's great servants could inscribe *Hic incipit vita nova* as a rubric to these verses.

Verse 10 *to* end. De Thou the younger (son of the historian and composer of the Edict of Nantes), recited the psalm *Credidi* at his execution, kneeling and shouting the words aloud fervently and joyfully, and paraphrasing them in French (*vide* Ps. cxviii. 21).

Liturgical use.—Churching of Women, before a Celebration.
Latins.—(Divide this after 9th verse); Monday Vespers; Apostles and Evangelists; Martyrs; All Saints.
Greeks.—Saturday morning.

PSALM CXVII. *Laudate Dominum.*

O PRAISE the Lord, all ye heathen : praise him, all ye nations.

2 For his merciful kindness is ever more and more towards us : and the truth of the Lord endureth for ever. Praise the Lord.

In the second part of the Paschal Hallel, and therefore sung at the Last Supper.
"At the foot of Doon Hill" (after Dunbar battle) "the Lord General" (Cromwell) "made a halt and sang Psalm cxvii., till our horse could gather for the chase." The Puritans called it the Dunbar psalm.

Liturgical use.—Introit to the Mass of St. Matthew (e).
Latins.—Monday Vespers; Christmas; Ascension-tide; Whitsuntide; Apostles and Evangelists; St. Michael and All Angels; All Saints.
Greeks.—Saturday morning; Evensong.

PSALM CXVIII. *Confitemini Domino.*

O GIVE thanks unto the Lord, for he is gracious : because his mercy endureth for ever.

2 Let Israel now confess, that he is gracious : and that his mercy endureth for ever.

3 Let the house of Aaron now confess : that his mercy endureth for ever.

4 Yea, let them now that fear the Lord confess : that his mercy endureth for ever.

5 I called upon the Lord in trouble : and the Lord heard me at large.

6 The Lord is on my side : I will not fear what man doeth unto me.

7 The Lord taketh my part with them that help me : therefore shall I see my desire upon mine enemies.

8 It is better to trust in the Lord : than to put any confidence in man.

9 It is better to trust in the Lord : than to put any confidence in princes.

10 All nations compassed me round about : but in the Name of the Lord will I destroy them.

11 They kept me in on every side, they kept me in, I say, on every side : but in the Name of the Lord will I destroy them.

12 They came about me like bees, and are extinct even as the fire among the thorns : for in the Name of the Lord I will destroy them.

13 Thou hast thrust sore at me, that I might fall : but the Lord was my help.

14 The Lord is my strength, and my song : and is become my salvation.

15 The voice of joy and health is in the dwellings of the righteous : the right hand of the Lord bringeth mighty things to pass.

16 The right hand of the Lord hath the pre-eminence : the right hand of the Lord bringeth mighty things to pass.

17 I shall not die, but live : and declare the works of the Lord.

18 The Lord hath chastened and corrected me : but he hath not given me over unto death.

19 "Open me the gates of righteousness : that I may go into them, and give thanks unto the Lord."

20 "This is the gate of the Lord : the righteous shall enter into it."

21 I will thank thee, for thou hast heard me : and art become my salvation.

22 The same stone which the builders refused : is become the head-stone of the corner.

23 This is the Lord's doing : and it is marvellous in our eyes.

24 This is the day which the Lord hath made : we will rejoice and be glad in it.

25 Help me now, O Lord : O Lord, send us now prosperity.

26 Blessed be he that cometh in the Name of the Lord : we have wished you good luck, ye that are of the house of the Lord.

27 God is the Lord who hath shewed us light : bind

the sacrifice with cords, yea, even unto the horns of the altar.

28 Thou art my God, and I will thank thee : thou art my God, and I will praise thee.

29 O give thanks unto the Lord, for he is gracious : and his mercy endureth for ever.

This psalm was the thanksgiving or recessional hymn after the Passover, and was therefore sung by Christ and the Apostles at the end of the Last Supper. It is most probably the hymn they sang on the way to the Mount of Olives, and our Lord no doubt precented it by singing the first half-verse alone.

This was Charles V.'s favourite psalm, as he told Marot.

Verse 6. St. Gordius sang this verse under torture, with Psalm xxiii. ; and many other martyrs with it on their lips, by faith stopped the mouths of lions, quenched the violence of the fire, and subdued kingdoms.

On St. Martin's journey into Italy, the Devil, in likeness of a fellow traveller, pointed out to him that he was bringing upon himself the enmity of all the lords of Hell. The saint wheeled round upon him and put him to flight with this verse.

This verse comforted poor William Cowper, and was his "first religious impression," when he was a much-bullied little boy at Market Street School, 1737.

Verse 10. St. Bernard and Henry Martyn were each of them in his sickness troubled by doubts lest God should not recognise them amid such a multitude of souls coming up for judgment. The latter was heartened by the words, "The Lord knoweth them that are His," the former, "with a far deeper insight," says Neale, by this verse.

Verse 12. The war cry of the Huguenots at the battle of Coutras, October 20, 1581, when they won their first victory after twenty-five years' fighting. Love of the psalms was traditional among these men, for, in the reigns of Francis I. and Henry II., they were gagged at the stake to prevent them singing psalms, but the fire often burnt the gags and they chanted with charred lips, this and other favourites. It was found safer to cut their tongues out, before burning them.

Whitfield mourned that this was his imprecation upon his schoolfellows who teased him. He lived at the Bell Inn then in Gloucester, but had not yet become a tapster or an evangelist.

Verse 18. "O Lord my God! such need is there of chastening and correcting with Thy holy Grace, that if it please Thy mercy that I may be removed from the turmoil of this life, I have remained long enough with this army." Baldwin, the crusading Archbishop of Canterbury, was overheard praying in these words, fifteen days before he died heartbroken at the coarseness of the Crusading army.

Verse 23. Queen Elizabeth's exclamation when she heard that Queen Mary was dead, and her fears were removed. She quoted the coin motto of the sovereigns of that time.

Verse 24. This is the old Easter Antiphon. It was cited by "blessed" William Thurkeld when sentence of death was passed upon him, 1579.

Liturgical use.—Easter Day evening.
Latins.—Sunday at Prime; Commendation of the dying.
Greeks.—Saturday morning.

PSALM CXIX. *Beati immaculati.*

BLESSED are those that are undefiled in the way : and walk in the law of the Lord.

2 Blessed are they that keep his testimonies : and seek him with their whole heart.

3 For they who do no wickedness : walk in his ways.

4 Thou hast charged : that we shall diligently keep thy commandments.

5 O that my ways were made so direct : that I might keep thy statutes!

6 So shall I not be confounded : while I have respect unto all thy commandments.

7 I will thank thee with an unfeigned heart : when I shall have learned the judgements of thy righteousness.

8 I will keep thy ceremonies : O forsake me not utterly.

Psalm cxix. is said to have been composed for the use of Jewish caravans on the way to the feasts at Jerusalem, and the gradual psalms which immediately follow it, were for the ascent to the Temple. It is a beautiful thought and an allegory, to picture the devout and dusty travellers, when they caught sight of the Holy City, breaking out into this great song. It has been used by many travellers to the "Mother of us all," the *Urbs Sion inclyta*, as they, too, caught glimpses of the Heavenly Jerusalem on their journey.

A sick man, who recited *Beati immaculati*, and said Our Father six times, was, by the English Canons of 963 A.D., loosed from one day's fast.

One or two writers have thought this psalm to be too legal in its constant dwelling upon the idea of Duty; but Duty is the flywheel of the spiritual machinery. It does not inspire the noble life, it regulates it; and the psalm is for the use of those who have already received inspiration from the sight of the City of God. *Verse* 5. The motto of Pope Pius V.

Liturgical use.—Introit to Mass for I. Sunday after Trinity (e).
Latins.—Daily at Prime; Christmas Prime; Commendation of a dying soul; Child's funeral, on the way to Church.
Greeks.—Saturday morning; Daily Nocturns; Burial of laymen, monks, and infants; and also of priests.

In quo corriget?

WHEREWITHAL shall a young man cleanse his way: even by ruling himself after thy word.

10 With my whole heart have I sought thee: O let me not go wrong out of thy commandments.

11 Thy words have I hid within my heart: that I should not sin against thee.

12 Blessed art thou, O Lord: O teach me thy statutes.

13 With my lips have I been telling: of all the judgements of thy mouth.

14 I have had as great delight in the way of thy testimonies: as in all manner of riches.

15 I will talk of thy commandments: and have respect unto thy ways.

16 My delight shall be in thy statutes: and I will not forget thy word.

Among the people who learnt this Psalm cxix. by heart were William Wilberforce, the philanthropist, who found it of much comfort; Mr. Ruskin, who began by thinking it the most repulsive, and ended by thinking it the most precious, of all the psalms his mother taught him; and Henry Martyn, the missionary, who translated it, with the rest of the Prayer-book, into Hindustani.

When Sir William Wallace was hung and drawn at Smithfield, he desired a priest who was standing by to take his Psalter, in which he much delighted, and to hold it before his eyes; which was done until he died under the executioner's hand. The priest would be almost sure to open it at the Commendatory psalms (August 23, 1305).

Liturgical use.—Introit to Mass for II. Sunday after Trinity (e).
Latins.—Daily at Prime; Christmas Prime; Commendation of the dying; at a child's funeral, on the way to Church.
Greeks.—Saturday morning; daily Nocturns; all funerals, clerical and lay.

Retribue servo tuo.

O DO well unto thy servant : that I may live and keep thy word.

17 Open thou mine eyes : that I may see the wondrous things of thy law.

19 I am a stranger upon earth : O hide not thy commandments from me.

20 My soul breaketh out for the very fervent desire : that it hath alway unto thy judgements.

21 Thou hast rebuked the proud : and cursed are they that do err from thy commandments.

22 O turn from me shame and rebuke : for I have kept thy testimonies.

23 Princes also did sit and speak against me : but thy servant is occupied in thy statutes.

24 For thy testimonies are my delight : and my counsellors.

Verse 17. St. Luxorius's verse (*vide* lxxxvi. 9).

Verse 23. When St. Thomas of Canterbury came to an open rupture with Henry II., and there was an evident conspiracy to insult and perhaps to kill him at the Assize of Northampton, he had to dedicate an altar to St. Stephen. Amid an immense throng of people he began the Mass for St. Stephen, *Etenim sederunt Principes*, with his strong clear voice. The sobs and tears of the worshippers showed that they applied the words to their own Archbishop (October 12, 1164).

Liturgical use.—Introit for Mass on III. Sunday after Trinity (e).

Latins.—Daily at Prime ; Christmas ; Commendation of the dying ; funeral of a child, on the way to Church.

Greeks.—Saturday morning ; daily Nocturns ; all funerals.

Adhæsit pavimento.

MY soul cleaveth to the dust : O quicken thou me, according to thy word.

26 I have acknowledged my ways, and thou heardest me : O teach me thy statutes.

27 Make me to understand the way of thy commandments : and so shall I talk of thy wondrous works.

28 My soul melteth away for very heaviness : comfort thou me according unto thy word.

29 Take from me the way of lying : and cause thou me to make much of thy law.

30 I have chosen the way of truth : and thy judgements have I laid before me.

31 I have stuck unto thy testimonies : O Lord, confound me not.

32 I will run the way of thy commandments : when thou hast set my heart at liberty.

When Theodosius the Emperor had, in violation of his promise, massacred 7,000 of the rebellious people of Thessalonica, St. Ambrose refused to admit him to the Holy Communion at Milan. For eight months he remained excommunicate. At Christmas (390 A.D.) he came, without his royal robes, and lay prostrate on the church floor, plucking out his hair and shedding tears, and repeating, *Adhæsit pavimento*. St. Ambrose gave him Absolution, but not before he had promised that all military executions should henceforth be delayed for thirty days, lest they might be done out of haste and tyranny. The whole psalm was a great favourite with St. Ambrose, who said of it that David shone here in his noonday light, without the imperfections of sunrise or abatement of sunset.

Adhæsit pavimento anima mea: with this "spiritual javelin" St. Hugh of Lincoln overcame a fierce temptation of the flesh.

Liturgical use.—Introit for the Mass on IV. Sunday after Trinity (e).

Latins.—Daily at Prime ; Christmas ; Commendation of the dying ; funeral of a child, on the way to Church.

Greeks.—Saturday morning ; daily Nocturns ; all funerals.

Legem pone.

TEACH me, O Lord, the way of thy statutes : and I shall keep it unto the end.

34 Give me understanding, and I shall keep thy law : yea, I shall keep it with my whole heart.

35 Make me to go in the path of thy commandments : for therein is my desire.

36 Incline my heart unto thy testimonies : and not to covetousness.

37 O turn away mine eyes, lest they behold vanity : and quicken thou me in thy way.

38 O stablish thy word in thy servant : that I may fear thee.

39 Take away the rebuke that I am afraid of : for thy judgements are good.

40 Behold, my delight is in thy commandments : O quicken me in thy righteousness.

St. Augustine had so great a reverence for Psalm cxix., that he hesitated to comment on it, because of its marvellous depth and apparent utter simplicity.

Liturgical use.—Introit for Mass of V. Sunday after Trinity (e).
Latins.—Daily at Tierce (9 o'clock); funeral of a child, on the way to Church.
Greeks.—Saturday morning; daily Nocturns; all funerals.

Et veniat super me.

LET thy loving mercy come also unto me, O Lord, even thy salvation, according unto thy word.

42 So shall I make answer unto my blasphemers : for my trust is in thy word.

43 O take not the word of thy truth utterly out of my mouth : for my hope is in thy judgements.

44 So shall I alway keep thy law : yea, for ever and ever.

45 And I will walk at liberty : for I seek thy commandments.

46 I will speak of thy testimonies also, even before kings : and will not be ashamed.

47 And my delight shall be in thy commandments : which I have loved.

48 My hands also will I lift up unto thy commandments, which I have loved : and my study shall be in thy statutes.

Among the most pathetic of metrical versions is the very bald one of James Maxwell. He died in great poverty in 1800, much disappointed and astonished that the Scotch Kirk men would not take to his doggerel instead of their own, for he had left out all mention of " brutal sacrifices and of instrumental music," and he hoped this would endear his book to all Scottish hearts.

Liturgical use.—Introit for the Mass on VI. Sunday after Trinity (e).
Latins.—Daily at Tierce; funeral of a child, on the way to Church.
Greeks.—Saturday morning; daily Nocturns; all funerals.

Memor esto servi tui.

O THINK upon thy servant, as concerning thy word : wherein thou hast caused me to put my trust.

50 The same is my comfort in my trouble : for thy word hath quickened me.

51 The proud have had me exceedingly in derision : yet have I not shrinked from thy law.

52 For I remembered thine everlasting judgements, O Lord : and received comfort.

53 I am horribly afraid : for the ungodly that forsake the law.

54 Thy statutes have been my songs : in the house of my pilgrimage.

55 I have thought upon thy Name, O Lord, in the night-season : and have kept thy law.

56 This I had : because I kept thy commandments.

Verse 54. From this verse the term "pilgrimage," used for "life," has passed into common life. Othello, for instance, "all his pilgrimage" dilates; Raleigh's poem, called "His Pilgrimage," and Bunyan's "Pilgrim's Progress" itself, refer ultimately to this, and to the use which St. Peter made of it (1 Peter ii. 11).

Liturgical use.—Introit to the Mass on VII. Sunday after Trinity.
Latins.—Daily at Tierce; funeral of a child, on the way to Church.
Greeks.—Saturday morning; daily Nocturns; all funerals.

Portio mea, Domine.

THOU art my portion, O Lord : I have promised to keep thy law.

58 I made my humble petition in thy presence with my whole heart : O be merciful unto me, according to thy word.

59 I called mine own ways to remembrance : and turned my feet unto thy testimonies.

60 I made haste, and prolonged not the time : to keep thy commandments.

61 The congregations of the ungodly have robbed me : but I have not forgotten thy law.

62 At midnight I will rise to give thanks unto thee : because of thy righteous judgements.

63 I am a companion of all them that fear thee : and keep thy commandments.

64 The earth, O Lord, is full of thy mercy : O teach me thy statutes.

Verse 59. Pascal, who declared that the whole psalm summed up the Christian virtues, said that this verse gives the turning-point to a man's character and career.

Verse 62. This is the origin of the midnight Hour being kept with prayer and praise. It is in all the midnight offices of both East and West. The Benedictine rule, which was next ancient in England to the Saxon (*vide* verse 164), and was the foundation of all others, divided the hours thus : (1) Cock-crow or *Nocturns* at 2 a.m., when Christ rose ; (2) *Matins* at 6 a.m., when the Jews offered the morning sacrifices, and the women heard from Angels that Christ was risen ; (3) *Tierce* at 9 a.m., when Christ was condemned and scourged ; (4) *Sext* at noon, when Our Lord was crucified, and the Sun was darkened ; (5) *None* at 3 p.m., when He gave up the ghost ; (6) *Vespers*, the time of the evening sacrifice, when Christ was taken from the cross ; (7) *Compline* at 7 p.m., when the agony in the garden began.

Liturgical use.—Introit for the Mass on VIII. Sunday after Trinity.

Latins.—Daily at Tierce ; funeral of a child, on the way to Church.

Greeks.—Saturday morning ; daily Nocturns ; all funerals.

Bonitatem fecisti.

O LORD, thou hast dealt graciously with thy servant : according unto thy word.

66 O learn me true understanding and knowledge : for I have believed thy commandments.

67 Before I was troubled, I went wrong : but now have I kept thy word.

68 Thou art good and gracious : O teach me thy statutes.

69 The proud have imagined a lie against me : but I will keep thy commandments with my whole heart.

70 Their heart is as fat as brawn : but my delight hath been in thy law.

71 It is good for me that I have been in trouble : that I may learn thy statutes.

72 The law of thy mouth is dearer unto me : than thousands of gold and silver.

Verse 71. Francis I. of France was taken prisoner at Pavia, 1525, and taken to the Church of the Certosa, where the choir were singing this psalm. He joined in loudly at this verse.

Liturgical use.—Introit for IX. Sunday after Trinity (e).
Latins.—Daily at Tierce; funeral of a child, on the way to Church.
Greeks.—Saturday morning; daily Nocturns; all funerals.

Manus tuæ fecerunt me.

THY hands have made me and fashioned me : O give me understanding, that I may learn thy commandments.

74 They that fear thee will be glad when they see me : because I have put my trust in thy word.

75 I know, O Lord, that thy judgements are right : and that thou of very faithfulness hast caused me to be troubled.

76 O let thy merciful kindness be my comfort : according to thy word unto thy servant.

77 O let thy loving mercies come unto me, that I may live : for thy law is my delight.

78 Let the proud be confounded, for they go wickedly about to destroy me : but I will be occupied in thy commandments.

79 Let such as fear thee, and have known thy testimonies : be turned unto me.

80 O let my heart be sound in thy statutes : that I be not ashamed.

Verse 78. *Confundantur superbi.* When Charlemagne was hearing Mass, an outland monk came who had not yet learnt to sing. The choir-master, seeing him silent, smote him with a staff and bade him join in the praises of God, which he did, out of tune, screwing his neck about very queerly, until the others laughed aloud. The Emperor in a loud voice stopped the Mass, sent for the strange monk, and thanked him for the pains he had taken to sing, and gave him money for his melody.

Liturgical use.—Introit for X. Sunday after Trinity (e).
Latins.—Daily at Tierce; funeral of a child, on the way to Church.
Greeks.—Saturday morning; daily Nocturns; all funerals.

Defecit anima mea.

MY soul hath longed for thy salvation : and I have a good hope because of thy word.

82 Mine eyes long sore for thy word : saying, O when wilt thou comfort me?

83 For I am become like a bottle in the smoke : yet do I not forget thy statutes.

84 How many are the days of thy servant : when wilt thou be avenged of them that persecute me?

85 The proud have digged pits for me : which are not after thy law.

86 All thy commandments are true : they persecute me falsely ; O be thou my help.

87 They had almost made an end of me upon earth : but I forsook not thy commandments.

88 O quicken me after thy loving-kindness : and so shall I keep the testimonies of thy mouth.

Dr. Johnson thus defended the prose version of the Psalter against the fashionable metrical translators: "Of sentiments purely religious, it will be found that the most simple expression is the most sublime. Poetry loses its lustre and its power because it is applied to something more excellent than itself. All that pious verse can do is to help the memory and delight the ear, and for these purposes it may be very useful, but it supplies nothing to the mind. The ideas of Christian theology are too simple for eloquence and too majestic for ornament ; to recommend them by tropes and figures is to magnify by a concave mirror the sidereal hemisphere."

Liturgical use.—Introit for the Mass on XI. Sunday after Trinity (e).

Latins.—Daily at Sext ; funeral of a child, on the way to Church.

Greeks.—Saturday morning ; daily Nocturns ; all funerals.

In æternum, Domine.

O LORD, thy word : endureth for ever in heaven.

90 Thy truth also remaineth from one generation to another : thou hast laid the foundation of the earth, and it abideth.

91 They continue this day according to thine ordinance : for all things serve thee.

92 If my delight had not been in thy law : I should have perished in my trouble.

93 I will never forget thy commandments : for with them thou hast quickened me.

94 I am thine, O save me : for I have sought thy commandments.

95 The ungodly laid wait for me to destroy me : but I will consider thy testimonies.

96 I see that all things come to an end : but thy commandment is exceeding broad.

Verse 92. The verse Luther selected as his motto for his own Bible, which is now in the museum at Berlin. He wrote to the Abbot of Nuremberg thus about the whole psalm : " I have more especially attached myself to this psalm, and have in truth a sort of right to call it my own. It has deserved well of me: it has saved me from many a difficulty whence neither the emperor nor king nor wise men nor saints could have extricated me. It is, my friend, dearer to me than all the honours, all the power of the earth. I would not exchange it for the whole earth if I could."

Verse 93. St. Theodore (*a studio*), who died in 826, begged his friends to sing him *Beati immaculati*, and died at this verse while they were doing so.

Verse 95. This is beautifully chosen as the introit to the Mass both for the holy St. Agnes and also for St. Mary Magdalen's Day, in the Latin use.

Verse 96. Dean Stanley's favourite verse. It is the epitaph above his wife's grave and his own.

Liturgical use.—Introit for XII. Sunday after Trinity (e).
Latins.—Daily at Sext ; funeral of a child, on the way to Church.
Greeks.—Saturday morning ; daily Nocturns ; all funerals.

Quomodo dilexi!

LORD, what love have I unto thy law : all the day long is my study in it.

98 Thou through thy commandments hast made me wiser than mine enemies : for they are ever with me.

99 I have more understanding than my teachers : for thy testimonies are my study.

100 I am wiser than the aged : because I keep thy commandments.

101 I have refrained my feet from every evil way : that I may keep thy word.

102 I have not shrunk from thy judgements : for thou teachest me.

103 O how sweet are thy words unto my throat : yea, sweeter than honey unto my mouth.

104 Through thy commandments I get understanding : therefore I hate all evil ways.

Quomodo dilexi was a passage particularly loved by Henry Martyn, the Indian missionary. He was a Cornishman, born at Truro, and became Fellow and Tutor at St. John's College, Cambridge. The influence of Charles Simeon sent him out to India, where he translated the Psalter and the New Testament into Hindustani and Persian, but died shortly afterwards (1781-1812).

Verse 103 is David's scroll-motto in the title-page of Coverdale's Bible (1535) "O hovv swete are thy vvordes vnto my throte : ye more then hony," etc. This Bible was the precursor of all English Bibles.

Liturgical use.—Introit for the Mass on XIII. Sunday after Trinity (e).
Latins.—Daily at Sext ; funeral of a child, on the way to Church.
Greeks.—Saturday morning ; daily Nocturns ; all funerals.

Lucerna pedibus meis.

THY word is a lantern unto my feet : and a light unto my paths.

106 I have sworn, and am steadfastly purposed : to keep thy righteous judgements.

107 I am troubled above measure : quicken me, O Lord, according to thy word.

108 Let the free-will offerings of my mouth please thee, O Lord : and teach me thy judgements.

109 My soul is alway in my hand : yet do I not forget thy law.

110 The ungodly have laid a snare for me : but yet I swerved not from thy commandments.

111 Thy testimonies have I claimed as mine heritage for ever : and why ? they are the very joy of my heart.

112 I have applied my heart to fulfil thy statutes alway : even unto the end.

Verse 105. The coin motto for the half-sovereigns of Edward VI. is *Lucerna pedibus meis verbum Tuum*. This represented not only the new-found delight in the use of the Bible in the English Church, but also the hope that the nation had passed its troubles, and would be quickened "according to Thy word."

Liturgical use.—Introit to the Mass on XIV. Sunday after Trinity (e).
Latins.—Daily at Sext ; funeral of a child, on the way to Church.
Greeks.—Saturday morning ; daily Nocturns ; all funerals.

Iniquos odio habui.

I HATE them that imagine evil things : but thy law do I love.

114 Thou art my defence and shield : and my trust is in thy word.

115 Away from me, ye wicked : I will keep the commandments of my God.

116 O stablish me according to thy word, that I may live : and let me not be disappointed of my hope.

117 Hold thou me up, and I shall be safe : yea, my delight shall be ever in thy statutes.

118 Thou hast trodden down all them that depart from thy statutes : for they imagine but deceit.

119 Thou puttest away all the ungodly of the earth like dross : therefore I love thy testimonies.

120 My flesh trembleth for fear of thee : and I am afraid of thy judgements.

Verse 116. " Receive me according to Thy loving-kindness, and let me not be disappointed of my hope." These were the last words of St. Eligius, the Bishop of Noyou, Vermondes and Tournay, who died November 30th, 659 A.D. His name is known to English folk chiefly because of Chaucer's Nonne Prioresse, whose heaviest oath was " but, by Saint Eloy."

Liturgical use.—Introit to the Mass on XV. Sunday after Trinity (e).

Latins.—Daily at Sext ; funeral of a child, on the way to Church.

Greeks.—Saturday morning ; daily Nocturns ; all funerals.

Feci judicium.

I DEAL with the thing that is lawful and right : O give me not over to mine oppressors.

122 Make thou thy servant to delight in that which is good : that the proud do me no wrong.

123 Mine eyes are wasted away with looking for thy health : and for the word of thy righteousness.

124 O deal with thy servant according unto thy loving mercy : and teach me thy statutes.

125 I am thy servant, O grant me understanding : that I may know thy testimonies.

126 It is time for thee, Lord, to lay to thine hand : for they have destroyed thy law.

127 For I love thy commandments : above gold and precious stone.

128 Therefore hold I straight all thy commandments : and all false ways I utterly abhor.

Verse 125. This verse expressed the aspirations of the Oxford Reformers of 1498, whose great plea was for thorough understanding rather than mechanical repetition of holy words. "The careful meditating and thorough understanding of one single verse only will profit more," says Erasmus, "than the being able to repeat the whole book of Psalms, but without knowing the meaning of one word thereof."

Liturgical use.—Introit for the Mass on XVI. Sunday after Trinity (e).
Latins.—Daily at Sext ; funeral of a child, on the way to Church.
Greeks.—Saturday morning ; daily Nocturns ; all funerals.

Mirabilia.

THY testimonies are wonderful : therefore doth my soul keep them.

130 When thy word goeth forth : it giveth light and understanding unto the simple.

131 I opened my mouth, and drew in my breath : for my delight was in thy commandments.

132 O look thou upon me, and be merciful unto me : as thou usest to do unto those that love thy Name.

133 Order my steps in thy word : and so shall no wickedness have dominion over me.

134 O deliver me from the wrongful dealings of men : and so shall I keep thy commandments.

135 Shew the light of thy countenance upon thy servant : and teach me thy statutes.

136 Mine eyes gush out with water : because men keep not thy law.

In 1632 George Wither published a double metrical version of the Psalms, encouraged by the late king, and dedicated with zealous loyalty to Elizabeth, Queen of Bohemia. He closes his preface thus : "If I have pleased my Readers I am glad : if not ; Yet I am glad I have honestly endeavoured it. And (being assured my labour shal not all be lost) I will sing and be Merry by myselfe, in the use of this Translation, untill others please to sing it with mee ; or untill a more exact Version shall be produced and allowed." He added to each psalm a pious meditation of his own. This is his comment on *Mirabilia:* "Sweet Jesus, though we desire to seeme wise; wee are very simple in the best knowledge: Oh encrease our understandings. Though wee professe great Affection to thee and thy Lawe; yet wee soone deny (yea forswear) both, if we are in danger to partake thy suffrings. O look upon us therefor, with such an aspect, as thou didst cast on thy Apostle St. Peter, that weeping bitterly for our Sinns and unkindnesses, as he did; we may obtaine the same forgiveness." Amen.

Liturgical use.—Introit to the Mass on XVII. Sunday after Trinity (e).
Latins.—Daily at Nones (3 o'clock afternoon); the funeral of a child, on the way to Church.
Greeks.—Saturday morning; daily Nocturns; all funerals.

Justus es, Domine.

RIGHTEOUS art thou, O Lord : and true is thy judgement.

138 The testimonies that thou hast commanded : are exceeding righteous and true.

139 My zeal hath even consumed me : because mine enemies have forgotten thy words.

140 Thy word is tried to the uttermost : and thy servant loveth it.

141 I am small, and of no reputation : yet do I not forget thy commandments.

142 Thy righteousness is an everlasting righteousness : and thy law is the truth.

143 Trouble and heaviness have taken hold upon me : yet is my delight in thy commandments.

144 The righteousness of thy testimonies is everlasting : O grant me understanding, and I shall live.

Justus es Domine et rectum judicium tuum was the frequent meditation of St. Augustine and his friends during the great siege of Hippo, during which he died : having lived to see the cities of his diocese overwhelmed in ruin with their builders, the inhabitants either fled, dead or scattered, the churches without priest or minister, the monks and nuns all dispersed; of the people some killed with tortures, some slain by the sword, and some captives, broken in mind, body, and faith, serving the enemy in evil and harsh fashion. Of the many thousand churches only three remained standing.

Verse 137. The Emperor Maurice, whose five sons were first slain before his face, died with these words on his lips (602 A.D.).

Verse 140. *Ignitum eloquium tuum vehementer.* Scripture itself "is like an apothecary's shop, wherein are all remedies for all infirmities of mind, purgatives, cordials, alteratives, corroboratives, lenitives, etc. 'Every disease of the soul,' saith Austin, 'hath a peculiar medicine in Scripture: this only is required, that the sick man take the potion which God hath already tempered.' Gregory calls it a glass wherein we may see all our infirmities, *ignitum colloquium;* Origen, a charm. And therefore Hierom prescribes Rusticus the monk continually to read the Scripture and to meditate on that which he hath read : ' for as mastication is to meat, so is meditation on that which we read'" (*Burton*).

Liturgical use.—Introit to the Mass on XVIII. Sunday after Trinity (e).
Latins.—Daily at Nones ; funeral of a child, on the way to Church.
Greeks.—Saturday morning ; daily Nocturns ; all funerals.

Clamavi in toto corde meo.

I CALL with my whole heart : hear me, O Lord, I will keep thy statutes.

146 Yea, even unto thee do I call : help me and I shall keep thy testimonies.

147 Early in the morning do I cry unto thee : for in thy word is my trust.

148 Mine eyes prevent the night-watches : that I might be occupied in thy words.

149 Hear my voice, O Lord, according unto thy loving-kindness : quicken me, according as thou art wont.

150 They draw nigh that of malice persecute me : and are far from thy law.

151 Be thou nigh at hand, O Lord : for all thy commandments are true.

152 As concerning thy testimonies, I have known long since : that thou hast grounded them for ever.

Dr. Richard Holdsworth, the Elizabethan Bishop of Bristol, made this meditation, when near to his "patient death." "I admire," said he, "at David's gracious heart, who so often in Scripture (but especially in the 119 Psalm) extolleth the worth and value of the word of God ; and yet *quantillum Scripturæ*, how little of the word of God, they had in that age, — the Pentateuch, the book of Job and some of the Hagiography ! How much have we now thereof since the accession of the Prophets, but especially of the New Testament ! And yet, alas!

the more we have of the word of God the less it is generally regarded."

The late Bishop Medley, when he was a child of six, learned the whole of Psalm cxix. at his mother's knee. He retained an ardent love for the psalms all his days, and used to say in his latest days that he was just beginning to comprehend something of their depth and beauty.

Liturgical use.—Introit to the Mass on XIX. Sunday after Trinity (e).
Latins.—Daily at Nones; funeral of a child, on the way to Church.
Greeks.—Saturday morning; daily Nocturns; all funerals.

Vide humilitatem.

O CONSIDER mine adversity, and deliver me : for I do not forget thy law.

154 Avenge thou my cause, and deliver me : quicken me, according to thy word.

155 Health is far from the ungodly : for they regard not thy statutes.

156 Great is thy mercy, O Lord : quicken me, as thou art wont.

157 Many there are that trouble me, and persecute me : yet do I not swerve from thy testimonies.

158 It grieveth me when I see the transgressors : because they keep not thy law.

159 Consider, O Lord, how I love thy commandments : O quicken me, according to thy loving-kindness.

160 Thy word is true from everlasting : all the judgements of thy righteousness endure for evermore.

"In the inner sanctuary," says Mr. Gladstone, writing of the Mosaic system, "provided for the most capable human souls, was reared the strong spiritual life, which appears to have developed itself pre-eminently in the depth, richness, tenderness and comprehensiveness of the Psalms. To the work they have here accomplished there is no parallel on earth."

Verse 160. This was a stronghold of orthodox people against the Arians. "Thy Word," of course, was used as meaning Christ, and rightly to understand the liturgical use of this psalm one must bear this constantly in mind.

Liturgical use.—Introit for the Mass on the XX. Sunday after Trinity (e).
Latins.—Daily at Nones; funeral of a child, on the way to Church.
Greeks.—Saturday morning; daily Nocturns; all funerals.

Principes persecuti sunt.

PRINCES have persecuted me without a cause : but my heart standeth in awe of thy word.

162 I am as glad of thy word : as one that findeth great spoils.

163 As for lies, I hate and abhor them : but thy law do I love.

164 Seven times a day do I praise thee : because of thy righteous judgements.

165 Great is the peace that they have who love thy law : and they are not offended at it.

166 Lord, I have looked for thy saving health : and done after thy commandments.

167 My soul hath kept thy testimonies : and loved them exceedingly.

168 I have kept thy commandments and testimonies : for all my ways are before thee.

Verse 164. This verse gave the seven-fold division of the day into the canonical hours. The seven gifts of the Holy Ghost were implored, one at each of these hours, and the choice is beautiful and appropriate. At 6 a.m., when Prime is said, we should implore the Spirit of Wisdom, as we enter upon the kingship of another day. At 9 a.m., when Tierce (Undern, the English called it) is said, as the light grows, we ask for Understanding. At noon, when Sext is said, and men meet for dinner, we ask for Counsel. At 3 o'clock, when Christ died, and the day declines and men begin to tire, Nones is due, and we ask for Strength. At 6 p.m. the day is full old, Compline comes, and we ask for Knowledge. At 9 p.m. is the Evensong, and we ask for the Piety which beautifies old age. At midnight is Nightsong, and all evil things are abroad. Then we ask for Holy Fear (see verse 62). The Roman hours are Matins (Lauds), Prime, Tierce, Sext, Nones, Vespers, and Compline.

Verse 165. This is the sundial motto of the cathedral at Padua.

Liturgical use.—Introt to the Mass on XXI. Sunday after Trinity (e).
Latins.—Daily at Nones ; funeral of a child, on the way to Church.
Greeks.—Saturday morning ; daily Nocturns ; all funerals.

Day 27 — PSALM CXIX — Morning Prayer

Appropinquet deprecatio.

LET my complaint come before thee, O Lord : give me understanding, according to thy word.

170 Let my supplication come before thee : deliver me, according to thy word.

171 My lips shall speak of thy praise : when thou hast taught me thy statutes.

172 Yea, my tongue shall sing of thy word : for all thy commandments are righteous.

173 Let thine hand help me : for I have chosen thy commandments.

174 I have longed for thy saving health, O Lord : and in thy law is my delight.

175 O let my soul live, and it shall praise thee : and thy judgements shall help me.

176 I have gone astray like a sheep that is lost : O seek thy servant, for I do not forget thy commandments.

A famous book in its day was William Cowper's "Holy Alphabet for Sion's Scholars," a dissertation upon this psalm. The author was Bishop of Galloway, and in 1613 dedicated his book to David (Murray), Lord Scone. He contends, with St. Ambrose, that this psalm is subdivided in order to be applied to different periods of man's life.

Liturgical use.—Introit for the Mass for the XXII. Sunday after Trinity (e).
Latins.—Daily at Nones ; funeral of a child, on the way to Church.
Greeks.—Saturday morning ; daily Nocturns ; all funerals.

PSALM CXX. *Ad Dominum.*

WHEN I was in trouble I called upon the Lord : and he heard me.

2 Deliver my soul, O Lord, from lying lips : and from a deceitful tongue.

3 What reward shall be given or done unto thee, thou false tongue : even mighty and sharp arrows, with hot burning coals.

4 Woe is me, that I am constrained to dwell with Mesech : and to have my habitation among the tents of Kedar.

5 My soul hath long dwelt among them : that are enemies unto peace.

6 I labour for peace, but when I speak unto them thereof : they make them ready to battle.

This is the first of the fifteen gradual psalms, or songs of degrees, which prepared the worshippers for the sacrifice. They are divided into three flights of five psalms each.

If Psalm cxix. was composed for the Jewish caravans, as they converged upon the Holy City, the songs of degrees (Pss. cxx.-cxxxiv.) were for the ascent up to the Temple, from the valleys to the summit. The Temple was said in the Middle Ages to have had fifteen steps up to it, as one may see in Titian's "Presentation of the Virgin Mary," for instance, and these fifteen or gradual psalms were a preparation for Sacrifice. They are said by the Latins in Lent on Wednesdays, with the antiphon *Requiem æternam*, etc.—" Grant them rest, O Lord, and lighten them with everlasting light." The first five are said without Gloria.

Verse 4. Isaac Walton uses this of Joan Churchman (Mrs. Richard Hooker), who, like Solomon's dripping house, caused her husband to say with the holy Prophet, "Woe is me, that I am constrained to have my habitation in the tents of Kedar."

This verse was quoted by " Blessed " Richard Kirkman, who was hung at Tyburn for saying Roman Mass, and refusing the oath of supremacy, 1579.

Verse 5. *Multum incola fuit anima mea*—a verse often in the mouth of Lord Bacon, *e.g.*, in the Essay of "Nature and Man"; the letter to Bodley, etc.

Liturgical use.—Introit to the Mass on the II. Sunday in Advent (e).

Latins.—Monday Vespers ; Maundy Thursday.

Greeks.—Friday evening.

PSALM CXXI. *Levavi oculos.*

I WILL lift up mine eyes unto the hills : from whence cometh my help.

2 My help cometh even from the Lord : who hath made heaven and earth.

3 He will not suffer thy foot to be moved : and he that keepeth thee will not sleep.

4 Behold, he that keepeth Israel : shall neither slumber nor sleep.

5 The Lord himself is thy keeper : the Lord is thy defence upon thy right hand ;

6 So that the sun shall not burn thee by day : neither the moon by night.

7 The Lord shall preserve thee from all evil : yea, it is even he that shall keep thy soul.

8 The Lord shall preserve thy going out, and thy coming in : from this time forth for evermore.

This second gradual psalm has been called the Traveller's psalm ; and Hooper, the Puritan Bishop of Gloucester, was accustomed, like many others, to use it when he set out upon a journey. Livingstone read it to his family before he left for Africa.

Henry Vaughan, the Silurist, loved this psalm, and meditated upon it in *Silex Scintillans:*

"Up to those bright and gladsome hills,
  Whence flowes my weal and mirth,
I look and sigh for Him, who fills
  Unseen both heaven and earth."

Miss Rossetti's meditation in our more subjective time upon the same begins :

"I am pale with sick desire,
  For my heart is far away
From this world's fitful fire,
  And this world's waning day."

Verse 2. *Auxilium meum a Domino*—a motto chosen by Edward the Black Prince for the English coins of 1362.

Verse 4. *Non dormit qui custodit* is the motto of the Coghill family.

Liturgical use.—Introit for the Mass on the Sunday after Christmas Day (e).
Latins.—Monday Vespers.
Greeks.—Friday evening ; daily Nocturns.

PSALM CXXII. *Lætatus sum.*

I WAS glad when they said unto me : We will go into the house of the Lord.

2 Our feet shall stand in thy gates : O Jerusalem.

3 Jerusalem is built as a city : that is at unity in itself.

4 For thither the tribes go up, even the tribes of the Lord : to testify unto Israel, to give thanks unto the Name of the Lord.

5 For there is the seat of judgement : even the seat of the house of David.

6 O pray for the peace of Jerusalem : they shall prosper that love thee.

7 Peace be within thy walls : and plenteousness within thy palaces.

8 For my brethren and companions' sakes : I will wish thee prosperity.

9 Yea, because of the house of the Lord our God : I will seek to do thee good.

A gradual psalm (*vide* cxx.).

Verse 1. When St. Richard, the Bishop of Lincoln, was told by the physicians that his end was near, he cried out these words. They asked him if he needed anything, and he answered with St. Philip, "Show us the Father, and it sufficeth us." Whereupon they showed him the crucifix, which he devoutly kissed, and presently died. This use of the psalm was not uncommon.

Dean Stanley when he preached the funeral sermon of Sir G. Gilbert Scott, chose this as the motto for his sermon, which was upon the religious aspect of Gothic Architecture.

Verse 7. *Fiat pax in virtute tua* (Peace be in thy strength) is the legend on English coins of 1422, when baby Henry VI. was crowned in Paris King of England and France.

Liturgical use.—Introit to the Mass for the Circumcision (e). Coronation Service.

Latins.—Tuesday Vespers ; Circumcision ; Festivals of our Lady.

Greeks.—Friday evening.

PSALM CXXIII. *Ad te levavi oculos meos.*

UNTO thee lift I up mine eyes : O thou that dwellest in the heavens.

2 Behold, even as the eyes of servants look unto the hand of their masters, and as the eyes of a maiden unto the hand of her mistress : even so our eyes wait upon the Lord our God, until he have mercy upon us.

3 Have mercy upon us, O Lord, have mercy upon us : for we are utterly despised.

4 Our soul is filled with the scornful reproof of the wealthy : and with the despitefulness of the proud.

A gradual psalm (*vide* cxx.).

This psalm was the last said at the gallows by "the blessed" William Hart, one of the many Romanist victims of Elizabeth's reign, who was hung at York, 1583, for denying the supremacy, and suspected treason.

It was not uncommonly used as an antidote to death. Vicars (*vide* lxiv.) paraphrased it, on the other hand, as a psalm of "thanksgiving for the great deliverance from the Popish Powder Plot."

Latins.—Tuesday Vespers.
Greeks.—Friday evening.

PSALM CXXIV. *Nisi quia Dominus.*

IF the Lord himself had not been on our side, now may Israel say : if the Lord himself had not been on our side, when men rose up against us;

2 They had swallowed us up quick : when they were so wrathfully displeased at us.

3 Yea, the waters had drowned us : and the stream had gone over our soul.

4 The deep waters of the proud : had gone even over our soul.

5 But praised be the Lord : who hath not given us over for a prey unto their teeth.

6 Our soul is escaped even as a bird out of the snare of the fowler : the snare is broken, and we are delivered.

7 Our help standeth in the Name of the Lord : who hath made heaven and earth.

This is the psalm of English Victory at Sea, and so almost the psalm of England herself. It ends the first division of the gradual psalms (see cxx.).

The proper psalms for the Restoration of Charles II. were cxxiv., cxxvi., cxxix., and cxviii.

Verse 6. The words with which the Duke of Gandia gave up his great possession to join the Society of Jesus (see Ps. cxiv); and the dying words of McCheyne, the Scotch Divine.

Liturgical use.—Introit for the Mass on XXIII. Sunday after Trinity (e); Thanksgiving for a Naval Victory.
Latins.—Tuesday Vespers.
Greeks.—Friday evening.

PSALM CXXV. *Qui confidunt.*

THEY that put their trust in the Lord shall be even as the mount Sion : which may not be removed, but standeth fast for ever.

2 The hills stand about Jerusalem : even so standeth the Lord round about his people, from this time forth for evermore.

3 For the rod of the ungodly cometh not into the lot of the righteous : lest the righteous put their hand unto wickedness.

4 Do well, O Lord : unto those that are good and true of heart.

5 As for such as turn back unto their own wickedness : the Lord shall lead them forth with the evildoers; but peace shall be upon Israel.

A gradual psalm (*vide* cxx.). In those old dramas, Coventry mysteries, the Blessed Virgin Mary enters and says the gradual psalms, with this preface:

"Now Lord God, dysspose me to prayour
That I may sey the holy psalmes of Davyth
Wheche book is clepyd the Sawtere ;
That I may preyse the, my God, therwith.

"Of vertuys thereof this is the pygth.
It mayketh sowles fayr, that doth it say :
Angelys besteryd to help us therwith ;
It lytenyth therknenesse, and pullyth divelys away."

In these dramas the gradual psalms are recommended to be said in memory of the maid Mary, and then *Maria* is the antiphon.

Liturgical use.—Introit to the Mass for the XXIV. Sunday after Trinity (e).
Latins.—Tuesday Vespers.
Greeks.—Friday evening.

PSALM CXXVI. *In convertendo.*

WHEN the Lord turned again the captivity of Sion : then were we like unto them that dream.

2 Then was our mouth filled with laughter : and our tongue with joy.

3 Then said they among the heathen : The Lord hath done great things for them.

4 Yea, the Lord hath done great things for us already : whereof we rejoice.

5 Turn our captivity, O Lord : as the rivers in the south.

6 They that sow in tears : shall reap in joy.

7 He that now goeth on his way weeping, and beareth forth good seed : shall doubtless come again with joy, and bring his sheaves with him.

A gradual psalm (see cxx.). In 1653 Jeremy Taylor wrote his "Life of Christ," "desirous to put a portion of the holy fire into a repository which might help to re-enkindle the Incense when it shall please God Religion shall return and all his servants shall sing *In convertendo captivitatem Sion* with a voice of eucharist."

This psalm was a favourite with the Abolitionists. Sir Thomas Fowell Buxton, the philanthropic brewer, quoted the second verse when he heard that the slaves were freed and the work accomplished.

Perhaps a favourite of Thackeray's (*vide* "Esmond," ii., chap. 6).

Latins.—Tuesday Vespers ; Apostles and Evangelists.
Greeks.—Friday evening.

PSALM CXXVII. *Nisi Dominus.*

EXCEPT the Lord build the house : their labour is but lost that build it.

2 Except the Lord keep the city : the watchman waketh but in vain.

3 It is but lost labour that ye haste to rise up early, and so late take rest, and eat the bread of carefulness : for so he giveth his beloved sleep.

4 Lo, children and the fruit of the womb : are an heritage and gift that cometh of the Lord.

5 Like as the arrows in the hand of the giant : even so are the young children.

6 Happy is the man that hath his quiver full of them : they shall not be ashamed when they speak with their enemies in the gate.

A gradual psalm (*vide* cxx.).

This was the psalm which Clement III. used in his exhortation to the English Bishops to succour the Holy Land. Upon this our Richard Cœur de Lion took the cross.

Nisi Dominus frustra is the motto of several noble families, *e.g.*, Baron Rawdon and the Moira family and of the Comptons. It is also a very common old house motto, *e.g.*, it is over the Cameronian Meeting House in Edinburgh. It is the motto of that city itself. It is the legend over the chaplain's door to the Tower Chapel dedicated to St. Peter ad Vincula. It is also a common ring and trencher motto.

When Ferdinand II. fled from his kingdom of Naples, he chanted this psalm again and again across the bay, and continued it until he came to Ischia.

Verse 3. Mrs. Browning's favourite verse.

"Of all the thoughts of God that are
Borne inward into souls afar,
Along the Psalmist's music deep,
Now tell me, if that any is
For gift or grace surpassing this—
'He giveth His beloved sleep'?"

Liturgical use.—Introt for the Mass on the XXV. Sunday after Trinity (e). The Churching of Women.
Latins.—Wednesday Vespers ; Circumcision ; Feasts of Our Lady.
Greeks.—Friday evening.

PSALM CXXVIII. *Beati omnes.*

BLESSED are all they that fear the Lord : and walk in his ways.

2 For thou shalt eat the labours of thine hands : O well is thee, and happy shalt thou be.

3 Thy wife shall be as the fruitful vine : upon the walls of thine house.

4 Thy children like the olive-branches : round about thy table.

5 Lo, thus shall the man be blessed : that feareth the Lord.

6 The Lord from out of Sion shall so bless thee : that thou shalt see Jerusalem in prosperity all thy life long.

7 Yea, that thou shalt see thy children's children : and peace upon Israel.

A gradual psalm (*vide* cxx.).

Verse 2. Piers Ploughman quotes this to the idle classes to show that God means all to work ; "in dyking or delving or travailling in prayers, contemplative life or active, Christ would men wrought. The 'freke' (or manly fellow) that feedeth himself with his faithful labour, he is blessed by the book in body and soul."

A certain monk, of good birth, thought it beneath him to scour the saucepans when it was his work to cook for the brethren. St. Bernard called him up, and gave him a tremendous rebuke, not only on the dangerous and outrageous sin of pride, but upon the absolute necessity of living by labour, enjoined upon all Christian men ; and pointed out this verse to him, as an evidence that it was a law, even before the Word took our flesh to serve us.

Liturgical use.—Introit to the Mass on St. Thomas's Day (e) ; a Marriage psalm.
Latins.—Wednesday Vespers.
Greeks.—Friday evening ; Marriages.

PSALM CXXIX. *Sæpe expugnaverunt.*

MANY a time have they fought against me from my youth up : may Israel now say.

2 Yea, many a time have they vexed me from my youth up : but they have not prevailed against me.

3 The plowers plowed upon my back : and made long furrows.

4 But the righteous Lord : hath hewn the snares of the ungodly in pieces.

5 Let them be confounded and turned backward : as many as have evil will at Sion.

6 Let them be even as the grass growing upon the house-tops : which withereth afore it be plucked up;

7 Whereof the mower filleth not his hand : neither he that bindeth up the sheaves his bosom.

8 So that they who go by say not so much as, The Lord prosper you : we wish you good luck in the Name of the Lord.

In the legends of the Holy Rood, the mediæval poets told how the History of Christ is the story of mankind. The Rood sprang from three seeds Adam brought with him from Paradise. Moses planted the little trees in Tabor, and David brought them with joy and melody into Jerusalem, singing the gradual psalms. There they grew into one great tree, under which he wrote *Miserere* and all the "sawter buke"; and would have built there the temple, had not God forbidden it. But he circled the tree with silver, and saw it wax very great in his day.

Liturgical use.—Introit for St. Andrew's Day (e).
Latins.—Wednesday Vespers.
Greeks.—Friday evening.

PSALM CXXX. *De profundis.*

OUT of the deep have I called unto thee, O Lord : Lord, hear my voice.

2 O let thine ears consider well : the voice of my complaint.

3 If thou, Lord, wilt be extreme to mark what is done amiss : O Lord, who may abide it?

4 For there is mercy with thee : therefore shalt thou be feared.

5 I look for the Lord; my soul doth wait for him : in his word is my trust.

6 My soul fleeth unto the Lord : before the morning watch, I say, before the morning watch.

7 O Israel, trust in the Lord, for with the Lord there is mercy : and with him is plenteous redemption.

8 And he shall redeem Israel : from all his sins.

This is the sixth penitential psalm — these are Nos. vi., xxxii., xxxviii., li., cii., cxxx., and cxliii.—and is the antidote to the deadly sin of Envy.

It is also a gradual psalm (see cxx.).

This is the last psalm of Mary Queen of Scots, of " Blessed " John Nelson, the Romanist, at Tyburn in 1578, and is also among the last words of the judicious Richard Hooker, the author of the " Ecclesiastical Polity."

Phineas Fletcher's (1581-1650) translation of (or rather meditation upon) this psalm is one of the best of that author's shorter pieces :

"As a watchman waits for day,
And looks for light and looks again,
When the night grows old and gray,
To be relieved he calls amain ;
So look, so wait, so long mine eyes,
To see my Lord, my Sun arise."

Jeremy Taylor quotes it as the psalm of psalms for the sick. His " Holy Dying " was the book which was read to the poet Keats in his last days.

Liturgical use.—Introit for the Mass on II. Sunday in Lent (e) ; Ash Wednesday evening.
Latins.—Wednesday Vespers ; going and returning from funerals ; 2nd Vespers for Christmas.
Greeks.—Friday evening ; daily Evensong.

PSALM CXXXI. *Domine, non est.*

LORD, I am not high-minded : I have no proud looks.

2 I do not exercise myself in great matters : which are too high for me.

3 But I refrain my soul, and keep it low, like as a child that is weaned from his mother : yea, my soul is even as a weaned child.

4 O Israel, trust in the Lord : from this time forth for evermore.

A gradual psalm (see cxx.).

Verse 2. In 1625, a pious but unpoetical silk merchant named Dod was forcibly reminded of this verse by the authorities. Wither notes it thus: "Dod the silkman's late ridiculous translation of the Psalms was, by authority, worthily condemned to the fire."

Liturgical use.—The Introit to the Mass on Lady Day (e).
Latins.—Wednesday Vespers.
Greeks.—Friday evening.

PSALM CXXXII. *Memento, Domine.*

LORD, remember David : and all his trouble.

2 How he sware unto the Lord : and vowed a vow unto the Almighty God of Jacob;

3 I will not come within the tabernacle of mine house : nor climb up into my bed;

4 I will not suffer mine eyes to sleep, nor mine eyelids to slumber : neither the temples of my head to take any rest;

5 Until I find out a place for the temple of the Lord : an habitation for the mighty God of Jacob.

6 Lo, we heard of the same at Ephrata : and found it in the wood.

7 We will go into his tabernacle : and fall low on our knees before his footstool.

8 Arise, O Lord, into thy resting-place : thou, and the ark of thy strength.

9 Let thy priests be clothed with righteousness : and let thy saints sing with joyfulness.

10 For thy servant David's sake : turn not away the presence of thine Anointed.

11 The Lord hath made a faithful oath unto David : and he shall not shrink from it;

12 Of the fruit of thy body : shall I set upon thy seat.

13 If thy children will keep my covenant, and my testimonies that I shall learn them : their children also shall sit upon thy seat for evermore.

14 For the Lord hath chosen Sion to be an habitation for himself : he hath longed for her.

15 This shall be my rest for ever : here will I dwell, for I have a delight therein.

16 I will bless her victuals with increase : and will satisfy her poor with bread.

17 I will deck her priests with health : and her saints shall rejoice and sing.

18 There shall I make the horn of David to flourish : I have ordained a lantern for mine Anointed.

19 As for his enemies, I shall clothe them with shame : but upon himself shall his crown flourish.

A gradual psalm (see cxx.).

Verses 4 and 5. The epitaph over good Bishop Hacket of Lichfield.

Verse 15. St. Thomas Aquinas was seized with a fever at Castle Maganza, but would not be stayed, and pushed on to Fossa Nuova, a Cistercian Abbey, near Terracina, to die there. As he was carried in he repeated these words with rapture. He mused also much upon St. Augustine's words : "Then shall I truly live, when I shall be fulfilled with Thy love : now I am a burden to myself, because, Lord, I am not full of Thee." He died on the floor on ashes, March 7, 1274.

Verse 18. *Paravi lucernam Christo meo.* I have ordained a lantern for my Christ. These were the last words of Cyril of Alexandria, whose warts Kingsley has drawn in strong relief in "Hypatia," rather adding to them than otherwise, and hardly even outlining the brave rugged face which they blemished. Perhaps St. Cyril used the words because they were a common motto then and since, for St. John the Baptist.

Verse 19. *Inimicos eius induam confusione.* These words were engraved on the English shilling of King Edward VI., minted in 1549. See in contrast (Psalm lii. 7) Edward III.'s motto.

Liturgical use.—Christmas evening.
Latins.—Thursday Vespers.
Greeks.—Last psalm for Friday evening.

PSALM CXXXIII. *Ecce quam, bonum !*

BEHOLD, how good and joyful a thing it is : brethren, to dwell together in unity.

2 It is like the precious ointment upon the head, that ran down unto the beard : even unto Aaron's beard, and went down to the skirts of his clothing.

3 Like as the dew of Hermon : which fell upon the hill of Sion.

4 For there the Lord promised his blessing : and life for evermore.

A gradual psalm (see cxx.). Christopher Smart, who wrote his Song to David in a madhouse, and printed it with a key on the panels of the wall (1754-6), thus alludes to this psalm:

"Sweet is the dew that falls betimes
And drops upon the leafy limes.
Sweet, Hermon's fragrant air:
Sweet is the lily's silver bell,
And sweet the wakeful tapers' smell
That watch for early prayer."

This is the psalm which the commander of the Greely Expedition read to his men, when they wintered in the dark Arctic regions for a night which lasted twenty weeks.

Liturgical use.—Introit to the Mass of SS. Philip and James (e).
Latins.—Thursday Vespers.
Greeks.—Friday morning.

PSALM CXXXIV. *Ecce nunc.*

BEHOLD now, praise the Lord : all ye servants of the Lord;

2 Ye that by night stand in the house of the Lord : even in the courts of the house of our God.

3 Lift up your hands in the sanctuary : and praise the Lord.

4 The Lord that made heaven and earth : give thee blessing out of Sion.

This is the last of the gradual psalms. The pilgrims have now reached the Temple, and hear the Levites intoning the praises of God.

On the morning of his death (February 28, 992), St. Oswald, Archbishop of York, washed the feet of the poor and recited the gradual psalms. As they rose to thank him and while he was still saying the *Gloria*, he fell dead at the altar, his last word being *Sancto*.

Liturgical use.—Introit to the Mass for the Purification (e).
Latins.—The last psalm in daily Compline.
Greeks.—Friday morning ; daily Nocturns.

PSALM CXXXV. *Laudate Nomen.*

O PRAISE the Lord, laud ye the Name of the Lord : praise it, O ye servants of the Lord ;

2 Ye that stand in the house of the Lord : in the courts of the house of our God.

3 O praise the Lord, for the Lord is gracious : O sing praises unto his Name, for it is lovely.

4 For why ? the Lord hath chosen Jacob unto himself : and Israel for his own possession.

5 For I know that the Lord is great : and that our Lord is above all gods.

6 Whatsoever the Lord pleased, that did he in heaven, and in earth : and in the sea, and in all deep places.

7 He bringeth forth the clouds from the ends of the world : and sendeth forth lightnings with the rain, bringing the winds out of his treasures.

8 He smote the first-born of Egypt : both of man and beast.

9 He hath sent tokens and wonders into the midst of thee, O thou land of Egypt : upon Pharaoh, and all his servants.

10 He smote divers nations : and slew mighty kings ;

11 Sehon king of the Amorites, and Og the king of Basan : and all the kingdoms of Canaan ;

12 And gave their land to be an heritage : even an heritage unto Israel his people.

13 Thy Name, O Lord, endureth for ever : so doth thy memorial, O Lord, from one generation to another.

14 For the Lord will avenge his people : and be gracious unto his servants.

15 As for the images of the heathen, they are but silver and gold : the work of men's hands.

16 They have mouths, and speak not : eyes have they, but they see not.

17 They have ears, and yet they hear not : neither is there any breath in their mouths.

18 They that make them are like unto them : and so are all they that put their trust in them.

19 Praise the Lord, ye house of Israel : praise the Lord, ye house of Aaron.

20 Praise the Lord, ye house of Levi : ye that fear the Lord, praise the Lord.

21 Praised be the Lord out of Sion : who dwelleth at Jerusalem.

On October 28, 1704, John Locke, the philosopher, died at Oates, in Essex, while the psalms for the day were being read to him, which had been done throughout his sickness. He interrupted Lady Masham, who was reading them to him, with, "Cease now," and suddenly died.

This psalm and the next form the Great Hallel of Jewish worship, as opposed to the (Mizric) Egyptian Hallel. Both are recited on the Passover evenings.

Latins.—Thursday Vespers.
Greeks.—Friday morning.

PSALM CXXXVI. *Confitemini.*

O GIVE thanks unto the Lord, for he is gracious : and his mercy endureth for ever.

2 O give thanks unto the God of all gods : for his mercy endureth for ever.

3 O thank the Lord of all lords : for his mercy endureth for ever.

4 Who only doeth great wonders : for his mercy endureth for ever.

5 Who by his excellent wisdom made the heavens : for his mercy endureth for ever.

6 Who laid out the earth above the waters : for his mercy endureth for ever.

7 Who hath made great lights : for his mercy endureth for ever ;

8 The sun to rule the day : for his mercy endureth for ever ;

9 The moon and the stars to govern the night : for his mercy endureth for ever.

10 Who smote Egypt with their first-born : for his mercy endureth for ever ;

11 And brought out Israel from among them : for his mercy endureth for ever ;

12 With a mighty hand, and stretched out arm : for his mercy endureth for ever.

13 Who divided the Red sea in two parts : for his mercy endureth for ever.

14 And made Israel to go through the midst of it : for his mercy endureth for ever.

15 But as for Pharaoh and his host, he overthrew them in the Red sea : for his mercy endureth for ever.

16 Who led his people through the wilderness : for his mercy endureth for ever.

17 Who smote great kings : for his mercy endureth for ever ;

18 Yea, and slew mighty kings : for his mercy endureth for ever ;

19 Sehon king of the Amorites : for his mercy endureth for ever ;

20 And Og the king of Basan : for his mercy endureth for ever ;

21 And gave away their land for an heritage : for his mercy endureth for ever ;

22 Even for an heritage unto Israel his servant : for his mercy endureth for ever.

23 Who remembered us when we were in trouble : for his mercy endureth for ever ;

24 And hath delivered us from our enemies : for his mercy endureth for ever.

25 Who giveth food to all flesh : for his mercy endureth for ever.

26 O give thanks unto the God of heaven : for his mercy endureth for ever.

27 O give thanks unto the Lord of lords : for his mercy endureth for ever.

On February 8, 358, as St. Athanasius was at Mass in the Church of St. Thomas, at Alexandria, the Arians burst in. He ordered this psalm to be sung, but before it was over the soldiers had begun a massacre, and with difficulty the saint was rescued by the clergy and escaped to the desert and its monks.

Perhaps Shakespeare had this psalm in mind when he wrote :

"Wilt thou draw near the nature of the gods?
Draw near them, then, in being merciful ;
Sweet mercy is nobility's true badge."

How magnificently Milton, when a lad of only fifteen years, paraphrased this psalm into his hymn, "Let us with a gladsome mind"! (1624).

Verse 27. The French Psalter is the only other one which contains this verse. It is not found, for instance, in the Authorized Version.

Latins.—Thursday Vespers.
Greeks.—Friday morning.

PSALM CXXXVII. *Super flumina.*

BY the waters of Babylon we sat down and wept : when we remembered thee, O Sion.

2 As for our harps, we hanged them up : upon the trees that are therein.

3 For they that led us away captive required of us then a song, and melody, in our heaviness : "Sing us one of the songs of Sion."

4 "How shall we sing the Lord's song : in a strange land ?"

5 If I forget thee, O Jerusalem : let my right hand forget her cunning.

6 If I do not remember thee, let my tongue cleave to the roof of my mouth : yea, if I prefer not Jerusalem in my mirth.

7 Remember the children of Edom, O Lord, in the day of Jerusalem : how they said, "Down with it, down with it, even to the ground."

8 O daughter of Babylon, wasted with misery : yea, happy shall he be that rewardeth thee, as thou hast served us.

9 Blessed shall he be that taketh thy children : and throweth them against the stones.

This was the favourite psalm of Camoens, of Crashaw, and of Sir Walter Scott.

In 1606, St. Vincent de Paul was a slave to the Turks, captured and bought by an apostate. The Turkish wife of his master asked him to sing the praises of his God, and, "being a man full of the spirit of the psalms," he sang with tears *Super flumina* and *Salve Regina*. The woman was so touched that she upbraided her husband with his apostasy, who not only set St. Vincent free, but embarked with him for Aigues-Mortes.

Sir John Digby, Earl of Bristol, who lost his estate and his country when he sided with the king, died an exile in 1653, and was buried in a Paris cabbage-garden. This psalm was a favourite of his—as it was with many pious royalists in their exile—and he turned it into verses beginning :

"Sitting by yᵉ streams that glide
Down by Babell's towering wall."

This was set to music, and published, after the Restoration, in Clifford's Services, among the "Anthems usually sung in Cathedrals."

Liturgical use.—Introit for St. Luke's Mass (c).
Latins.—Thursday Vespers.
Greeks.—Friday morning.

PSALM CXXXVIII. *Confitebor tibi.*

I WILL give thanks unto thee, O Lord, with my whole heart : even before the gods will I sing praise unto thee.

2 I will worship toward thy holy temple, and praise thy Name, because of thy loving-kindness and truth : for thou hast magnified thy Name, and thy Word, above all things.

3 When I called upon thee, thou heardest me : and enduedst my soul with much strength.

4 All the kings of the earth shall praise thee, O Lord : for they have heard the words of thy mouth.

5 Yea, they shall sing in the ways of the Lord : that great is the glory of the Lord.

6 For though the Lord be high, yet hath he respect unto the lowly : as for the proud, he beholdeth them afar off.

7 Though I walk in the midst of trouble, yet shalt thou refresh me : thou shalt stretch forth thy hand upon the furiousness of mine enemies, and thy right hand shall save me.

8 The Lord shall make good his loving-kindness toward me : yea, thy mercy, O Lord, endureth for ever ; despise not then the works of thine own hands.

In Antioch of Syria there was an order of monks, in the days of Eusebius, who were founded to keep up the *laus perennis* of ceaseless psalmody. Day and night throughout the year the Psalms were chanted without interruption by relays of these monks. At the end of the fourth century Corbilla, a Syrian monk, probably one of them, founded a similar monastery on Psalmody Island, in the diocese of Nismes.

Liturgical use.—Introit to the Mass of the Conversion of St. Paul (e).
Latins.—Friday at Vespers ; St. Michael and All Angels.
Greeks.—Friday morning.

PSALM CXXXIX. *Domine, probasti.*

O LORD, thou hast searched me out, and known me : thou knowest my down-sitting, and mine uprising ; thou understandest my thoughts long before.

2 Thou art about my path, and about my bed : and spiest out all my ways.

3 For lo, there is not a word in my tongue : but thou, O Lord, knowest it altogether.

4 Thou hast fashioned me behind and before : and laid thine hand upon me.

5 Such knowledge is too wonderful and excellent for me : I cannot attain unto it.

6 Whither shall I go then from thy Spirit : or whither shall I go then from thy presence ?

7 If I climb up into heaven, thou art there : if I go down to hell, thou art there also.

8 If I take the wings of the morning : and remain in the uttermost parts of the sea ;

9 Even there also shall thy hand lead me : and thy right hand shall hold me.

10 If I say, " Peradventure the darkness shall cover me " : then shall my night be turned to day.

11 Yea, the darkness is no darkness with thee, but the night is as clear as the day : the darkness and light to thee are both alike.

12 For my reins are thine : thou hast covered me in my mother's womb.

13 I will give thanks unto thee, for I am fearfully and wonderfully made : marvellous are thy works, and that my soul knoweth right well.

14 My bones are not hid from thee : though I be made secretly, and fashioned beneath in the earth.

15 Thine eyes did see my substance, yet being imperfect : and in thy book were all my members written ;

16 Which day by day were fashioned : when as yet there was none of them.

17 How dear are thy counsels unto me, O God : O how great is the sum of them !

18 If I tell them, they are more in number than the sand : when I wake up I am present with thee.

19 Wilt thou not slay the wicked, O God : depart from me, ye blood-thirsty men.

20 For they speak unrighteously against thee : and thine enemies take thy Name in vain.

21 Do not I hate them, O Lord, that hate thee : and am not I grieved with those that rise up against thee ?

22 Yea, I hate them right sore : even as though they were mine enemies.

23 Try me, O God, and seek the ground of my heart : prove me, and examine my thoughts.

24 Look well if there be any way of wickedness in me : and lead me in the way everlasting.

In many parts of the country there is a good and ancient custom among the old wives, of reading this psalm to women in labour. Our grandmothers and great-grandmothers were no doubt strengthened and calmed by its words in their hours of need and peril.

It was a favourite psalm of

the great Emperor Charlemagne, who had, like many other soldiers, a special devotion to the Holy Ghost. Both the collect, "Almighty God, unto whom all hearts be opened," and the great hymn, *Veni Creator* ("Come, Holy Ghost, our souls inspire"), are said to have been made by him. They both have echo this psalm.

"I shall conclude my essay" (says Addison, in the *Spectator*, June 7, 1712) "with observing that the two kinds of hypocrisy I have here spoken of, namely, that of deceiving the world and that of imposing on ourselves, are touched with wonderful beauty in the 139th psalm. The folly of the first kind of hypocrisy is there set forth by reflections on God's omniscience and omnipresence, which are celebrated in as noble strains of poetry as any other I ever met with, either sacred or profane. The other kind of hypocrisy, whereby a man deceives himself, is intimated in the two last verses, where the Psalmist addresses himself to the great Searcher of hearts in that emphatical petition, 'Try me,' etc."

So the *Observer* (60): "Where can we meet a more touching description of God's omnipresence and providence than the 139th Psalm?"

Verse 9. A favourite verse of the poor missionary Captain Gardiner (*vide* Ps. xvii.).

Latins.—Friday Vespers.
Greeks.—Friday morning.

PSALM CXL. *Eripe me, Domine.*

DELIVER me, O Lord, from the evil man : and preserve me from the wicked man.

2 Who imagine mischief in their hearts : and stir up strife all the day long.

3 They have sharpened their tongues like a serpent : adder's poison is under their lips.

4 Keep me, O Lord, from the hands of the ungodly : preserve me from the wicked men, who are purposed to overthrow my goings.

5 The proud have laid a snare for me, and spread a net abroad with cords : yea, and set traps in my way.

6 I said unto the Lord, "Thou art my God" : hear the voice of my prayers, O Lord.

7 O Lord God, thou strength of my health : thou hast covered my head in the day of battle.

8 Let not the ungodly have his desire, O Lord : let not his mischievous imagination prosper, lest they be too proud.

9 Let the mischief of their own lips fall upon the head of them : that compass me about.

10 Let hot burning coals fall upon them : let them be cast into the fire, and into the pit, that they never rise up again.

11 A man full of words shall not prosper upon the earth : evil shall hunt the wicked person to overthrow him.

12 Sure I am that the Lord will avenge the poor : and maintain the cause of the helpless.

13 The righteous also shall give thanks unto thy Name : and the just shall continue in thy sight.

"The Nicolaitans, Gnostics, and Manichæans," says Philostratus, "denied David altogether to be a prophet ; and Paul of Samosata suppressed the Psalms and those hymns which the Christians sang in praise of Christ. He wished to substitute poems in his own honour, it was said."

Professor Robertson Smith, who thinks it a question more curious than important, whether David had a hand in any of the Psalms, is yet "unable to fit in any with his life" ; but Professor Kirkpatrick, in his summary of critical work, applauded by Dr. Salmond in the *Critical Review*, still assigns "the foundation of the Psalter to David."

Liturgical use.—Introit to the Mass for St. Matthew's Day (e).
Latins.— Friday Vespers ; Maundy Thursday.
Greeks.—Friday morning ; Mesorion of the Ninth hour.

PSALM CXLI. *Domine, clamavi.*

LORD, I call upon thee, haste thee unto me : and consider my voice when I cry unto thee.

2 Let my prayer be set forth in thy sight as the incense : and let the lifting up of my hands be an evening sacrifice.

3 Set a watch, O Lord, before my mouth : and keep the door of my lips.

4 O let not mine heart be inclined to any evil thing : let me not be occupied in ungodly works with the men that work wickedness, lest I eat of such things as please them.

5 Let the righteous rather smite me friendly : and reprove me.

6 But let not their precious balms break my head : yea, I will pray yet against their wickedness.

7 Let their judges be overthrown in stony places : that they may hear my words, for they are sweet.

8 Our bones lie scattered before the pit : like as when one breaketh and heweth wood upon the earth.

9 But mine eyes look unto thee, O Lord God : in thee is my trust, O cast not out my soul.

10 Keep me from the snare that they have laid for me : and from the traps of the wicked doers.

11 Let the ungodly fall into their own nets together : and let me ever escape them.

This has been called the Evening hymn of Early Christendom. It seems to have been in daily use in the African Church.

Verses 2, 3, *and* 4. The words used for censing the altar. The Christian use of incense dates from the catacombs, where sweet gums had to be burnt, as disinfectants.

Verse 3. This was and is the last verse of the last service of the day (Compline) for the Benedictine monks, after which silence is straitly enjoined upon all.

Liturgical use.—Introit for St. Mark's Mass (e).
Latins.—Friday Vespers ; Maundy Thursday.
Greeks.—Friday morning ; daily Evensong.

PSALM CXLII. *Voce mea ad Dominum.*

I CRIED unto the Lord with my voice : yea, even unto the Lord did I make my supplication.

2 I poured out my complaints before him : and shewed him of my trouble.

3 When my spirit was in heaviness thou knewest my path : in the way wherein I walked have they privily laid a snare for me.

4 I looked also upon my right hand : and saw there was no man that would know me.

5 I had no place to flee unto : and no man cared for my soul.

6 I cried unto thee, O Lord, and said: "Thou art my hope, and my portion in the land of the living.

7 "Consider my complaint : for I am brought very low.

Day 29 PSALM CXLIII *Evening Prayer*

8 " O deliver me from my persecutors : for they are too strong for me.

9 " Bring my soul out of prison, that I may give thanks unto thy Name " : which thing if thou wilt grant me, then shall the righteous resort unto my company.

On October 4, 1226 A.D., St. Francis of Assisi was dying, naked, upon the bare earth.

" At last, though Death he saw and felt him full strong,
Voce meâ he began, one psalm of evensong ;
And said forth the same all out, and held up his hands on high,
And with the last word of the same, he began to die !"
(*South English Legendary.*)

Verse 9. In 1548 the learned Protestant Beza (Theodore) was sick with a sore disease, which his conscience told him was a punishment come upon him for having " privately married " his wife. He prayed this prayer to God, and was restored. He then honourably and openly married her.

Liturgical use.—Introit to St. Barnaby's Mass (e).
Latins.—Friday Vespers ; Maundy Thursday.
Greeks.—Friday morning ; daily Evensong.

PSALM CXLIII. *Domine, exaudi.*

HEAR my prayer, O Lord, and consider my desire : hearken unto me for thy truth and righteousness' sake.

2 And enter not into judgment with thy servant : for in thy sight shall no man living be justified.

3 For the enemy hath persecuted my soul ; he hath smitten my life down to the ground : he hath laid me in the darkness, as the men that have been long dead.

4 Therefore is my spirit vexed within me : and my heart within me is desolate.

5 Yet do I remember the time past ; I muse upon all thy works : yea, I exercise myself in the works of thy hands.

6 I stretch forth my hands unto thee : my soul gaspeth unto thee as a thirsty land.

7 Hear me, O Lord, and that soon, for my spirit waxeth faint : hide not thy face from me, lest I be like unto them that go down into the pit.

8 O let me hear thy loving-kindness betimes in the morning, for in thee is my trust : shew thou me the

way that I should walk in, for I lift up my soul unto thee.

9 Deliver me, O Lord, from mine enemies : for I flee unto thee to hide me.

10 Teach me to do the thing that pleaseth thee, for thou art my God : let thy loving Spirit lead me forth into the land of righteousness.

11 Quicken me, O Lord, for thy Name's sake : and for thy righteousness' sake bring my soul out of trouble.

12 And of thy goodness slay mine enemies : and destroy all them that vex my soul; for I am thy servant.

This is the seventh penitential psalm (these are vi., xxxii., xxxviii., li., cii., cxxx., and cxliii.), and an antidote to the deadly sin of Sloth or Indifference.

Charles the Good, Count of Flanders, was slain at the Lady Altar, as he recited this psalm March 2, 1127.

One of Gerson's prayers contains this sentence : "Grant me, O Lord, that this sevenfold group of penitential psalms may be a remedy against the sevenfold group of deadly sins, and help to the sevenfold group of the principal virtues, and the sevenfold group of spiritual gifts, to the sevenfold beatitudes, and to the seven petitions contained in the Lord's Prayer" (*ob.* 1429).

Liturgical use.—Introt for the Mass on the Nativity of St. John Baptist (e) ; Ash Wednesday.
Latins.—Friday Lauds.
Greeks.—Friday morning ; Dawn ; the late Evensong ; and also in Lent.

PSALM CXLIV. *Benedictus Dominus.*

BLESSED be the Lord my strength : who teacheth my hands to war, and my fingers to fight;

2 My hope and my fortress, my castle and deliverer, my defender in whom I trust : who subdueth my people that is under me.

3 Lord, what is man, that thou hast such respect unto him : or the son of man, that thou so regardest him ?

4 Man is like a thing of nought : his time passeth away like a shadow.

5 Bow thy heavens, O Lord, and come down : touch the mountains, and they shall smoke.

6 Cast forth thy lightning, and tear them : shoot out thine arrows, and consume them.

7 Send down thine hand from above : deliver me, and take me out of the great waters, from the hand of strange children ;

8 Whose mouth talketh of vanity : and their right hand is a right hand of wickedness.

9 I will sing a new song unto thee, O God : and sing praises unto thee upon a ten-stringed lute.

10 Thou hast given victory unto kings : and hast delivered David thy servant from the peril of the sword.

11 Save me, and deliver me from the hand of strange children : whose mouth talketh of vanity, and their right hand is a right hand of iniquity.

12 That our sons may grow up as the young plants : and that our daughters may be as the polished corners of the temple.

13 That our garners may be full and plenteous with all manner of store : that our sheep may bring forth thousands and ten thousands in our streets.

14 That our oxen may be strong to labour, that there be no decay : no leading into captivity, and no complaining in our streets.

15 Happy are the people that are in such a case : yea, blessed are the people who have the Lord for their God.

Benedictus Dominus Deus meus. A not uncommon sword-motto, alluding to the whole psalm, which is one of the war psalms. St. Bernard made much use of it, when he preached the Crusades.

Verse 3. Richard Baxter on his death-bed admired the Divine condescension to us, often saying: "Lord, what is man? What am I, vile worm, to the Great God?"

Verse 4. The dial motto of St. Brelade, Jersey, is "L'homme est semblable à la vanité : ses jours sont comme une ombre qui passe."

Verse 7. This was the text of courteous Bishop Bedell's last sermon. He had just been released from captivity by the Irish rebels of 1641. He translated our Prayer-book into Italian, and had it translated into Irish. He was a great reformer of the Irish Church, and that not only in his see of Kilmore.

Liturgical use.—Introit to St. Peter's Mass (e).
Latins.—Saturday Vespers.
Greeks.—Friday morning.

PSALM CXLV. *Exaltabo te, Deus.*

I WILL magnify thee, O God, my King : and I will praise thy Name for ever and ever.

2 Every day will I give thanks unto thee : and praise thy Name for ever and ever.

3 Great is the Lord, and marvellous, worthy to be praised : there is no end of his greatness.

4 One generation shall praise thy works unto another : and declare thy power.

5 As for me, I will be talking of thy worship : thy glory, thy praise, and wondrous works.

6 So that men shall speak of the might of thy marvellous acts : and I will also tell of thy greatness.

7 The memorial of thine abundant kindness shall be shewed : and men shall sing of thy righteousness.

8 The Lord is gracious, and merciful : long-suffering, and of great goodness.

9 The Lord is loving unto every man : and his mercy is over all his works.

10 All thy works praise thee, O Lord : and thy saints give thanks unto thee.

11 They shew the glory of thy kingdom : and talk of thy power;

12 That thy power, thy glory, and mightiness of thy kingdom : might be known unto men.

13 Thy kingdom is an everlasting kingdom : and thy dominion endureth throughout all ages.

14 The Lord upholdeth all such as fall : and lifteth up all those that are down.

15 The eyes of all wait upon thee, O Lord : and thou givest them their meat in due season.

16 Thou openest thine hand : and fillest all things living with plenteousness.

17 The Lord is righteous in all his ways : and holy in all his works.

18 The Lord is nigh unto all them that call upon him : yea, all such as call upon him faithfully.

19 He will fulfil the desire of them that fear him : he also will hear their cry, and will help them.

20 The Lord preserveth all them that love him : but scattereth abroad all the ungodly.

21 My mouth shall speak the praise of the Lord : and let all flesh give thanks unto his holy Name for ever and ever.

This psalm must have been in Milton's mind when he wrote the last speech of Adam, the exile, in " Paradise Lost " :

"Henceforth I learn, that to
    obey is best,
And love with fear the only
    God, to walk
As in His presence, ever to
    observe
His providence and on Him
    sole depend,
Merciful over all His works,
    with good
Still overcoming evil, and by
    small
Accomplishing great things,
    by things deemed weak
Subverting worldly strong,
    and worldly wise
By simply meek ; that suffer-
    ing for truth's sake
Is fortitude to highest victory,
And to the faithful Death the
    Gate of Life :
Taught this by His example,
    whom I now
Acknowledge my Redeemer
    ever blest."

Liturgical use.—Whit-Sunday evening.
Latins.—Saturday at Vespers.
Greeks.—Friday morning.

PSALM CXLVI. *Lauda, anima mea.*

PRAISE the Lord, O my soul ; while I live, will I praise the Lord : yea, as long as I have any being, I will sing praises unto my God.

2 O put not your trust in princes, nor in any child of man : for there is no help in them.

3 For when the breath of man goeth forth he shall turn again to his earth : and then all his thoughts perish.

4 Blessed is he that hath the God of Jacob for his help : and whose hope is in the Lord his God ;

5 Who made heaven and earth, the sea, and all that therein is : who keepeth his promise for ever ;

6 Who helpeth them to right that suffer wrong : who feedeth the hungry.

7 The Lord looseth men out of prison : the Lord giveth sight to the blind.

8 The Lord helpeth them that are fallen : the Lord careth for the righteous.

9 The Lord careth for the strangers ; he defendeth

Evening Prayer   PSALM CXLVII   *Day* 30

the fatherless and widow : as for the way of the ungodly, he turneth it upside down.

10 The Lord thy God, O Sion, shall be King for evermore : and throughout all generations.

A dirge psalm (see Ps. v.).

In 1621 the Protestant leader, Andrew Willet, of Cambridge and Ely, was thrown from his horse and broke his leg. He was carried to a bone-setter's and had it attended to. When it was set he leaned on his staff and repeated "this most sweet psalm," dwelling especially on the eighth verse ; then suddenly fainted away and died.

Verse 2. Aptly quoted by Strafford, when he heard that his master, King Charles I., had thrown him to the wolves, by signing the Bill of Attainder.

Verse 7. The motto of the Trinitarian friars of Mottingden, Kent, who raised money to ransom Christian captives from the Saracens.

Liturgical use.—Introit for St. Mary Magdalen's Mass (e).
Latins.—Saturday Vespers.
Greeks.—Friday morning.

PSALM CXLVII. *Laudate Dominum.*

O PRAISE the Lord. for it is a good thing to sing praises unto our God : yea, a joyful and pleasant thing it is to be thankful.

2 The Lord doth build up Jerusalem : and gather together the out-casts of Israel.

3 He healeth those that are broken in heart : and giveth medicine to heal their sickness.

4 He telleth the number of the stars : and calleth them all by their names.

5 Great is our Lord, and great is his power : yea, and his wisdom is infinite.

6 The Lord setteth up the meek : and bringeth the ungodly down to the ground.

7 O sing unto the Lord with thanksgiving : sing praises upon the harp unto our God ;

8 Who covereth the heaven with clouds, and prepareth rain for the earth : and maketh the grass to grow upon the mountains, and herb for the use of men ;

9 Who giveth fodder unto the cattle : and feedeth the young ravens that call upon him.

10 He hath no pleasure in the strength of an horse : neither delighteth he in any man's legs.

11 But the Lord's delight is in them that fear him : and put their trust in his mercy.

12 Praise the Lord, O Jerusalem : praise thy God, O Sion.

13 For he hath made fast the bars of thy gates : and hath blessed thy children within thee.

14 He maketh peace in thy borders : and filleth thee with the flour of wheat.

15 He sendeth forth his commandment upon earth : and his word runneth very swiftly.

16 He giveth snow like wool : and scattereth the hoar-frost like ashes.

17 He casteth forth his ice like morsels : who is able to abide his frost?

18 He sendeth out his word, and melteth them : he bloweth with his wind, and the waters flow.

19 He shewed his word unto Jacob : his statutes and ordinances unto Israel.

20 He hath not dealt so with any nation : neither have the heathen knowledge of his laws.

Verse 4. A favourite verse of Sir Thomas Browne, the author of "Religio Medici."

Verse 8. "Look up to the higher hills, where the waves of green roll silently into long inlets among the shadow of the pines, and we may perhaps know the meaning of those quiet words of the 147th Psalm, 'He maketh the grass to grow upon the mountains'" (*Ruskin*).

Latins.—Saturday at Vespers ; Dedication of a Church (verses 12-20) ; Feasts of Our Lady.

Greeks.—Friday morning.

PSALM CXLVIII. *Laudate Dominum.*

O PRAISE the Lord of heaven : praise him in the height.

2 Praise him, all ye angels of his : praise him, all his host.

3 Praise him, sun and moon : praise him, all ye stars and light.

4 Praise him, all ye heavens : and ye waters that are above the heavens.

5 Let them praise the Name of the Lord : for he spake the word, and they were made ; he commanded, and they were created.

6 He hath made them fast for ever and ever : he hath given them a law which shall not be broken.

7 Praise the Lord upon earth : ye dragons, and all deeps ;

8 Fire and hail, snow and vapours : wind and storm, fulfilling his word ;

9 Mountains and all hills : fruitful trees and all cedars.

10 Beasts and all cattle : worms and feathered fowls ;

11 Kings of the earth and all people : princes and all judges of the world ;

12 Young men and maidens, old men and children, praise the Name of the Lord : for his Name only is excellent, and his praise above heaven and earth.

13 He shall exalt the horn of his people ; all his saints shall praise him : even the children of Israel, even the people that serveth him.

Perhaps St. Francis derived his hymn of all creatures from this psalm. In it he calls all creation to bless God (*propter honorabilem fratrem nostrum solem*) for our noble brother the Sun, etc.

Verses 1 and 2. St. Bernard's brother Gerard died with these words of triumph. "At that moment, my brother, day dawned on thee, though it was night for us. Just as I reached his side I heard him utter aloud those words of Christ, *Pater in manûs tuas.* Then repeating the verse over again, and resting on the word 'Father ! Father !' he turned to me and, smiling, said, 'O how gracious of God to be the Father of men, and what an honour for men to be His children !'"

Verse 2. The "Angel Psalms" are viii., xxxiv., xxxv., lxviii., lxxviii., xci., ciii., civ., and this one. The Angelicals are divided into three choirs and nine orders. The Contemplative Choir is made up of Seraphim, who behold ; Cherubim, who veil with wings ; and Thrones, who upbear God in his glory. The Middle Choir consists of Dominations, who order the stars ; Virtues, who uphold qualities ; and Powers, who hold evil spirits in leashes. Below these are Principalities, who keep us human ; Archangels, who guard our nationality and our Church ; and Angels, who maintain our individuality, and set our soul's food before us, and bring us at last to the judgement.

Liturgical use.—Introit for St. James's Mass (e).
Latins.—Daily at Lauds ; at burial of children, on the way to Church and to the grave.
Greeks.—Friday morning ; Dawn ; burial of priests.

PSALM CXLIX. *Cantate Domino.*

O SING unto the Lord a new song : let the congregation of saints praise him.

2 Let Israel rejoice in him that made him : and let the children of Sion be joyful in their King.

3 Let them praise his name in the dance : let them sing praises unto him with tabret and harp.

4 For the Lord hath pleasure in his people : and helpeth the meek-hearted.

5 Let the saints be joyful with glory : let them rejoice in their beds.

6 Let the praises of God be in their mouth : and a two-edged sword in their hands;

7 To be avenged of the heathen : and to rebuke the people;

8 To bind their kings in chains : and their nobles with links of iron.

9 That they may be avenged of them, as it is written : such honour have all his saints.

This war psalm was used by Caspar Sciopius to rouse the Romanist Princes to the thirty years' war, as it had been by Thomas Munzer to rouse the peasants in the great German Jacquerie, which followed in the wake of the Reformation.

Verses 5 and 6. A curious use of these verses, and the next psalm, is given by Alexander Neckan, a mediæval medical writer. They are a charm against the flying and the travelling evil, or, as we should say, contagion and epidemics. If this were mere superstition, at least it was not as harmful as the superstitious use made of this psalm by the fanatics of the xvi. and xvii. centuries.

Verse 5. This verse suggested to Richard Baxter and Margaret, his wife, their habit of singing psalms in bed the last thing at night and the first in the morning. They probably used Baxter's own "far from contemptible version"; but at last were driven out of the practice by the derision of the neighbouring wags.

Liturgical use.—Introit for Hallowmas (e).
Latins.—Daily at Lauds; burial of children, between the house and Church, and the Church and grave.
Greeks.—Friday morning; Dawn; burial of priests.

PSALM CL. *Laudate Dominum.*

O PRAISE God in his holiness : praise him in the firmament of his power.

2 Praise him in his noble acts : praise him according to his excellent greatness.

3 Praise him in the sound of the trumpet : praise him upon the lute and harp.

4 Praise him in the cymbals and dances : praise him upon the strings and pipe.

5 Praise him upon the well-tuned cymbals : praise him upon the loud cymbals.

6 Let every thing that hath breath : praise the Lord.

It is thanks to this psalm above others that the use of instrumental music has been continuously preserved in the Church, although some of the severer Fathers looked upon it with distrust. It is one of the psalms in which not only Christian musicians, but artists of all sorts, delight. Fra Angelico, for instance, so often refers to it that we may call it his favourite psalm. His well-known Angels of the Tabernacle, the dances of the blessed, in the " Day of Judgment," and the musical instruments in the Uffizzi Madonna, are instances. Orcagna's " Day of Judgment," Raphael's "St. Cecilia," and countless other pictures, illustrate the same. To this day in Seville ten little boys dance before the altar in the Cathedral in direct reference to *verse* 4. The word "pipe" in the same verse is in the Latin and Greek versions "organ," and the organ was used even in the Catacomb services, and in St. Augustine's time, though perhaps not North of the Alps till the eighth century.

Clement of Alexandria once tried to explain away this psalm into an allegory of the human body : the tongue being the lute, the face the harp, the lips cymbals, and so on. He could not bear to think of the Church using what had excited the heathen to lust or war.

Verse 6. *Omnis spiritus laudet Dominum* is the sundial motto of Great Smeaton Church, Yorks.

Liturgical use.—Introit to the Mass for SS. Simon and Jude (e).

Latins.—Daily at Lauds ; burial of children, on the road to Church, and from Church to the grave.

Greeks.—Friday evening ; late Evensong ; burial of priests.

Laus Deo.

INDEX

The numbers refer to the Psalms.

ABOLITIONISTS, 10
Abraham, 89
Adam, 92
Addison, 19, 23, 139
Adhelm, 68
Agincourt, 114
St. Agnes, 110
Albertus Magnus, 28, 58
Alfred, 72
St. Ambrose, 6, 7, 43, 44, 64, 78, 119 (p. 184)
Anastasius IV., 17
Andrewes, 82, 85
Angelo, 148
Angelico, Fra, 150
St. Anno, 112
St. Anselm, 27, 53
St. Anthony, 9, 20, 68
St. Thomas Aquinas, 53, 59, 84, 102, 132
Argyle, 74
Arians, 45, 48, 119 (p. 196)
Armada, 3, 76
Arnold, M., 49, 77
Arnold, T., 51
Arthur, King, 31
Arundel, Lady, 46
Ascension psalms, 8, 11, 15, 19, 21, 24, 30, 47, 93, 97, 99, 103, 108, 117
Ash Wednesday: see " Penitential "
Aske, R., 74

Asperges, 51
St. Athanasius, 2, 5, 45, 62, 79, 89, 104, 116, 126
St. Augustine H., 4, 12, 32, 33, 79, 87, 101, 119 (pp. 185, 194)
St. Augustine C., 84

St. Babylas, 96
Bacon, 14, 101, 104, 120
Baker, H., 23
Baldwin, 118
Balsamus, 27, 115
St. Basil, the Great, 15, 31
Bauhinus, 104
Baxter, 2, 91, 144, 149
Beauchamp, 16
Bede, 24, 42, 113
Bedell, 144
Bell, 115
St. Benedict A., 37
St. Benedict Bis., 83
Berkeley, 8
St. Bernard, 12, 13, 51, 107, 116, 118, 128
De Berulle, 9
Beza, 64, 142
Blackmore, 64
Black Prince, 7, 28, 121
Blake, 85
St. Bonaventura, 17, 76
St. Boniface, 6, 69
Bosanquet, M., 27
Boy-bishop, 91

231

INDEX

Brian, 51
Bristol, Ld., 137
Browne, T., 2, 147
Browning, E. B., 127
Browning, R., 39, 55, 68
Bunyan, 119 (p. 186)
Burial psalms, 23, 24, 39, 51, 84, 90, 91, 113, 116, 119, 130, 139, 146, 148, 149, 150
Burleigh, Ld., 55
Burnet, 22
Burns, 90
Burton, R., 1, 119 (p. 195)
Butchers' Company, 8
Buxton, 126
Byrom, 23
Byzantine wars, 20

Caird, 53
Calmet, 64
Calvin, 6, 13, 39
Calvinists, 97
Campion, 31
Canterbury, St. Thomas of, 37, 119 (p. 183)
Capgrave, 7, 45, 51
Caravans, 119, (p. 181)
Carlyle, J., 6
Carlyle, Th., 21, 72, 84
Carnovale, Fra, 91
Catherine de Medici, 6
Cealchythe, 15
St. Chad, 18
Chalice motto, 116
Charlemagne, 4, 26, 68, 119 (p. 189), 139
Charles the Bad, 11
Charles I., 9, 52, 56, 83
Charles V., 90, 102, 118
Charles VIII., 65
Chaucer, 81, 119 (p. 192)
Christ, 82, 110, 118
Christmas psalms, 2, 8, 19, 45, 48, 72, 85, 89, 96, 98, 110, 111, 112, 113, 117, 132
St. Chrysostom, 24, 61, 62, 116
Circumcision, 12
Clement Alex., 150
Cloveshoo, 1
Clovis, 18, 29
Cœnobites, 55

Colet, 51
St. Columba, 34, 45, 78, 84
Columbus, 19, 31
Commendation, 12, 118, 119 (p. 182)
Commentators, eighteenth century, 105
Composite psalm, 71
Constantine, 82
Contrition, 51
Corbilla, 138
Cosin, 90
Cottam, 71
Coutras, 118
Coverdale, 119 (p. 191)
Cowper, Bp., 119 (p. 198)
Cowper, W., 101, 118
Cranmer, 44, 51
Crashaw, 137
St. Crispin, 79
Cromwell, 68, 117
Cuthbert, 60
St. Cyprian, 6
St. Cyril, 132

Dante, 9, 51, 92, 114
Darnley, 55
David, 140
De Civitate Dei, 87
Defensor, Bp., 8
Descartes, 53
Dial mottoes, 74, 80, 89, 90, 102, 113, 119 (p. 197), 150
Didymus, 88
Dies Iræ, 19, 97, 102, 110
Digby, E., of Bristol, 137
Dionysius, Ar., 24
Dirge, 5, 27, 30, 41, 42, 71, 116, 146
Dod, 131
Donatists, 26
Drumclog, 76
Dunbar, 68, 117
Duns Scotus, 53
Dunstan, 51, 68, 111
Dürer, 90
Durham University, 87
Duty, 119 (p. 181)

Easter psalms, 2, 57, 62, 111, 112, 113, 114, 117, 118

INDEX

Easter text, 110
St. Edmund, 72
Edward III., 6, 52, 112
Edward VI., 119 (p. 191), 132
Elfric, 25, 26, 51
St. Eligius, 119 (p. 192)
Eliot, G., 85
Elizabeth, 14, 90, 118
Elohists, 53
St. Elphege, 3
England, 125
St. Epiphanius, 31
Epiphany, 29, 46, 47, 66, 72, 86, 87, 95, 96, 97
Erasmus, 1, 15, 119 (p. 193)
Essex, 55
Ethelbert, 29
Evelyn, 14

Fabricius, 12
Fifth Monarchy, 7
Filbie, 51
Fisher, 6, 34, 71, 116
Fletcher, Ph., 130
Forrest, 62
Fortunatus, 96
Fox, 106
Francis I., 119 (p. 188)
St. Francis S., 40
St. Francis A., 23, 142, 148
Franklin, 107
Fuller, T., 8, 37, 52, 109

Gandia, Duke, 114, 124
Ganging, 103, 104
Gardiner, Allen, 17, 139
Gaudfridus, 106
Gentleman, 15
Gerard, 148
Gerson, 143
Giraldus, C., 55
Gladstone, Mr., 98, 119 (p. 196)
Gnostics, 140
Good Friday, 2, 22, 27, 38, 40, 54, 59, 69, 88, 94
St. Gordius, 118
St. Gorgonia, 4
Gradual, 120-134
Gregory Dec., 13
St. Gregory Gt., 1, 33, 69, 72
St. Gregory N., 4, 49

Grote, 112
Guardian, 40
Gunpowder plot, 64, 123

Habington, 19
Hacket, 24, 41, 132
Hall, J., 60, 79
Hallel, 113-118, 135
Hampton, C. C., 106
Handel, 24
Hare, 17
Harrington, 7, 38
"Harrowing of Hell," 24, 107
Hart, the, 42
Hart, 123
Hatton, 92, 108
Heine, 23
Helmore, 47
Henry II., 6
Henry III., 85
Henry V., 51, 114
Henry VI., 122
Henry VII., 43
Heraldry, 127
Herbert, G., 1, 11, 23, 29, 31, 38, 71
St. Hilarion, 20
Hildebrand, 45
Hobbs, Ab., 79
Holdsworth, 119 (p. 195)
Holland, 64
Hooker, 35, 55
Hooper, 77, 88, 121
Horne, 106
Hours, 119, (pp. 187, 197)
House motto, 127
Howard, P., 8
St. Hugh, 10, 58, 68, 119 (p. 184)
Humboldt, 19, 104
"Hundredth, Old," 100
Hunnis, 6, 102
Huss, 31

Incense, 141
Innocent VIII., 26
Invitatory, 95
Iscariot, 41
St. Isidore, 39

Jackson, T., 116
James I., 68, 83

233

INDEX

Japan, 113, 114
St. Jerome, 1, 17, 55
Jerusalem, Siege of, 2
Jewel, 71
Jewish lament, 79
Jocelyn, 84
St. John Baptist, 132
John VIII., 67
St. John Evangelist, 69
Johnson, R., 51
Johnson, S., Dr., 119 (p. 189)
Julian Ap., 68, 96, 115
Justinianus, 19
Justin Martyr, 96

Keble, 39, 51, 86
Ken, 8
Kethe, 100
King, H., 80
Kingsley, 76
King's psalm, 20
King's evil, 102
Kirkman, 120
Kirkpatrick, Pro., 140
Knox, 31, 51, 103
Kyrie, 51

Lamb, 1
Laud, 9, 21, 90
Laus perennis, 138
Lawrence, Lady, 27
Lazarus, 94
Leicester, 73
Leighton, 39
Le Long, 64
Lightfoot, 78
Lincoln Coll., 80
Lincoln, Pres., 11
Livingstone, 37, 121
Locke, J., 135
Lok, 49
Longfellow, 100
St. Louis, 25, 32
Luther, 2, 31, 46, 100, 119 (p. 190)
Lux Mundi, 110
Luxorius, 86, 119 (p. 183)
Lyte, 84

McCheyne, 124
Magic, 50

Maine, C., 31
Manoel, 37
Margaret of Scotland, 1
Margaret of Richmond, 6
Marriage psalms, 67, 128
Marseilles, Bp. of, 91
St. Martin, 8, 118
Martyn, H., 118, 119 (p. 191)
Martyrs, 115
Blessed Virgin Mary, 8, 19, 24, 45, 46, 87, 96, 97, 98, 110, 113, 122, 127, 131, 147
Mary Queen of Scots, 18, 71, 130
Matheson, 92
Matilda, 92
Maundy Thursday, 69, 70, 71, 72, 73, 74, 75, 76, 77, 116, 120, 140, 141, 142
St. Maur, 42
Maurice, Emp., 119 (p. 194)
Maxwell, 119 (p. 185)
Medley, Bp., 119 (p. 196)
Melchizedek, 110
Merks, 105
Methodius, 67
Midnight hour, 119 (pp. 187, 197)
Midwife's psalm, 139
Milman, 25
Milton, 19, 114, 136, 145
Molinos, 18
Monica, 101
Monkish vows forbidden, 54
Montanists, 26
More, T., 51
Morley, Ld., 94
Moses, 100
Munzer, 149
Musical psalms, 30
Mutiny, Indian, 79
Mysteries, Coventry, 125
Mystics, 18

Naseby, 47
Neale, 96
Neckan, 149
Necromancy, 50
Nelson, Jn., 31, 130
Newman, 90, 104, 112
Newton, 21

INDEX

Nicene Creed, 36
Nicholas III., 57
Nicholson, Bp., 70
Norris, Jn., 18
Northernmost grave, 51
Notker, 22

Observer, 139
Oldcastle, 94
Oratorians, 9
Organ, 150
Origen, 50, 65, 80, 102
Oswald, Bp., 16, 134
Oxford University, 27

St. Pambo, 39
Paris, M., 92
Parker, Arch., 47
Pascal, 119 (p. 187)
Paula, 84
Pauline psalms, 32
Pelican, 102
Penitential psalms, 6, 32, 38, 51, 102, 130, 143
Philostratus, 140
Piano, 33
Pico della Mirandola, 16, 26
Pierson, 87
Piers Ploughman, 32, 36, 37, 112, 128
Pilgrimage of Grace, 74
Pius V., 119 (p. 182)
St. Polycarp, 31
St. Pontius, 115
Pope, Alex., 18, 64
Porphyrius, 52, 78
Prime, A.-S., 71, 80, 85, 88
Publia, 68, 115
Pygot, 106

Raleigh, W., 75
Restoration, 124
Reynolds, Dr., 105, 106
Reynolds, R., 27
Richard I., 22, 127
St. Richard, 122
Richard de Bury, 116
Romaine, 107
Rood, 129
Rossetti, Miss, 121
Rudd, 90

Ruskin, 19, 23, 36, 147
Russell, W., 42

Salmond, 142
Sancroft, 32
Sandys, 80
Saunderson, R., 57, 103
Savonarola, 2, 51, 66, 68
Sciopius, C., 149
Scott, G., 122
Scott, W., 16, 114, 137
Secreta, 43
Shakespeare, 18, 19, 22, 89, 93, 100
Shallow, 89
Sidney, P., 10
Small books, 40
Smart, C., 133
Smart, P., 31
Smith, R., 140
Socrates S., 39
Sparkes, Dr., 105
Spenser, 37, 91
Stanley, A., 78, 112, 119 (p. 190), 122
Strafford, 25, 146
Strathmore, 31
Sundial : see "Dial"
Supremacy, Papal, 105
Swedenborg, 74
Sword motto, 144
Syllogism, false, 66

Tait, 17
Talmud, 100
Tasso, 31
Tate and Brady, 10, 34
Taylor, J., 126
Taylor, R., 51
Templars, 95
Tennyson, 86
Thackeray, 37, 126
Theodolf, 51
St. Theodore, 119 (p. 190)
St. Theodore Mop., 18, 79
St. Theodore M., 34
Theodoret, 78
Theodosius, 119 (p. 183)
St. Thomas à Kempis, 85
St. Thomas of Canterbury, 37, 119 (p. 183)

235

INDEX

Thomson, 19
De Thou, 116, 118
Thring, 78
Thurkeld, 118
Titian, 120
Torquemada, 35
Traveller's psalm, 121
Trench, 86
Trinitarian friars, 146
Trinity psalms, 8, 19, 24, 47, 48, 67, 72, 96, 97, 98

Utrecht Psalter, 106

Vane, Sir H., 7
Van Mildert, 87
Vaughan, H., 65, 104, 121
Verney, E., 105
Vicars, 64, 123
St. Vincent de P., 137
Vincentius L., 46
Vindicatio, 59
Vindictive psalms, 59, 69, 79, 109

Visconti, B., 51
Visitation of Sick, 6, 23, 27, 32, 51, 55, 61, 71, 102

Waddell, 10
Wallace, 119 (p. 182)
Walton, I., 2, 32, 120
Watts, 90
Wesley, C., 72
Wesley, J., 38
White, K., 18
Whitfield, 118
Whitgift, 105
Whitsuntide, 33, 48, 68, 100, 101, 104, 117, 145
Wilberforce, 119 (p. 182)
Wilfred of York, 104
Willet, A., 146
Wither, 119 (p. 193)
Wolsey, W., 106
Wordsworth, 19, 88, 113

Xavier, 31, 114
Ximenes, 115

THE END.

Elliot Stock, Paternoster Row, London.

www.ingramcontent.com/pod-product-compliance
Lightning Source LLC
Chambersburg PA
CBHW020807230426
43666CB00007B/902